THE UNIVERSITY OF TOULOUSE
IN THE MIDDLE AGES

The University of Toulouse in the Middle Ages

ITS ORIGINS AND GROWTH TO 1500 A.D.

CYRIL EUGENE SMITH

Associate Professor of History at Marquette University

THE MARQUETTE UNIVERSITY PRESS

Milwaukee   1958   *Wisconsin*

PREFACE

The research for materials upon which to base this work was undertaken in France and Italy as long ago as 1926 and 1927. Some of the materials were used in a doctoral dissertation submitted in 1928 to the University of California at Berkeley under the direction of Louis John Paetow shortly before his untimely death. The typescript copies of this dissertation are on file in that university library.

In the intervening years, the materials unused in the dissertation were worked into additional chapters far more numerous than the original seven which covered only the foundation of the University of Toulouse and surveyed the history of its first hundred years. The first four chapters of this present volume are reworked from the dissertation, the others are new. Indeed, eight further chapters have been completed which do not appear in this work, but are reserved for future publication. This is possible because the whole project falls readily into two parts of about equal length. The first part — the present volume — is concerned with the origin and external history of the university to 1500, while the second analyzes aspects of its constitutional and administrative growth and the organization and administration of its collegiate institutions. Thus the chronological narrative chapters have been separated from the topical chapters which describe the basic university organizational features such as general congregations, officers, servants, financial administration and various aspects of the growth and activities of the university's colleges. This is mentioned to explain what otherwise must appear as obvious lacunae. It is hoped that the publication of the remaining chapters may not be too long delayed and that chapters on masters and students can be included to complete the second part of the project.

Contents

CHAPTER 1

INTRODUCTION

THE history of a medieval university whose origins go back to the early thirteenth century requires a preliminary sketch of the regional and cultural features that form its background. Since at that time institutions for higher learning were comparatively few, a tendency toward standardization had not as yet set in, so each new *studium* retained the particular flavor and charm of its own locale.

Situated at about a mid-point between the rugged walls of the Pyrenees and the picturesque but less formidable highlands of the Auvergne, and between the marshy shores of the Gulf of the Lion and the sombre *landes* of the Bay of Biscay, is Toulouse. Actually the geographical center of the great sub-Pyrenean region, it tended to become the political center.[1]

Civilization in this area stretches back through long ages. Even in Paleolithic times there were evidences of a not inconsiderable artistic skill, examples of which are still to be seen in its caves. The daring Hellenic seamen from Asiatic Phocaea, who pushed to the far west in the pursuit of trade, established a colony at Massilia toward 600 B.C. in the midst of the aborginal Ligurians. From this center the new cultural element spread gradually, to be given a serious rival within half a century in the less advanced but exceptionally virile Celtic invader. Celts and Ligurians later mingled to such an extent that after a century it was almost impossible to distinguish conqueror from conquered.[2] Roman writers of later date took note of this fusion by applying to the peoples between the Garonne and the Pyrenees the term Aquitanian to distinguish them from the other Celts.

To protect her new Spanish colonies acquired during the Second Punic War, Rome not only occupied the Mediterranean

---

[1] Vidal de la Blache in his *Tableau de la géographie de la France,* which forms the first volume of Lavisse, *Histoire de France,* neatly summarizes the development of this region.

[2] Camille Jullian, *Histoire de la Gaule* (Paris, 1908), I, chap. iv-vi.

litoral of Gaul but also extended her sphere of influence far inland. The coastal areas were soon organized as a flourishing province with its capital at Narbonne, a city not far distant from the Tectosage center of Toulouse.[3] At some epoch, before 100 B.C., the latter city became the ally of Rome. Under that date Dio Cassius records its revolt and attempted union with the Cimbres, a Germanic tribe that had defeated Silanus and had entered Gaul. By Caesar's time, the inhabitants had become so Romanized that warriors from Toulouse could be summoned to aid even in fighting the more independent neighboring Celts.[4]

Of Toulouse itself during the Roman era comparatively little is known. The few evidences there are as to the physical aspects of the city indicate a presumably prosperous urban center divided into four or five parts and surrounded by thoroughly characteristic brick walls.[5] References to *Palladian Toulouse* by no less a poet than Martial—with echoes in Apollinarius Sidonius—seem to indicate that literature flourished, and this is in some measure corroborated by the vogue of its rhetor, Lucius Statius Ursulus. Even after the catastrophic invasion of barbarians from across the Rhine in 276 A.D., which disrupted for some years the placid tenor of provincial life, Toulouse retained her scholastic reputation, for Ausonius of Bordeaux in writing the biographies of noted teachers of his time included several of this city.[6]

[3] References to the early history of this region are to be found in Polybius and Caesar. For the former see Edmund Cougny (ed.), *Extraits des auteurs grecs concernant la géographie et l'histoire des Gaules* (Paris, Société de l'histoire de France, 1879) II, 122-133; and for the latter consult the *de bello Gallico*, I. Passages from Strabo concerning Toulouse are also to be found in Cougny: Book IV, chap. i (Cougny, I, 64-65) Book IV, chap. vi and xiii (Cougny, I, 80-81, and 100-101), and Book IV, Part II, chap. i (Cougny, I, 108-111).

[4] See the long notes of Edward Barry on the Gallic city of Veille-Toulouse in Dom Claude De Vic et Dom Joseph Vaisette, *Histoire générale de Languedoc* (new edition; Toulouse, 1872-1904), I, 167, n. 2; and on Toulouse itself in *ibid.*, II, n. cxvii, 528-549. For the Romans, consult Jullian, III, 63; and Dio Cassius, fragment cclxx of the remains of Books I-XXXVI (Cougny, IV, 221); Justin, XXXII, chap. i (Dom Martin Bouquet, *Recueil des historians des Gaules et de la France* [Paris, 1869-1904], I, 483); and Caesar *de bello Gallico* III, chap. xx.

[5] Ausonius, *Urbes*, 99 (Bouquet, I, 80). "Tolosam, coctilibus muris quam circuit ambitus ingenus." See also Adrien Blanchet, *Les enceintes romaines de la Gaule* (Paris, 1907), pp. 199-202, for a description of these walls. For fragments of sculpture found in the region consult Emile Espernadieu, *Recueil générale des bas-reliefs de la Gaule romaine* (*Collection des documents inédits*, Paris, 1907), I, 472-478; and II, 29-106, who reproduces photographs of these works; and Ernest Roschach, *Histoire graphique de l'ancienne province de Languedoc* (Toulouse, 1904), pp. 211, 225, 227, and 231.

[6] Martial, *liber* IX, epigram 101. Apollinarius, *carmen* vii, 436 (Bouquet,

Tradition brings Christianity to Toulouse about the middle of the third century with Saint Saturninus as its patron. Aside from the details of his martyrdom and the early veneration of the saint there, little is known of its growth. Toulouse, however, has a place of importance in French ecclesiastical annals as one of five sees whose foundations can be traced to this epoch. By the opening years of the fifth century its bishop, Exsuperius, is credited with having completed a basilica to Saint Saturninus and with having carried thither the relics of the martyr.[7]

Through a letter of this same prelate to Jerome, the ravages of the barbarians at Toulouse in 409 have been recorded, for the Vandals before occupying Spain had passed through the area. A few years later another group of invaders, the Visigoths, arrived to make Toulouse one of their principal centers. The Emperor Honorius, who was unable to cope with them otherwise, tacitly recognized the situation, and a kingdom was set up with that city as capital. The Visigothic realm had endured there for about a century when the more enterprising Frankish barbarians drove out their Gothic kinsmen and annexed it to their growing empire.[8] Clovis is reported to have captured Toulouse in 507, seizing the treasure of Alaric which was stored there. Afterwards, under his sons and grandsons, it was apparently ruled by officers responsible to Merovingian kings.

Glimpses of the early history of Toulouse during this chaotic period of Frankish history are to be found in the pages of poets and historians, particularly in those of Fortunatus of Poitiers and Gregory of Tours. The city became the capital of Charibert, a short-lived Merovingian, but thereafter nearly a century elapses before it is again mentioned.[9] It was besieged for a time by a

I, 808). Jullian, VI, 124, n. 9. For Ausonius on the provincial teachers, see *ibid.*, 248, n. 2; and 263-264. For a map of the region during the Roman domination, consult the *Histoire graphique de Languedoc,* plate II.

[7] Gregory of Tours, *Historia francorum,* I, chap. xxx; Jullian IV, 338-339; *Histoire générale de Languedoc,* I, 335-339, and II, p. 58, n. xxxi; Louis Duchesne, *Fastes épiscopaux de l'ancienne Gaule* (2nd ed., Paris, 1907), I, 32, and 306-309.

[8] "Non possum absque lacrymis Tolosae facere mentionem," Jerome, epistle xci (Bouquet, I, 744). For the Visigoths at Toulouse, consult the *Chronicon Moissiacense* (*ibid.*, II, 648); the *Chronicon Idatii episcopi* (*ibid.*, I, 618); and Auguste Longnon, *Géographie de la Gaule au VIe siècle* (Paris, 1878), pp. 39-51.

[9] For Toulouse in the Merovingian era, consult Gregory of Tours, *Historia francorum, liber* III, *cap.* xxxvii; *liber* VII, *cap.* xxvii; *liber* X, *cap.* xxxi; Longnon, pp. 534-537; and the *Chronicon Fredegarii scholastici* (Bouquet, II, 436). See also Fortunatus, *carmen ix.* The shifting divisions of

Saracen leader in 720, and fifty-seven years later King Pepin in
royal progress included it in his itinerary. Toulouse was the seat
of a count in the reign of Louis the Pious, and that monarch held
court there when treating with the Mohammedans in establishing
a frontier. Charles the Bald spent some time in the city during
843 and 844, judging from the number of his charters dated from
there that are extant. In the latter year Toulouse was also visited
by the Northmen who ascended the Garonne, although no mention is made of its capture.[10]

During the early Feudal age a local dynasty of counts developed at Toulouse who soon came to govern almost the whole of
Languedoc. They bore various titles—Duke of Narbonne and
Marquis of Provence—but an unfortunate scheme of inheritance
whereby the patrimony was frequently divided between two sons
weakened the incipient strength of this feudal state. The house
of Toulouse, however, proved sturdy enough to protect itself
against the encroachments of the threatening counts of Barcelona
and dukes of Aquitaine. One of the best known members of
this family was the notable Raymond of Saint Gilles, prominent
as leader of the southern hosts on the First Crusade. In the course
of the twelfth century the area was brought into the conflict that
grew out of the rivalries of Capetian with Norman and Angevin
dynasts. Louis the Young besieged Toulouse in 1141, trying to
make good his wife's claim to it as heiress of the duchy of Aquitaine, while a few years later Eleanor's second husband was
found pressing the same claim.[11]

Gaul in the sixth century may be traced in the series of eleven maps in
the plates at the end of Longnon's volume.

[10] For Carolingian Toulouse, consult the *Chronicon Moissiacense* (Bouquet,
II, 654); the *Annales francorum* (*ibid.*, V, 18); the *Vita Ludovici pii
imperatoris* (*ibid.*, VI, 89, 90-91); the charters in *ibid.*, VIII, 441, 442,
457-459, 461-462, and 464-466. Capitularies were made at Toulouse in
843, (*ibid.*, VII, 598). See also the *Annales Bertiniani* (*ibid.*, VII, 63);
and the note on the Northmen at Toulouse in the *Histoire générale de
Languedoc*, II, n. xcviii, cols. 362-364.

[11] For the feudal epoch, see the *Genealogia comitum Tolosae* of Bernardus
Gui (Bouquet, XII, 372); the *Chronicon S. Maxentii* (*ibid.*, XI,
219); Ordericus Vitalis, *Historia ecclesiastica, liber* XIII, *cap.* xliii
(edited by Prevost, *Société de l'histoire de France*, 1838), V, 132; the
Continuatio historiae Aimonii, ad an. 1159 (Bouquet, XII, 123); William
of Newburgh, *Historia rerum Anglicarum, liber* II, *cap.* x (*Chronicles of
the Reigns of Stephen, Henry II and Richard I* [edited by Hewlett, Rolls
Series, 1876], I, 353); Benedict of Peterborough, *Gesta regis Henrici
secundi* (edited by Stubbs, Rolls Series, 1876), I, 353; the *Histoire générale de Languedoc*, II, n. lxxxvii, pp. 214-233, 295-300; and Luchaire, in
Lavisse, *Histoire de France*, II:II, 304-305. For a map of Languedoc at
this epoch, see the *Histoire graphique de Languedoc*, plate V.

Toulouse was also prominent in the ecclesiastical history of southern France during the early Feudal epoch. Several church councils were held there during the eleventh century, the one in 1090 being designed for the restoration of Christianity at Toledo only recently recaptured from the Mohammedans. Six years later Urban II himself passed through the city where he presided at the consecration of the church of Saint Sernin. In 1119 Calixtus II toured France celebrating a series of councils, one of which was held in Toulouse. In 1161 it was the seat of a very important council for the question was one of papal schism. The decision was there reached to recognize Alexander III.[12] The importance of Toulouse as a religious center is also emphasized in another fashion. The basilica of Saint Sernin, just outside the city walls, had early become a pilgrimage center. One of the most frequented routes to Compostella led through the city, and the many bands of pilgrims would naturally include a visit to the rose brick edifice on their way to the Spanish shrine. An account of the quarrel between the canons of Vioux and the bishop of Albi gives further evidence of the monastic importance of the city. The bishop wanted to expel the ignorant canons and install some monks from Orléans in their place, but the canons persuaded him to give them a period in which to reform their chapter, and then sent some of their members to Toulouse to be taught the rules and customs of community life.[13]

There is no indication, however, of any active intellectual life in the religious establishments of the whole southern section of France. A few twelfth-century catalogues of local monastic houses show a paucity of books that implies a decided lack of

---

[12] *Narratio de instaurato Lactorensi episcopi* (Bouquet, XIV, 28); Bertholdus Constant in his additions to the *Chronicon* of Hermanus Contractus (*ibid.*, p. 676); *Chronicon breve Tolosanum, ad an.* 1096, (*ibid.*, XII, 373 ff.); *Chartularium album Aucensis ecclesiae, cap.* 56 (*ibid.*, XIV, 321); *Chronicon Mauriniacense* (*ibid.*, XII, 73-74); *Gesta in concilio Tholosano* (*ibid.*, XIV, 198); *Chronicon S. Maxentii* (*ibid.*, XII, 406); and Gerhohus Reicherspergensis praepositus, *de revelatione Antichristi, liber* 1 (*ibid.*, XIII, 104, n. 8).

[13] Louis VII, in 1154, commenced a charter, "Ego autem Ludovicus Dei gratia Francorum rex, rediens a Sancto Jacobo et per Tolosam transiens . . ." *Histoire générale de Languedoc*, V, no. 601-CCCCXCIV, col. 1175. See also Joseph Bédier, *Les légendes épiques* (2nd ed., Paris, 1914, 1, 364-429; the *Codex de saint Jacques de Compostelle* (edited by Fita and published at Paris, 1882). A Latin *miraculum* from this codex is quoted in the *Acta Sanctorum* (Bollandists), July, VI, 50, in which two German pilgrims were arrested for bearing off valuables which their host had hidden in their luggage. This is localized at Toulouse with the date 1090. See also the *Notitia de ecclesia S. Eugenii de Viancio* (Bouquet, XIV, 51).

interest in literature in general.[14] Among the notable philoso-
phers and theologians of the eleventh and twelfth centuries, not
one was native to Languedoc. Even the monastic historians are
few in number and of poor quality. On the other hand, charters
and chartularies are exceedingly numerous, testifying to a knowledge of and interest in legal forms. In fact a council held at Montpellier in 1162 found it necessary to forbid monks, regular canons,
and other religious to occupy themselves with secular law or
medicine. This was reconfirmed later at the Council of Tours,
and in 1188 the provost of Maguelonne was authorized to constrain his canons from delving in law, worldly studies or secular
business.[15]

Although the clergy of the region were for the most part intellectually languid, the laity were quite active, particularly
where law, medicine, and vernacular poetry were concerned. The
legal and medical schools at Montpellier were prominent in the
twelfth century, and lawyers and doctors frequently figure in
charters and other documents. For their lyrics the troubadours of
the Midi were justly renowned through all western Europe. Their
verses reflected primarily the life of the nobles and catered to
their taste in a rather stereotyped formalism, but for facility and
beauty of expression these poets were unsurpassed. The theme
of this école courtoise was almost exclusively chivalric love,
which early became a conventionalized system sung with elaborate variations. The writers and singers of these songs, when not
actually noble themselves, were always closely allied with seig-
norial courts, as it was only there that audience and recompense
could be found for their labors. Hagiographic and didactic
poetry in the vernacular were not so popular as in the north
where culture was primarily ecclesiastical. This type of medieval
literature is but feebly represented in Provençal by an eleventh

---

[14] There are two fragmentary catalogues for Moissac published in Léopold
   Delisle, Le Cabinet des manuscrits de la bibliothèque nationale (Paris,
   1874), II, 440-441; a catalogue for Saint-Aphrodise de Béziers of 1162
   ibid., 504-505; and for the priory of Saint Martin de la Canourge in
   Gévaudan for the same century, ibid., 505-506. Neither of the latter
   shows forty titles all told.
[15] The Chronicon S. Saturnini Tolosae is a contemporary chronicle of the
   twelfth century, but does not rise above purely annalistic form. See the
   edition in the Histoire générale de Languedoc, V, 49-54; and Molinier,
   Sources de l'histoire de France, II, no. 1543, p.124. Raymond d'Aguilers,
   the chaplain-historian of the crusading count of Toulouse, was deacon of
   Adhemar du Puy, the papal legate, so cannot be considered a representative Languedocian. For Raymond, see the Histoire littéraire, VIII, 622.
   Molinier remarks the "languishing" interest of Languedoc in historiography up to the thirteenth century, Les sources, II, 118. There is one

century *Life of Saint Foy* of apparent Languedocian origin and by several other *vitae* of inferior merit.[16]

The counts of Toulouse did not figure so prominently as many of the lesser nobles of the Midi as patrons of vernacular literature, but still there is some evidence that troubadours frequented their courts. Several of the more noted poets are connected in one way or another with Alphonse-Jourdain and Raymond V. Among those so connected were Marcabrun, Bernard de Ventadour, and Peire Roger. Peire Ramon, Peire Vidal, and Guiredos lo Ros were actually natives of Toulouse. But in spite of all this indirect evidence of poets at the court of Toulouse—the vernacular biographies from which our information is drawn are not contemporary —there remains not a single verse addressed to a member of the dynasty as corroboratory proof of their patronage. This seems the more strange because panegyric verse was a most respected custom of the age.[17]

In the fields of architecture and plastic art as well as in literature, Languedoc was rising to prominence during the twelfth century. French interest in the struggling efforts of Christian Spain, fostered most sedulously by Cluny, seems to have played an outstanding rôle in spreading certain forms of Romanesque architecture. All along the routes of pilgrimage that led to Spain are found architectural types more or less related but of infinite local variety. Among these regional schools that of Languedoc was influenced both by its Poitevan and Auvergnat neighbors. Although at times it is accused of a lack of originality, it produced monuments of the first order, and had early learned the art of vaulting. One section of this region, that around Toulouse itself, had the further distinction of building extensively in brick, using stone almost exclusively as decoration.[18] The out-

reference to Latin verse-making at Toulouse in a letter of Pierre le Vénérable, *liber* IV, *ep.* 23 (*Historie générale de Languedoc,* III, 757). He praises the verses sent him by a monk of his order as revivifying the ancient art of Toulouse. For the worldly interests of religious of the area, see Molinier, *Les sources,* II, 118; Mansi, *Concilia,* XXI, 1159 and 1176. "Ad leges aut mundana studia aut negotia secularia" in Jaffe, *Regesta,* II, no. 15818, p. 516; no. 16218, p. 544, citing the *Mémoirs de la société de Montpellier,* V, 542.

[16] Alfred Jeanroy, "La littérature de langue française dès origines à Ronsard," in Hanotaux, *Histoire de la nation française,* XII, 249-270.

[17] Paul Meyer, "Les troubadours à la cour des comtes de Toulouse" in the *Histoire générale de Languedoc,* VII, n. lvii, 441-448. The biographies of the troubadours in Provençal, edited by C. Chabaneau, are to be found in *ibid.,* X, n. xxxviii, 218, 261, 270, 271 and 271-273.

[18] See Louis Gillet, *Histoire des arts* in Hanotaux, *Histoire de la nation française,* XI, 73-80; Jose Pijoan, *Historia del arte* (Barcelona, 1915), II,

standing example of this type is the great basilica of Saint Sernin, whose choir, consecrated in 1096, was under construction during the first decades of the twelfth century. In general arrangement it is similar to the churches of the Auvergne which slightly antedate it, but as a whole it bears the greatest resemblance to the cathedral of Santiago de Compostella. The exterior of this vast edifice, where stone is employed so sparingly for buttresses and frames for the round-arched windows—in striking contrast to its rose brick walls—conveys an impression of massive solidity that is unforgettable. The shallow breadth of the double aisles whose successively rising roof levels aid in resisting the thrust of the stone-vaulted nave even heightens the sturdiness of its aspect. The massive, dim interior is of extraordinary height and length, while the reiterated succession of pier and arch to support the barrel vault and the confining strictures of the double collaterals and triforium galleries, which prevent the direct entry of light into the nave, render it even more tunnel-like and heavy. The atmosphere within this sombre structure is dark and oppressive, which is the more remarkable in contrast to its smiling fenestrated exterior.[19]

Little remains of the other early medieval constructions in Toulouse. One much-restored, thirteenth century residence, with two large arches giving entrance to tiny shops on the ground floor and paired windows separated by colonettes on the floor above, gives some idea of the domestic architecture of the region.

279-282; Camille Enlart in André Michel, *Histoire de l'art*, I:II, 558 ff.; Robert de Lasteyrie, *L'architecture religieuse en France à l'époque romane* (Paris, 1912); Emile Mâle, *L'art religieux du XIIe siècle en France* (2nd ed.; Paris, 1924); and Arthur K. Porter, *Romanesque Sculpture and the Pilgrimage Roads* (Boston, 1923). See the chart illustrating the radiation of the architectural school of southern France in Brunhes *Géographie humaine,* in Hanotaux, *Histoire de la nation française,* II, 641-649. Consult also Camille Enlart, *Manuel d'archéologie française* (2nd ed.; Paris, 1919), I:I, 227; Jean A. Brutails, *Précis d' archéologie du moyen âge* (2nd ed.; Paris, 1924), p. 108; Anton Springer, *Handbuch der Kunstgeschichte* (7th ed.; Leipzig, 1904), II, 180; Paul Frankel, *Die Frühmittelalterliches und Romanische Baukunst* (Potsdam, 1926), p. 155; and Eugène Viollet-le-Duc, *Dictionnaire raisonné de l'architecture française* (Paris, 1859), II, 250.

[19] For dating the work on the basilica of St. Sernin, see the selection from the "Vita sancti Raimundi, Sancti Saturnini Tolosani canonici" in Victor Mortet, *Recueil de textes relatifs à l'histoire de l'architecture et à la condition des architectes en France au moyen âge (Collection des textes pour servir à l'étude et l'enseignement de l'histoire,* Paris, 1911), 262. For photographs and plates of St. Sernin and its closely related structures, see Brutails, 110; Viollet-le-Duc, IX, 221; Enlart, I:I, 286; Pijoan, *Outlines of the History of Art* (English translation of his *Historia*) II, 257; de Lasteyrie, pp. 299 and 447; Frankel, pp. 157-158.

It is typical of Toulouse in that it is constructed of flat, rose-colored brick, but it did not have the soaring tower that so frequently distinguished the dwellings of the local nobility. In addition to these existing remains, literary sources mention the famous church of the Daurade, whose primitive octagonal form bore witness to yet more ancient origin, and the double-towered fortress of the Narbonnais which dominated the southern confines of the city and served as a residence for the counts when they sojourned there.[20]

The figurative art of the school of Toulouse was even more distinctive than its architecture. The earliest extant sculpture dates from the end of the eleventh century and consists of three bas-reliefs on the screen between choir and ambulatory in the basilica of Saint Sernin. One of these panels represents a rather oriental, unbearded Christ, seated on a cushioned throne, displaying on His knee an open book, and extending a two-fingered, Roman blessing—the whole enclosed in a mandorla with the winged symbols of the evangelists filling the corners. In this panel and in two others which accompany it, the figures are a trifle stocky and rude, the postures awkward, and the folds of the draperies most conventional. Great advance, however, is shown by the workmanship in the tympanum-relief over the south portal, a representation of the Ascension. Here movement and vivacity are effectively portrayed in graceful gesture and agitation of draperies. The Abbey of Moissac on the Tarn, which at the beginning of the twelfth century was intimately connected with Toulouse through an abbot-bishop, contains several low reliefs of this school and epoch. Decorating one of the mid-point pillars of the cloister is a likeness of this abbot-bishop dressed in pontifical vestments, so exact in detail and of such individuality that it is assuredly a portrait. The celebrated tympanum of the porch of the abbey-church—the extreme date for which is 1115—is a truly magnificent conception, based on the verses describing

---

[20] For the house at Toulouse, see Brutails, p. 218. The soaring tower of one residence is described in a document of 1152, recording the transfer of a piece of property. The house is listed as "inter domum Arnaldi de Vilela et altam domum Arnaldi Fabri," Alexandre Teulet, *Layettes du trésor des chartes* (Paris, 1863), I. no. 122, p. 69. The flat, rose-colored bricks are mentioned in a municipal statute of 1205, which sets the fine for its violation at a thousand flat tiles for the walls of the city. "Et qui contra hos stabilimentum fecerit, det I miliare tegularum planarum nomine pene ad clausuram ville," *Histoire générale de Languedoc*, VIII, no. 126, col. 515. For the plan of the Daurade, see Frankel, p. 9; and for the *Narbonnais*, Viollet-le-Duc, I, 331.

the vision of Saint John. A dignified, bearded Christ, enthroned
in glory and accompanied by the evangelistic symbols and attending angels, is flanked by the twenty-four old men of the
Apocalypse, playing upon their instruments and gazing in en-
thralled rapture at the beatific vision. The majesty and serenity
of the central figure, the vivacity and grace of the animal symbols
and angels, and the remarkable humanity of the twenty-four di-
minutive instrumentalists, make it a veritable masterpiece. The
exquisite intagliated roses of the lintel, showing a decided classic
feeling, the strikingly elongated apostles on the door-frames, and
the characteristic interlaced gazelles of the central pier of the
portal, even heighten the beauty of the composition. Equally
striking are the sculptured apostles from the destroyed cloister of
Saint Etienne, the cathedral church of Toulouse, and the enigmatic female figures bearing shields embossed with the zodiacal
lion and ram, now at the museum of Toulouse. These figures
like many others of the region are notable for the fashion in
which their legs are crossed and the little marks of tiling beneath
their feet—peculiarities which the eminent French archeologist,
Emile Mâle, has traced to Spanish illuminated manuscripts of a
very early date. A twelfth century Annunciation group in full
relief, of life size and rather severe beauty is yet another example
of the versatility of this school. The figures in this work have lost
the exceptional stockiness of the earlier examples, and are more
spiritual and less agitated.[21]

In the minutiae of decoration as well as in the more monumental types of sculpture, the school of Toulouse developed an
extraordinary delicacy and versatility. Especially characteristic
is its narrative art. The storied capitals of the cloister of Moissac,
of the Daurade and of Saint Etienne are marvels of ingenuity
and felicity of expression. One of them, conserved today in the
museum of the Augustins, depicts the banquet of Herod with a
richness of detail that is astounding in consideration of its very
moderate size. Even lovelier are the capitals of a frankly decorative nature. The sculptors seem to have reached highest perfec-

[21] For reproductions of the St. Sernin sculptures, see Brutails, plate III
(opposite p. 111); Michel, I:II, 614 and 616; de Lasteyrie, pp. 641 and
642. For Moissac, consult Michel, I:II, 616 and 619-620; de Lasteyrie,
pp. 640 and 645; Viollet-le-Duc, VIII, 109; Mâle, p. 3; Pijoan (English
translation) II, plate XXIXA; and the selections from the *Chronicon
Aymerici de Peyraco* in Mortet, pp. 146-149. For the museum pieces at
Toulouse, see Mâle, pp. 16-18; Michel, I:II, plate VII; de Lasteyrie, pp.
643-644; Viollet-le-Duc, I, 18, figs.; and Pijoan (English edition) II, 268.

tion in the intertwined foliage, pudics, and grotesques with which these cloisters were ornamented. Mermaids pursuing winged, human-headed lions, centaurs armed with bows and arrows attacking birds with women's heads, and a hunting scene where one huntsman has been seized by the infuriated animal while two of his companions try to extricate him, are among the most striking examples of this type. The figures and foliage in this sculpture are undercut for the most part, and appear almost totally detached from the solid background of stone which they decorate.[22] The sculptors of Languedoc showed great originality in their art even though the elements were borrowed at random far and wide. Byzantine ivories and the local Gallo-Roman sarcophagi seem to have had a most potent influence on the decorative details, while Spanish illuminated manuscripts inspired the tympanum ensembles.[23] The influence of this school of Toulouse radiated quite broadly in southern France; while northern church builders, especially Suger of Saint Denis, sought skilled workmen from the scaffolds of Languedoc, from whence can be traced the earliest steps in the evolution of Gothic art.[24]

It is not surprising, therefore, amid all this flourishing of architecture and art in the early twelfth century to learn that the city of Toulouse itself had been growing. With that century the city entered actively into the communal movement and soon acquired local self-government from its count. He conferred certain privileges on the people and city of Toulouse and the neighboring suburb of Saint Sernin in 1141, but the earliest reference to the *capitouls* or local councillors is not found until eleven years later. At first these officers were six in number, but by 1175 they had been augmented to twelve, six each for city and suburb. A few years later they were increased to twenty-four. Police, local administration, and justice inside the walls were included among the functions they supervised in conjunc-

[22] For the narrative capitals see the reproductions in Viollet-le-Duc, VIII, 125; Mâle, pp. 98, 132 and 181; Henry Revoil, *Architecture romane du Midi de la France* (Paris, 1874), III, plate LXIII; and Roschach, *Histoire graphique*, p. 333. For the grotesques, see Pijoan (English edition), II, 269; and Roschach, pp. 305 and 331. The hunting incident is pictured in Viollet-le-Duc, II, 502.

[23] Michel, I:II, 614. Compare the rather corpulent non-bearded Christ of the sarcophagus picture in Edmond Le Blant, *Les sarcophages chrétiens de la Gaule* (*Documents inédits*, Paris, 1886), plate XXXIX, with the Christ of the choir of St. Sernin. Note also the similarity of the vine used as decorative motive on the sarcophagus in plate XXXVIII, with some of the later floral decoration.

[24] Mâle, pp. 16-18 and 178; Michel, I:II, 632-633.

tion with the count's vicar. General police regulations and market rules were enacted by the *capitouls*, and on many occasions they acted as judges in law suits, confirmed creditors' sales, and drew up elaborate schemes for drainage in the city. Besides maintaining a police force they also seem to have had the direction of the local militia, for in several instances during the wars of Raymond VI the communal army is mentioned. At times the city waged war on its own account, for between 1202 and 1204 there were numerous engagements between the *capitouls* and neighboring lords and communes.[25]

Like all medieval communes, Toulouse was for the most part economically self-sufficient. The town dwellers had landed property in the region from which they received supplies of grain and wine. Practically all foodstuffs were thus secured in the neighborhood, as numerous market regulations bear witness.[26] Among the industries of Toulouse, milling was probably the most important as water power was easily obtainable for this purpose both above and below the city. Here again statutes and the records of lawsuits give data as to the situation of the mills and their practices. Some of the mills were constructed along the banks of the Garonne, while others were operated on boats in

---

[25] See the note on the commune of Toulouse by Roschach in the *Histoire générale de Languedoc*, VII, n. xlvii, 213-253, where he disproves the formerly popular theory of the persistence of Roman municipal government in the city and develops in detail the evolution of the medieval commune. The documents illustrating this growth are to be found in *ibid.*, V, no. 549, cols. 1051-1053; nos. 595-596, cols. 1163-1165; *ibid.*, VIII, no. 24, cols. 315-316; no. 41, col. 356; no. 44, cols. 360-363; no. 46, cols. 364-365; no. 50, cols. 373-374; and no. 52, cols. 376-377. References to vicar and *capitouls* acting in conjunction are found in *ibid.*, V, no. 595, cols. 1163-1165; and *ibid.*, VIII, no. 114, cols. 485-487. For market rules, see *ibid.*, V, no. 596, cols. 1165-1168; *ibid.*, VIII, no. 46, cols. 364-365; and no. 50, cols. 373-374. For the jurisdiction in lawsuits, see no. 24, cols. 315-316; no. 48, cols. 369-371 and no. 100, cols. 455-458. A creditor's sale is authorized in no. 169 and in no. 170, cols. 639-642. No. 41, cols. 356-358 and no. 126, cols. 513-516 have to do with the drainage of the city. For the communal army, see no. 109, col. 478; and no. 122, col. 504; and for the treaty privileges, see no. 109, cols. 476-478; no. 111, cols. 480-483; no. 116, cols. 491-492; no. 117, cols. 493-495; no. 118, cols. 496-497; no. 120, lols. 500-502; no. 121, cols. 502-504; and no. 122, cols. 504-506. See also John Hine Mundy, *Liberty and Political Power in Toulouse, 1050-1230* (New York, 1954).

[26] The landed property of the citizens is referred to in documents in the *Histoire générale de Languedoc*, V, no. 549, cols. 1051-1053; no. 596, cols. 1165-1168; *ibid.*, VIII, no. 64, cols. 392-393; no. 80, cols. 419-421; and no. 108, cols. 475-476. Market regulations are to be found in *ibid.*, V, no. 596, cols. 1165-1168; and no. 165-CXLI, cols. 351-352. Weights and measures are regulated in *ibid.*, VIII. no. 93, cols. 440-441. Prices are set on various articles in no. 46, cols. 364-365. Reference to animal husbandry is to be had in *ibid.*, V, no. 596, cols. 1165-1168.

the stream, or attached to the two principal bridges.[27] Butchers and tanners were also important within the city. The latter agreed to provide gratis all leather necessary in making catapults for the count and "good men" of Toulouse for the privilege of operating within the city. A butcher even attained to the *capitoulate* in 1214.[28] Bakers, wool carders, wool clippers, garment makers, glove makers, fuel and lumber merchants, barrel makers, rope makers, candle makers, harness makers, and cutlers are among the crafts listed in the municipal collection of guild statutes of Toulouse that dates from the end of the thirteenth century, and many of these were no doubt in existence at a much earlier time. Those catering to luxuries rather than to the necessities of life were the workers in buckskin and chamois and the dice makers.[29]

As a commercial center, Toulouse was only of minor importance since it was not situated upon a principal route between the Mediterranean and the North, and the east-west traffic from Narbonne could hardly have been very great. However, the *via Tolosana* which brought so many pilgrims to the city made the keeping of hostelries rather profitable, for in 1205 there is

[27] *Histoire générale de Languedoc*, V, no. 596, cols. 1165-1168; *ibid.*, VIII, no. 48, cols. 369-371; no. 76, cols. 414-416; Teulet, I, no. 416, p. 177; *Histoire générale de Languedoc*, VIII, no. 100, cols, 455-458; and Teulet, I, no. 399, p. 169. There is a reference to a miller in the *Histoire générale de Languedoc*, VIII, no. 41, col. 356. The text reads, "et aque de cornu domus Depratz farinam qui fuit" which is obviously a misreading for *farinarii*. The new editors of this work have advanced the date of no. 48 from 1192 to 1182 upon the authority of a copy in Register JJ, XXI of the *Archives nationales*. This register was made in 1305. See the *Etat somaire par séries des documents conservés aux archives nationales* (Paris, 1891), p. 194. It is to be noted, however, that another document from the same register, bearing the same month and day of the week, and with the same twenty-three *capitouls* named in only slightly different order, is dated and placed by the new edtiors under 1192 in no. 77, cols. 416-417. Yet another document from the same register — unfortunately with the names of the *capitouls* omitted — is the other lawsuit with the same defendant, and also bears the date 1192, no. 76, cols. 414-416. It seems probable that the copy in the register should be in error for the date 1182. Vaisette dated the new edition's no. 48 in the original edition on the authority of a manuscript in private hands, *ibid.*, III, no. LIV, col. 171.

[28] *Histoire générale de Languedoc*, V, no. 624-DXI, cols. 1218-1220; VIII, no. 50, cols. 373-374; and Teulet, I, no. 413, p. 176. "Petrus Vitalis macellarius" is encountered as *capitoul* in the *Histoire générale de Languedoc*, VIII, no. 170, col. 640.

[29] *Histoire générale de Languedoc*, V, no. 549, cols. 1051-1053, no. 596, cols. 1163-1168; VIII, no. 41, cols. 356-357; and Teulet, I, no. 413, p. 176. See the reproductions of the marginal drawings used as symbols for the various crafts in Roschach, *Histoire graphique*, 357. See Sr. M. Ambrose Mulholland, *Early Guild Records of Toulouse* (New York, 1931).

a municipal statute for the protection of the pilgrim from a too grasping inn-keeper. For a municipal inquiry of 1205 the *capitouls* recorded the customs barriers of the region. Of all the toll stations, that at Castelsarrasin on the Garonne seems to have been the most important, for its assessments are extremely varied. From this may be presumed that a considerable part of Toulouse's commerce was with Bordeaux and down-river ports. The route to Spain up the Ariège by way of Foix and Tarascon was marked by three customs stations, at Pamiers, Ax, and Marens, while the overland route to the Mediterranean by way of the gap of the Lauragais had a customs barrier at Castelnaudary. Land routes east to Lavaur and northeast to Rabestans were evidently not so much travelled as no one had set up a toll station along them. The road north to Montauban had a barrier at Saint Jory within eight miles of the city gates, while for continuing north to Moissac another toll had to be paid at Saint Martin de Bellecasse, just outside Castelsarrasin. A well defined highway for importation of salt is marked by the toll stations at Avignonet on the route to Castelnaudary, and at Peixora and Besplas, two villages a few miles to the southeast of the latter city. The merchants of Toulouse were a progressive group, for they actively sought trading privileges and the abatement of tolls in neighboring towns throughout this period. Boatmen of the city were active between Auterive on the Ariège and Martres-Tolosanes on the upper Garonne as far north as the *point* of Moissac—evidently the junction of the Tarn and the Garonne.[30]

This flourishing city of varied and active interests—apparently so ready at the turn of the twelfth century for a continued advance in political power and material civilization—was destined for a long, bitter struggle, which resulted ultimately, after trying transitional years, in its complete absorption into the ever-expanding Capetian realm of France. The underlying cause of this struggle lay in the appearance of the Albigensian heresy. For it was in this rich agricultural region, rimmed by the distant Pyrenees and warmed by a southern sun whose summer rays cast

[30] *Histoire générale de Languedoc,* VIII, no. 126, cols. 513-516; no. 130, cols. 527-530; and no. 123, cols. 507-509. Vidal de la Blache, *Tableau de la géographie de la France,* map opposite page 54, shows a salt mine at Sougraine, a little to the southeast of Couize in the *département* of the Aude. Perhaps it was from there that the salt routes led. For the activities of the boatman, see Teulet, II, no. 2130, pp. 202-203. For the toll-abatements, see *Histoire générale de Languedoc,* VIII, no. 117, cols. 493-495; and no. 122, cols. 504-506.

heavy, humid shadows of ominous languor—conducive perhaps to a certain freedom and laxness—that even in the fourth century there was cause for concern on the part of ecclesiastical authority. Priscillianism, an Iberian heresy, spread through Gaul when its founder traversed this area seeking Rome in an attempt to justify himself. There was a persecution at Bordeaux in 384 but nothing more was heard of it.[31]

Real ecclesiastical difficulties began early in the eleventh century when a wave of Manichaean doctrines entered Gaul, perhaps by way of Armenia, Bulgaria, and Italy. At any rate Ralph Glaber attributed the appearance of heresy to a woman who had come from the last named country. These beliefs spread rapidly in Aquitaine and in the Toulousain, for there is record of the destruction of Manichaeans at Toulouse as early as 1021.[32] Heresy obviously persisted in the area as attested by the reiteration of the canon against Manichaeans in a council of 1119. Further action had to be taken against other types of heresy within a few years. Henricians and Peter Brusians were spreading their doctrines through Provence, Duphiné, and Languedoc. At the request of Alberic of Ostia, the papal legate, Saint Bernard was prevailed upon to make a tour of the Midi in 1147.[33] In a letter to Count Alphonse, the great abbot expressed his astonishment at the headway made by the Henricians in the former's domain.

> The churches are without people, the people without priests, and the priests without due reverence, and indeed the Christians are without Christ. The churches are reputed to be synagogues and the holy sanctuary of God is denied; the sacraments are no longer deemed holy and the feast days are lacking in solemnities. Men die in their sins; their souls are hurried directly before the terrible

[31] For general works on the Albigensian heresy, consult Achille Luchaire, *Innocent III: la croisade des albigeois* (Paris, 1911); and Charles Henry Lea, *A History of the Inquisition in the Middle Ages* (New York, 1906), I, chap. ii-iv, pp. 57-208. Saint Augustine refers to the heretics of this area in his *de natura bona contra Manicheos*. See also the *Histoire générale de Languedoc*, I, 366-367.

[32] *Historiarum libri quinque* of Ralph Glaber (edited by Prou, Paris, 1886), III, chap. viii, pp. 26 and 74. *Chronicon Ademari Cabanensis, ad an.* 1021, "Nichilominus apud Tolosam inventi sunt Manichaei, et ipsi destructi," (Bouquet, X, 159). See also the *Histoire générale de Languedoc*, III, 259.

[33] Mansi, *Sacrorum conciliorum nova et amplissima collectio* (Reproduction in facsimile of the 1784 edition, Paris and Leipzig, 1903), XXI, cols. 226-227; *Vita S. Bernardi auctore Guillelmo abbate S. Theodorici* (Bouquet, XIV, 373); and *Histoire générale de Languedoc*, III, 741-743.

tribunal, alas, neither reconciled by penance nor fortified
with holy communion. The life of Christ is precluded to
the children of Christians since the grace of baptism is
denied.[34]

At Toulouse the noted missionary found only a few weavers
who professed heretical doctrines, and was well received, in
contrast to his less sympathetic reception elsewhere in the
region. Returning to Clairvaux he wrote again to Alphonse,
urging him to persevere in the work of extirpating heresy, for
evidently the saint realized that his efforts there had not been
entirely successful.[35]

The rather heterodox beliefs of the large group of heretics
now classed under the name Albigensian are known only through
the writings of their orthodox opponents. According to one of
these writers, Arian as well as Manichaean errors were found
among them, while there were other heretics—more specifically
the Waldensians—who seemed to have differed from the current
beliefs on points of a puritan nature only.[36] Even the staunch
supporter of Simon de Montfort, Pierre de Vaux-Cernay, admitted that the Waldensians were much less perverse than the
others, and that in many things they were even in accord with
the church.[37] Their chief errors to his mind were in wearing
sandals after the manner of the apostles, in denying oath-taking
and justified homicide, and in asserting that anyone so long as
he wore sandals could in case of necessity consecrate the
Eucharist. The Albigensians were accused of much graver
errors. They believed, it was said, in two creators: one invisible
whom they called the benign god; and the other visible, the
malign. To the benign god, they attributed the New Testament,
and to the malign, the Old Testament, which they repudiated
entirely except for certain parts incorporated in the former and
accepted as worthy because of their reverence for it. The author
of the Old Testament they branded as a murderer because he
was the author of the Deluge, and had destroyed Sodom and
Gommorrah and the Egyptians in the Red Sea. They denied

---

[34] *Epistola* ccxli (Bouquet, XV, 597).
[35] *Histoire générale de Languedoc*, III, 744-746, citing the *Vita S. Bernardi,
liber* III, *cap.* i. The letter is found in Bouquet, XV, 609.
[36] Guillaume de Puylaurens, *Historia Albigensium, prologus* (Bouquet, XIX,
193).
[37] Petrus Vallium Sarnaii monachi, *Hystoria Albigensis* (edited by Pascal
Guébin and Ernest Lyon, *Société de l'histoire de France*, Paris, 1926-
1930), I, 18-19. "Hi quidem mali erant, set comparatione aliorum here-
ticorum longe minus perversi; in multis enim nobiscum conveniebant."

the Incarnation and averred that the "good" Christ had never
been in the world except spiritually in the body of Paul. Other
heretics believed in one creator who had two sons, Christ and
the Devil, and denounced the church as a "den of thieves,"
denying the efficacy of its sacraments. The ranks of these sec-
tarians were divided into the "perfect" or "goodmen" and the
"believers of heretics." The former, who were a group of the elect,
wore black garments, abominated any oath-taking, and refrained
from eating meat, eggs, and cheese. In their asceticism the most
rigid dualists prohibited marriage and shunned the reproduction
of animal life. In these respects they were far superior to the
mere "believers of heretics," who lived secular lives and did not
attain to the austerities of the "perfect," but hoped to be saved
through their faith. The latter were accused of sinning the
more unrestrainedly because they believed that without the
restitution of stolen goods, and without confession and penance,
they would be saved, if only in the hour of death they could
say the *Pater Noster* and receive the imposition of hands from
certain officers knowns as deacons and bishops. This rite was
known as the *consolamentum*.[38] The extreme repugnance in
which they held all that was earthly or of the flesh caused them
to consider the mortification of the body, especially toward the
end of life, as the highest good. For this reason suicide by
starvation—the *endura*—or by poison or blood-letting, was common among them.[39]

As the twelfth century advanced, the heretics grew more and
more numerous. At the Council of Tours in 1163, where Alexander III presided, a canon was directed against them forbidding
any commerce with them and urging the clergy to seek out
and break up their conventicles. It would appear from this
document that it was common opinion that heresy had first
been manifested at Toulouse, and that from there it had spread
to Gascony and other provinces.[40] In 1173 Pons of Narbonne
besought King Louis to take action against the ever-growing
heresy, but warned him not to allow the king of England to
invade France under pretense of settling Toulouse. At the Third

[38] Petrus Vallium Sarnaii, I, 9-18. Corroboratory citations for most of the
statements of Pierre are given in the footnotes, as well as references to
the latest modern authorities on this subject.
[39] For a detailed account of these sects, see Charles H. Lea, *A History of
the Inquisition in the Middle Ages*, I, chap. III, 89-129.
[40] Mansi, XXI, col. 1177, "In partibus Tolosae damnanda haeresis dudum
emersit."

Lateran Council in 1179, anathema was directed against the heretics in Gascony and in the regions of Albi and Toulouse.[41] Etienne de Tournai, writing to his friend the bishop of Poitou, rejoiced that the latter had been translated to the see of Lyon from that of Narbonne to which he had been elected, giving as reason the desperate straits to which the south had been reduced.

> I have seen, formerly in passage when the lord king sent me to Toulouse, a frequent, fervent and terrible image of death; half-ruined walls of churches, charred sites of sacred edifices, uprooted foundations, and — where were once the habitations of men — the uncultivated domiciles of beasts.[42]

This dismal report was further corroborated by Raymond himself. He wrote to the general chapter of Cîteaux for aid in 1177 and pictured the heresy as very prevalent. Aside from the request for counsel and prayers, the count reported that he had already urged his king to come to assist him. Evidently the plea to his suzerain did not fall on deaf ears, for in the following year Louis VII and Henry of England decided to form a joint expedition to extirpate heresy. Upon more mature deliberation, the two monarchs reached a decision that a missionary embassy would be more efficacious, so the pope was petitioned to name a commission of prelates. For that purpose Pietro, cardinal of San Chrysogono and legate of the Holy See, the bishops of Poitiers and Bath, and Henry, abbot of Clairvaux, were selected.[43]

Although they went to Toulouse, their measures to eradicate heresy proved unavailing. In 1191 its bishop was ordered to correct the dissipation in the spiritual and temporal of his church on the pain of ecclesiastical censure. According to Guillaume de Puylaurens, a chaplain of Count Raymond, ecclesiastics did not dare to appear in public with their tonsures visible and heretics were held in such esteem that cemeteries were permitted in which the hereticated could be publicly buried. The bishop himself was reduced to living as a burgher in the episcopal mansion on the little he received from his mill

---

[41] The letter of Pons is in Bouquet, XVI, 159; the canon of the council is to be found in Mansi, XXII, cols. 231-232.

[42] Letter in Bouquet, XIX, 283.

[43] Gervase of Canterbury, *Opera historica* (edited by Stubbs, Rolls Series, London, 1879), I, 270; and Benedict of Peterborough, *Gesta regis Henrici secundi* (edited by Stubbs, Rolls Series, London, 1876), I, 198. The letter of Henri de Clairvaux is quoted in the latter at p, 215.

and oven, for he could collect no share of the tithe, and was compelled even to beg an escort from the nobility when he went on parochial visitations. [44] The problem of simony also appeared at Toulouse in 1201 when Raymond de Rabestens, an archdeacon of Agen, was elected to fill a vacancy in the see. "Because he hastened in the beginning," writes Guillaume, "for the vice of simony he lost the blessing in the end." He squandered the little remaining revenue most recklessly in the course of three years of litigation, engaging even his mills and ovens to creditors.[45] Quite obviously such a candidate was not agreeable to the reforming zeal of Innocent III, who in 1205 sent his legates to Toulouse to depose its bishop for having arranged a pact with several officers of the chapter prior to his election.[46] It was also about this epoch that Diego, bishop of Osma, passed through Toulouse, accompanied by Dominic, then a canon of his church.[47]

To fill the vacancy in the see of Toulouse caused by the deposition of Raymond, Folques de Marseille, a Cistercian abbot from the diocese of Fréjus, was designated. This prelate had been a Provençal poet of some note before entering upon the religious life. According to his biography in the vernacular, he was born in Marseille, the son of a rich Genoese merchant, upon whose death he set himself to the service of the nobility. When Alphonse of Castile was sorely beset by the king of Morocco, this courtly poet made great pleas for his friend to persuade the chivalry of Christendom to come to his aid. Thereafter, wearied of the world, he entered the order of Cîteaux, and was chosen abbot for the house of Toronet.[48] As an ecclesiastic, Folques

---

[44] The letters of Innocent to the bishop of Toulouse are found in Migne, *Patrolgia Latina*, CCXIV, *epistolae* lxxix-lxxxi, cols. 70-71; and in Jaffe, *Regesta*, II, Supplement, no. 1668a, p. 771, citing Douais, *Cartulaire de Saint Sernin*, p. lxi. For the sad state of the See of Toulouse, Guillaume de Puylaurens, *Historia Albigensium, prologus* (Bouquet, XIX, 194) gives much information. Documents witnessed by Guillaume in his capacity of chaplain to the count are to be found in Teulet, II, no. 3467, pp. 603-604; no. 3508, pp. 611-612; and no. 3531, p. 629. They date from 1245 and 1246.

[45] *Historia Albigensium, prologus* (Bouquet, XIX, 199-200).

[46] See the letter depriving one of these canons of the provostship, Migne, CCXV, col. 683. The prelate although suspended was permitted to exercise his former office on solemn feasts when especially invited by the clergy and was provided with an annuity from the episcopal revenues, *ibid.*, col. 682. Raymond is last mentioned as bishop in August of 1205, Teulet, I, no. 780, p. 295. A document of September is dated "Tolosa era senes bisbe," *ibid.*, no. 781, p. 295.

[47] Constantinus Urbevetanus in *Acta sanctorum*, August, I, 395.

[48] Folques is mentioned as bishop-elect in a document of November 6, 1205,

could not have been proud of his colorful past. Verses put into the mouth of the count of Foix by the author of the continuation of the *Chanson de la Croisade,* reproached Folques for his lying songs and verses which caused the eternal ruin of all who sang or recited them.[49] According to Robert de Sorbon, whenever the bishop heard one of his songs sung he fasted on bread and water, upon one occasion even at the table of the king.[50] He was consecrated at Arles in 1206, and entered upon the duties of his office Sexagesima Sunday of the same year, preaching his first sermon on the text from Saint Luke's gospel: "The sower went out to sow his seed" — one quite appropriate, remarks Guillaume de Puylaurens, for a bishop with less than one hundred *solidi* in his treasury, since his bishopric was surely dead and in need of reviving. The degraded state of the episcopal establishment was even further emphasized by the fact that there was no one to lead to the common watering place the four mules which the bishop had brought with him, while the prelate himself was even cited to appear before the municipal court by the creditors of the see.[51] Folques threw himself whole-heartedly into his duties, the most pressing of which were the combatting of heresy and the reëstablishment of his diocese, and went about preaching. His zeal in this work cannot be denied, for he actively supported Simon de Montfort later in the prosecution of the crusade; but the reproaches of bad faith, perfidy, and personal ambition hurled at him by the continuator of the *Chanson* are obviously due to the latter's strong partisanship for the houses of Foix and Toulouse.[52] Guillaume de Tudèle, author of the first portion of the same poem, speaks of him to the contrary in glowing terms; and Guillaume de Puylaurens, friendly to the counts of Toulouse, has also recognized his sterling qualities.[53]

Teulet, no. 784, p. 296. See his biography in the *Histoire générale de Languedoc,* X, n. xxxviii, cols. 289-291.

[49] Canto clxv, ll. 3311-3312 (edited by Paul Meyer, Paris, 1875), I, 147; and II, 178.

[50] "Sermones Roberti de Sorbona" in Hauréau, *Notices et extraits des manscrits,* XXIV, 2nd part, 286.

[51] Bull of consecration, Potthast, *Regesta,* I, no. 2778, p. 238. Guillaume de Puylaurens cites as authority certain sermons of Folques that had been recounted to him (Bouquet, XIX, 199-200).

[52] For support of the character of Folques, consult Stanislaw Stronski, *Le troubadour Folquet de Marseille* (Cracow, 1910), pp. 99-100, where an edition of his works is prefixed by a critical biography.

[53] "L'evesque de Tholosa Folquets cel de Maselha,
    Que degus de bontat ab el no s'aparelha,"
        Lines 1026-1027 (edition of Paul Meyer, I, 48).

In the meantime, other measures were being taken to combat heresy in Languedoc. Diego of Osma, having been refused permission at Rome to resign his see in order to preach the gospel to pagans, returned as far as Montpellier where he met Arnaud, abbot of Cîteaux, with Pierre de Castelnau and Raoul, two Cistercian monks. The legate and his companions were wearied from their fruitless endeavors and were on the point of relinquishing their legation, but the bishop encouraged them and suggested that they go about on foot in imitation of the apostles, and by pious example teach and preach to the people. This Arnaud's companions did while he set off for Cîteaux to hold a chapter general, from which he soon returned with twelve Cistercian abbots to assist in the work. After a period of renewed activity, however, even these returned to the north disheartened, and the death of the bishop of Osma deprived the orthodox of their most active supporter.[54] Meanwhile Count Raymond was doing nothing to assist the Cistercians in their legatine mission of uprooting heresy. Pierre de Vaux-Cernay reports that he even declared to the bishop that Cistercian monks could not be saved and invited the prelate to come to his palace by night to hear the preaching of the heretics.[55] A noble knight of the region, when asked by Folques why he did not expel heretics from his domain, since he acknowledged that their arguments had no strength against orthodox objections, responded that he could not because he had been nursed among them, and plainly saw that they lived honestly.[56] In May of the year 1207, Innocent wrote Raymond reproaching him for his laxity and accused him of refusing to maintain peace with his neighbors and of joining with the enemies of the faith. At the same time the pope confirmed the sentence of excommunication and interdict recently laid on the count by Castelnau, the legate, and Raymond was urged to take immediate steps to arrange for his absolution.[57] This he did and peace was re-established, but matters were fast approaching a crisis. It is

"Erat quippe pro suae bonitatis fama et laboris quem pro fide sustinuerat omnibus reverendus," chap. xxxvi (Bouquet, XIX, 217).
[54] Petrus Vallium Sarnaii (Guébin and Lyon), I, 21-27, 41-49; and Guillaume de Puylaurens, chaps. viii and ix (Bouquet, XIX, 200-201). Diego of Osma died December 30, 1207; Eubel, *Hierarchia catholica medii aevi* (Münster, 1898-1910) I, 382.
[55] *Hystoria Albigensis* (Guébin and Lyon, I, 34). Pierre claims to have had this on the authority of the bishop himself.
[56] Guillaume de Puylaurens, chap. viii (Bouquet, XIX, 200).
[57] Migne, CCXV, cols. 1166-1168.

conceivable that the heresy was so widespread and that the local clergy was so debased in public opinion that the count could take no very active part in opposing the heretics; but his refusal to keep the peace and truce of God, his open persecution of monasteries and his failure to observe other solemn engagements were open flaunts in the eyes of the pontiff.

Innocent had tried everything short of actual military force, and now he began to look even to that eventuality. As early as 1204 he had appealed to Philip Augustus to visit the Midi or to send his son there to constrain its recalcitrant nobles to act more vigorously against heresy, but the king was then interested in seizing Normandy from his powerful neighbor and unruly vassal, John of England.[58] In 1205 and again in 1207 came further appeals from the pope, but the king insisted on a settlement and truce with John as preliminary to any action in the South.[59] Indeed, all such appeals would probably have come to naught, had there not occurred soon after a most unfortunate event which aroused the zeal of all France. Pierre de Castelnau was brutally murdered. The act was committed by a retainer of Count Raymond after an ineffectual conference between the count and Pierre at Saint Gilles. As their relations had been extremely strained for some time it was but natural that the count be accused of connivance. Innocent took decisive action. He ordered the bishops of all ecclesiastical provinces of southern France to excommunicate and anathematize all who aided, received, or defended the murderer, and to place their lands under interdict. He released the vassals of Raymond from all fidelity to their lord, and again besought Philip to take the sword. The king again demurred but finally agreed to permit the duke of Burgundy and the count of Nevers to begin a crusade against the heretics with the proviso that only knights from Burgundy might accompany them.[60]

When Raymond heard of the preparations being made against him in the north, he first hastened to Philip to confer on the matter. Then he sought the legate, the abbot of Cîteaux,

---

[58] Migne, CCXV, cols. 361-362.

[59] The first letter is to be found in Migne, CCXV, cols. 526-528. The other, from the *fonds* Ottoboni of the Vatican Library, is printed in the *Histoire générale de Languedoc*, VIII, no. 138, cols. 557-558.

[60] Guillaume de Tudèle, 11. 79-96 (edition of Paul Meyer, I, 5-6 and II, 5-6); Guillaume de Puylaurens, *Historia Albigensium*, chap. ix (Bouquet, XIX, 201); and the letters of Innocent in Migne, CCXV, cols. 1354-1360. A letter of the King to the Pope from the *fonds* Ottoboni is published in the *Histoire générale de Languedoc*, VIII, no. 138, col. 558.

and begged to be released from his excommunication, which was refused for lack of special instructions from Rome. Finally Raymond turned to his friends the archbishop of Auch and to the former bishop of Toulouse, Raymond de Rabestens, sending them to Rome to plead his cause. They succeeded in having special legates sent out, who solemnly absolved the count at Saint Gilles, whereat he too took the cross with the hope, as Pierre de Vaux-Cernay ascribed it, of protecting his lands from the crusaders.[61]

Meanwhile Innocent had continued to direct the active preparations in France and had conferred special privileges on all who would take part in the expedition to combat heresy. So much enthusiasm was aroused in France by the exhortations of the pope and the preaching of the legates that the proviso of Ph'lip Augustus soon became a dead letter. In fact, the copy of the letter in the chartulary of the king is cancelled, and the presence of the count de Montfort and Gillaume des Roches, seneschal of Anjou, in the crusading army offered ample proof that its dictates were not followed.[62]

Count Raymond, having failed to organize a united front among his own very independent vassals, came to meet the crusaders as they approached Valence. The main body had descended the Rhone from Lyon, and thence was led overland to Montpellier by the count himself. Another group followed a more westerly route southwards and commenced the conquest of the Agenais. Thus the stronghold of heresy was encompassed on two sides. After the capture of Béziers and a cruel massacre of its inhabitants who refused to turn over to the crusaders the heretics listed by their bishop, the main army continued its march to Carcasonne which was also captured. At an assembly of crusading leaders to select a new lord for the conquered cities, Count Simon de Montfort was chosen, and agreed to accept the fief on condition that all nobles there present would come to his aid at any time he saw fit to summon them. Almost immediately, however, the crusading hosts began to dissolve —

[61] Guillaume de Puylaurens, chap. xiii (Bouquet, XIX, 202); Guillaume de Tudèle, canto IX, 11.184-201 (Paul Meyer edition, I, 9-10; and II, 9-10); canto X, 11. 221-223 (Meyer, I, 11; and II, 13); and canto XI, 11. 240-245 (Meyer, I, 12; and II, 14); and Petrus Vallium Sarnaii (Guébin and Lyon, I, 67 ff., and 72 ff.)

[62] Letters of Innocent are found in Migne, CCXV, *epistola* clvi, col. 1469; *epistola* clviii, cols. 1469-1470; and *epistola* ccxxxii, cols. 1546-1547. The cancelled letter of the royal chartulary is printed in the *Histoire générale de Languedoc*, VIII, no. 142, col. 563, footnote 2.

their *quarantaine* of service over — and the new viscount of Béziers and Carcasonne was left to maintain himself as best he could in the midst of his ever-augmenting enemies.[63]

The city of Toulouse along with its count was placed under ban of interdict in 1209 for failure to turn over for judgment the citizens whom Arnaud, the legate, had designated as abettors of heretics. The ban was only rescinded by the pope after special messengers had been sent to Rome for this purpose, and Bishop Folques had interceded with the legate for his city. But apparently Toulouse was not so uniformly orthodox as its citizens had tried to make it appear, for Guillaume de Tudèle recounts how the bishop and legate still went about preaching, exhorting the people to aid in the suppression of heresy and in the combatting of usury. Folques even founded a confraternity for the latter purpose in the city itself, which resulted only in rioting and the foundation of a counter-organization in the quarter of Saint Sernin. Only half of the contributions promised by the city for the cause of the crusaders was collected because of this turmoil, which resulted in the re-excommunication of the *capitouls*. This was relaxed only on new promises and the giving of hostages by the city. In this state of affairs, heresy, loyalty to count, and local patriotism soon became closely identified, in opposition to orthodoxy and the church which had summoned to their aid the detested "foreigner."[64] Indeed, when Count Raymond had entirely failed to gain absolution from the legates and journeyed through his domains publishing broadcast their demands, he was everywhere greeted by the sympathetic indignation of his subjects. Yet the count did not definitely break with his enemies until after the next season's campaigning had well begun, for his presence is noted in the camp of the besiegers at Lavaur, though he quite openly forbade the citizens of Toulouse to furnish them with siege machinery. Despite the obstructions that the count tried to lay in his way, Bishop Folques appeared at Lavaur with a great host of burghers to

---

[63] Petrus Vallium Sarnaii (Guébin and Lyon, I, 85-119); Guillaume de Tudèle canto IX, 11. 195-201 (Meyer edition, I, 10; and II, 11-12); and cantos XV-XXXVIII, 11. 342-886 (Meyer edition, I, 17-41; and II, 20-48). The letters of Innocent and his legates are in Migne, CCXVI, cols. 97-100, and cols. 137-142.

[64] Correspondence between Pope and legates is in Migne, CCXVI, col. 128, cols. 158-160, and cols. 174-175. Letter of the *capitouls* to the King of Aragon is in the *Histoire générale de Languedoc*, VIII, no. 161-CV, cols. 612-619; and also in Teulet, I, no. 968, pp. 368-371. Guillaume de Tudèle, canto XXXIX, 11. 886-891 (Meyer edition, I, 41-42; and II, 48);

assist in the siege.[65] On the capture of Lavaur the crusaders determined that it was time to break with Raymond and concentrate on unruly Toulouse to which he had retired. Bishop Folques, who had remained with the army after his confraternity had returned to the city, now ordered all the clergy to quit Toulouse. Despite the protests of the citizens, the city was put to siege for maintaining its fidelity to Count Raymond, but lack of supplies and the dispersion of the pilgrim-helpers finally forced the northerners to disperse.[66]

Although Innocent had apparently allowed his legates free rein, a letter to Philip indicates that perhaps he was growing a little dubious as to the aim of the crusading forces that he had called into being; for he informed the king that he had warned his legates to guard diligently the rights of the suzerains of Count Raymond. Nevertheless, the pope rewarded prominent ecclesiastics for their services by election to the various sees of Languedoc. Gui, abbot of Vaux-Cernay and uncle of the monk whose *Historia Albigensis* is such an important source for the actions of the crusaders, was elected to Carcasonne in 1211, and Arnaud of Cîteaux, head of the legates for such a long period, was raised soon after to the archbishopric of Narbonne, the most important of all Languedoc. Although such advancement was naturally repellent to the Midi, it must be admitted that there were few among the natives of Languedoc from whom to choose. The incompetency of the former archbishop of Narbonne and his colleague of Auch, which had so scandalized Innocent that he had finally to depose them after long litigations, was perhaps an object lesson in the choice of their successors. It was unfortunate but apparently unavoidable that these offices should be thus filled by those who were so closely identified

and canto XLVII, 11. 1038-1085 (Meyer, I, 49; and II, 56-57); Guillaume de Puylaurens, chap. xv (Bouquet, XIV, 203); and Petrus Vallium Sarnaii (Guébin and Lyon, I, 143) also give information on these matters.

[65] Guillaume de Tudèle, canto LXXVII, 11. 1408-1426 (Meyer edition, I, 65-66; and II, 78-79); and Petrus Vallium Sarnaii (Guébin and Lyon, I, 216-220). The part played by Bishop Folques and his confraternity at Lavaur is described in Guillaume de Puylaurens, chap. xi (Bouquet, XIX, 201-202); and in Petrus Vallium Sarnaii (Guébin and Lyon, I, 220-222).

[66] Guillaume de Tudèle, canto LXXVII, 11. 1731-1741 (Meyer edition, I, 80-81 and II, 95); Petrus Vallium Sarnaii (Guébin and Lyon, I, 232-237); and the letter of the *capitouls* to the King of Aragon, in the *Histoire générale de Languedoc*, VIII, no. 161-CV, cols. 612-619.

with the crusading hosts; but with the medieval attitude toward heresy little else could have been expected.[67]

Affairs went badly for Count Raymond in 1212, for the few gains he had made in the summer of the previous year were soon lost again to Simon. The resumption of the crusade had been preached in France by Jacques de Vitry, Folques of Toulouse, and the Abbot Gui de Vaux-Cernay. As a result, Simon was able to resume the offensive in the following spring. Unable to impede his triumphant progress, Raymond fled to Pedro of Aragon to engage his support, while the northerners ravaged up to the walls of Toulouse itself. Through the mediation of Pedro, one more attempt at reconciliation was made. The pope ordered Arnaud, now archbishop of Narbonne, to hear the complaints of Pedro on behalf of Raymond and the counts of Foix and Comminges. Simon was ordered to restore the lands he had seized from the vassals of King Pedro lest he appear to be acting for his own private gain, and Arnaud was directed to arrange truces in Provence and to desist from convoking armies against the heretics without the special mandate of the pope.[68] Obviously Innocent had decided that affairs in Languedoc had gone far enough, but evidently he did not yet realize that they were beyond his control so long as the existing legates remained in power. Pedro submitted briefs for his vassals and the count of Toulouse to Arnaud who was presiding at a church council at Lavaur. To these a very unsatisfactory reply was returned. The clergy had apparently decided on the utter extermination of the local dynasties with whom they could not get along. They were so embroiled in the heat of the conflict that in their eyes any intervention on behalf of their enemies convicted the intercessor of grave misdemeanor, even though he be such a staunch friend of the papacy and as renowned a fighter of Saracens as Pedro of Aragon fresh from his victory at Las Navas.[69] The pope succeeded, however, in stopping the inflow of crusaders from the north by deflecting them to the Holy Land, and Pedro retired to Aragon where he mortgaged a part of his land and collected an army for the inevitable conflict with Simon. Messengers from the clergy of Languedoc finally convinced the pope

---

[67] Letter of Innocent to the King in Migne, CCXVI, cols. 524-525; and Petrus Vallium Sarnaii, (Guébin and Lyon, I, 292-293).

[68] Petrus Vallium Sarnaii (Guébin and Lyon, I, 281-283; II, 56-58). The letters of the Pope are in Migne, CCXVI, cols. 739-743; and 744-745.

[69] Petrus Vallium Sarnaii (Guébin and Lyon, II, 66-95). The pleas of Pedro to the prelates are found in Migne, CCXVI, cols. 839-840.

that heresy was more prevalent in the Midi than the messengers of King Pedro would have him believe, whereafter he directed reproving letters to the king, ordering him to keep strict peace with Count Simon.[70]

The defeat of Pedro and his vassals and allies at Muret in 1213 was a crushing blow to the fortunes of Count Raymond. Pedro of Aragon was killed and the excommunicated counts were dispersed. A new host was recruited in the North, and at a church council held in Montpellier it was proposed that the lands of Raymond be conferred on Simon. The pope, however, reserved decision on the details of the disposition of these lands for the imminent general council. Raymond, who journeyed in person to Rome, found in Innocent a much more sympathetic judge than any of his legates had ever been. The legates were even ordered to provide for the count out of revenues from his sequestered estates though their custody had been turned over to Count Simon. When the Fourth Lateran Council finally assembled in Rome in 1215, among other matters of equal or greater importance, the affairs of the count of Toulouse were also settled. Simon de Montfort was confirmed in his possession of the major part of Languedoc, including the county of Toulouse, but Raymond's lands in Provence were reserved as a patrimony for his heir, and the exiled count was guaranteed a pension of four hundred pounds annually. The old count retired into exile in Spain, leaving behind him in Provence a very determined young Raymond whose intention was to wrest back from the invader all the lands of his patrimony. Between Simon and the young Raymond there was soon war on the banks of the Rhone.[71]

Nor did Count Simon, now that the relative positions of defender and invader of the county of Toulouse had been ex-

[70] See the letters of the Pope in Migne, CCXVI, cols. 817-822, 827-828, and 849-852. See also Petrus Vallium Sarnaii (Guébin and Lyon, II, 128-135); the *Gesta comitum Barcinonensium et Aragoniae regum* (Bouquet, XIX, 233); and Guillaume de Tudèle, canto CXXI, ll. 2756-2768 Meyer edition, I, 125; and II, 151).

[71] Petrus Vallium Sarnaii (Guébin and Lyon, II, 138-176, 236-275); the *Chanson de la croisade*, now the work of a continuator, cantos CXXXVII-CXLI, ll. 2931-3134, and cantos CXLIII-CL, ll. 3161-3593 (Meyer edition, I, 131-140, and II, 158-169; and I, 141-158, and II, 171-193); Guillaume de Puylaurens, chaps. xxi-xxii, and xxvi (Bouquet, XIX, 206-209, and 211); Migne, CCXVI, cols. 959-960; Teulet, I, no. 1099, pp. 410-411, no. 1113, pp. 413-414, nos. 1115-1116, pp. 415-416, and no. 1153, p. 420; and the *Histoire générale de Languedoc*, VIII, no. 186-cxix, cols. 681-682.

changed with Raymond, find it any easier to protect his domains. The two Raymonds timed operations well, for the young count besieged Beaucaire while Toulouse got into communication with the old count in Spain. Enraged at the threatened defection of Toulouse, Simon negotiated in Provence and hastened back to his capital city, which he reduced to submission before returning to the Rhone with a vast multitude of hostages and a huge indemnity with which to continue war. But despite these precautions, the city of Toulouse received its old count with transports of joy when he crossed the Pyrenees and reëntered it in triumph. The French garrison took refuge in the Narbonnais while Raymond and the burghers prepared the city for siege. Their efforts were successful for Count Simon never regained Toulouse. After nine months of siege he was killed by a stone hurled from a machine on its walls. With this the siege was raised and the crusading host dispersed to their homes in France.[72]

Once again the crusade was revived. Amauri de Montfort was confirmed by Pope Honorius III in the possessions of his father, and Philip Augustus and his son Louis were urged to take the field in person. In 1219 Louis of France actually appeared in Languedoc at the head of a crusading army, but his siege of Toulouse was also a failure. The succeeding years were filled with activity for Raymond, and with growing discouragement for Amauri. Each year saw Raymond in possession of a few more of the cities of his patrimony and Amauri clinging more precariously to his in spite of the aid of pope and legate who confirmed him in his possessions.[73] Under 1221 the chronicle of Aubri des Trois Fontaines records the loss of the greater part of all the lands acquired from the Albigensians in the course of

[72] For Simon as count of Toulouse, see Guillaume de Puylaurens, chap. xxvi (Bouquet, XIX, 211). A document of October 22 of this year carries his name as count, (Teulet, I, no. 1193, p. 434). For the continued campaigns, see Petrus Vallium Sarnaii (Guébin and Lyon, II, 275-280, and 293-319); Guillaume de Puylaurens, chaps. xxix-xxx (Bouquet, XIX, 212-213); and the *Chanson*, cantos CLXXI-CLXXIX, ll. 4965-5651, cantos CLXXXI-CLXXXIII, ll. 5709-5975, and cantos CXCIX-CCVI, ll. 7670-8548 (Meyer edition, I, 213-239, and II, 260-290; I, 242-252, and II, 295-307; and I, 314-345, and II, 385-424). The letters of Honorius are found in Bouquet, XIX, 641-649.

[73] The efforts of Honorius to revive the crusade are to be found in Petrus Vallium Sarnaii (Guébin and Lyon, II, 321); Teulet, I, no. 1331, p. 475; and Bouquet, XIX, 664-667 and 669-672. Affairs in Languedoc are described in Guillaume de Puylaurens, chap. xxxii (Bouquet, XIX, 214); the *Chanson*, cantos CCIX-CCXIV, ll. 8790-9578 (Meyer edition, I, 335-384 and II, 434-478); and Aubri des Trois Fontaines, *Chronica, ad*

fifteen years.[74] Amauri and Raymond continued the struggle a few years longer, each styling himself "Duke of Narbonne, Count of Toulouse, and Marquis of Provence," but the power of perseverance and vigorous action had changed sides since the death of Simon, and success finally went to Count Raymond, owing to the genius of his young son. The latter appears to have been director and leading spirit in all the moves since the siege of Toulouse in 1218. He soon proved himself a rather clever strategist in weakening the hold of Amauri on Languedoc. In 1224 the end came. Amauri withdrew to Paris, where soon after he ceded to his king all rights over the county.[75]

Raymond had meanwhile been sounding out the court of Rome. Honorius replied by promising a new legate, Romano, cardinal-deacon of San Angelo, and in ordering the archbishop of Narbonne to investigate matters toward a reconciliation. In 1225 the promised legate was sent to France and a council held at Bourges in November on the subject of heresy, but the attempted reconciliation between Raymond and Amauri proved a failure. The clergy then decided to appeal once again to Louis for his support, and voted a tithe on all their property for a resumption of the crusade. Evidently Romano pressed matters actively, for in January of 1226, at a great council held in Paris, twenty-nine of the chief barons of the realm petitioned Louis to undertake a crusade, and the legate and prelates, in the same month, announced that the king had taken the cross.[76]

an. 1219 (*Monumenta Germaniae historica,* XXIII, 909). Further efforts of Honorius to aid Amauri are found in Guillaume de Puylaurens, chaps. xxxiii-xxxiv (Bouquet, XIX, 214-216); and the texts of papal letters in Bouquet, XIX, 686 and 696; and in Teulet, I, no. 1435, p. 511, and no. 1456, pp. 518-519; and in the *Histoire générale de Languedoc,* VIII, no. 211-CXXXIV, i-vi, cols. 738-742.

[74] *Op. cit.,* (*Monumenta Germaniae historica,* XXIII, 912). Further efforts of the Pope to renew the crusade are attested by letters in Bouquet, XIX, 715, 716-717, and 719; and in Teulet, I, no. 1534, pp. 544-545; and Bouquet, XIX, 740-742.

[75] Amauri used the title, apparently for the last time, in a document dated January 15, 1224, to be found in the *Histoire générale de Languedoc,* VIII, no. 230-CXLIX, ii, cols. 781-782. In February he ceded his claims to Louis, *ibid.,* no. 233-CLII, cols. 789-790.

[76] Concerning the new legate, see the *Histoire générale de Languedoc,* VIII, no. 228-CXLVII, iii-vi, cols. 775-778; and Bouquet, XIX, 764-766; and Teulet, II, no. 1695, p. 47. For the Council of Bourges, see Aubri des Trois Fontaines, *ad an.* 1225 (*Monumenta Germaniae historica,* XXIII, 917); the quotation from a manuscript of the queen of Sweden as given in the *Histoire générale de Languedoc,* VIII, no. 242-CLX, cols. 815-816; the letter of Romano in *ibid.,* no. 267-CLXXXI, cols. 866-868; the proceedings of the council in Mansi, XXII, cols. 1213-1220, after the *Chronicon Turonense* and Matthew Paris; selections from the former in

When the news of the proposed expedition reached the south, letters of submission and fidelity and proffers of aid soon came pouring into the royal chancery from nobles great and small; and several cities renounced their connections with Raymond and made peace with the king and the church. Even Jaime of Aragon forbade his subjects to receive any refugees from across the mountains.[77] With the arrival of summer, the expedition proceeded down the Rhone until it was arrested by a defiant Avignon that refused free entry to the king. After a siege of three months, Avignon submitted. Thereafter there were submissions by other cities and the hosts directed their route to the west. Skirting Toulouse they turned north; but before they could reach Paris, Louis VIII had died, leaving his kingdom to a youthful son and regency to his Spanish widow. The disorders accompanying the minority of Louis IX delayed further expeditions, although hostilities continued fitfully through 1228.[78]

Romano, returning from Rome where he had consulted with the pope on Albigensian affairs and had been confirmed in his legation, had been advised to make one more effort toward peace. Gregory IX at the same time requested the general chapter of the Cistercian order to pray most particularly for the success of the endeavors of his legate, while Romano was authorized to make certain dispensations so that all foreign complications might be settled and the way left clear to put an end to the troubles in the south. In case the count of Toulouse would consider a reconciliation, it was left to the discretion of the legate even to issue dispensation for the marriage of the king's brother with Johanna, the daughter of Raymond. So armed, the legate was soon able to reach an understanding with the count and people of Toulouse, after the abbot of Grandselve,

Bouquet, XVIII, 309; and a letter of Honorius in the Histoire générale de Languedoc, VIII, no. 228-CXLVII, vii, cols. 778-779. The Council of Paris is reported in Teulet, II, no. 1742, pp. 68-69; no. 1743, pp. 69-70; the Histoire générale de Languedoc, VIII, no. 244-CLXII, cols. 817-818; the Chronicon Turonense (Bouquet, XVIII, 309); and a letter of Honorius in ibid., XIX, 771-772.

77 Teulet, II, no. 1747, pp. 71-72; nos. 1752-1757, pp. 73-74; nos. 1759-1760, pp. 75-76; nos. 1766-1767, pp. 78-79; no. 1775, p. 81; no. 1776, pp. 81-82; no. 1788, p. 87; nos. 1785-1786, pp. 84-85; and no. 1758, p. 75.

78 Teulet, II, no. 1790, p. 89; no. 1787^2, pp. 648-649; no. 1788^2, pp. 649-650; no. 1794, p. 90; nos. 1777-1778, pp. 82-83; Histoire générale de Languedoc, VIII, no. 250-CLXVII, cols. 832-834; Guillaume de Puylaurens, chaps. xxxv and xxxvi (Bouquet, XIX, 216-217); Aubri des Trois Fontaines, (Monumenta Germaniae historica, XXIII, 918-919); and the Gesta Ludovici VIII, ad an. 1226 (Bouquet, XVII, 310).

Hélie, had been sent to the south with an offer. The terms of the treaty with the king, which were confirmed later by Raymond, were arranged at Meaux in January, where the abbot acted as the count's attorney.[79] These permitted him to retain all of his lands lying in the bishoprics of Toulouse, Agen, Rodez, and Albi, with certain minor exceptions, on condition that he make his daughter sole heir and consent to her marriage with Alphonse of Poitiers. In case the two should die without issue, the lands in Languedoc were to go unconditionally to the king, and those beyond the Rhone in Provence, to the legate in the name of the church. For what remained of the once vast, almost independent county, Raymond was to swear homage to Louis, to whom were also to be given in pledge many of his strongest castles. Such was the cost, after nearly twenty years of warfare, of peace with king and church. Raymond and Languedoc, exhausted, were helpless to do other than accept, so on April 12, 1229, before the doors of the cathedral of Paris, after signing the treaty in its definitive form, Raymond was solemnly absolved by the legate and an epoch of war and strife was officially closed.[80]

[79] Guillaume de Puylaurens, chaps. xxxvii-xxxix (Bouquet, XIX, 218-219); Aubri des Trois Fontaines, *ad an.* 1228 (*Monumenta Germaniae historica*, XXIII, 921); Potthast, *Regesta*, I, no. 8151, p. 702; Auvray, *Les régistres de Grégroire IX* (Paris, 1896-1908) I, no. 232, col. 143; no. 233, col. 144; nos. 229-230, cols. 139-143; no. 234, col. 144; no. 238, col. 146; no. 236, col. 145; no. 237, col. 145; and Teulet, II, no. 1969, pp. 140-141. The preliminary arrangements for the peace were made at Toulouse in December, *Histoire générale de Languedoc*, VIII, no. 270-CLXXXIII, i, cols. 878-879. Definite provisions were drawn up at Meaux, no. 270-CLXXXIII, ii, cols. 879-883.

[80] The treaty in final form is given in the *Histoire générale de Languedoc*, VIII, no. 271-CLXXXIV, cols. 883-893; and in Teulet, II, no. 1992, pp. 147-152; another copy of the treaty is indicated in the note which follows the text in Teulet, II, pp. 152, and is also found at the end of one of the registers of Gregory IX, Auvray, II, no. 4784, cols. 1274-1282, dated April 10. Yet another text is found in *ibid.*, no. 4785, cols. 1282-1284. See also Guillaume de Puylaurens, chap. xl (Bouquet, XIX, 219).

CHAPTER 2

THE ORIGINS OF THE UNIVERSITY

HIDDEN away among the territorial arrangements, promises to extirpate heresy and respect the rights of the church, and provisions for indemnities and enforcement of the Treaty of Paris of 1229, there was a clause to which the University of Toulouse owed its birth.

> Likewise, four thousand marks shall be set aside by us for four masters of theology, two decretists, six masters of the liberal arts and two grammarians, teaching at Toulouse, which shall be divided in this manner: each of the masters of theology shall have fifty marks a year for ten years; each of the masters of decrees shall have thirty marks a year for ten years; similarly each master of arts shall have twenty marks annually for ten years; and each of the masters of the grammatical art shall likewise have ten marks annually for ten years.

Although no mention was made of such a clause in the preliminary arrangements dating from January of that year, the treaty in final form included it along with many others applying more directly to the church and repression of heresy.[1] This idea was due probably to the legate, for it was to him that John of Garland, one of the original professors of the University of Toulouse, attributed the activity behind its founding.[2]

Before the thirteenth century it had apparently not occurred to kings and princes that institutions of higher learning could be artificially propagated. In fact most of the great medieval universities that can prove their existence at an earlier epoch

[1] *Histoire générale de Languedoc,* VIII, no. 270-CLXXXIII, ii, cols. 879-883; and no. 271-CLXXXIV, cols. 883-892.
[2] John of Garland, *De triumphis ecclesiae libri octo,* edited by Thomas Wright, (London, 1856), p. 73. Cited also in Marcel Fournier, *Les statuts et privilèges des universités françaises* (Paris, 1890-1892), I, no. 508, p. 442. "Romanus studium sanxit in urbe novum."

owed their prosperity to the fame of their masters — the physicians of Salerno, the lawyers of Bologna, and the logicians of Paris. Thus it was of vital importance to the sometimes inappreciative townsmen when masters of a well-established *studium* migrated to another locality and gave birth, temporarily at least, to a new academic center. These migrations became very frequent by the first quarter of the thirteenth century and were particularly numerous in Italy where Vicenza, Arezzo, and Padua appeared as offshoots of Bologna before the quarter-century mark had been reached.[3] Indeed, even earlier than prelates and magnates, the burghers of northern Italian cities realized the advantages from a purely mercenary point of view of a university within their walls, and their rivalry soon extended to furtive attempts at luring particularly brilliant teachers from the schools of neighbors. For this purpose attractive offers of privileges were made which occasionally even included promises to pay magisterial salaries, or what today would be called the endowment of chairs.[4] This rapid and more or less spontaneous multiplication of *studia* during the early years of the thirteenth century may have suggested to the rulers of more extensive realms that they might actually found universities to compete with distant and renowned centers of learning, and thereby keep at home their ambitious subjects who sought the stamp of Paris or Bologna as prerequisite to an ecclesiastical or legal career. About 1212, at the suggestion of his councillor, the bishop of Palencia, Alfonso VIII of Castile invited masters from France and Italy to the already existing cathedral school at Palencia and endowed them with salaries. His successor gained the permission of Honorius III in 1220 to divert a fourth part of the ecclesiastical revenues devoted to the maintenance of churches for the payment of professorial salaries. A university was also created at Naples in 1224 by Fredrick II for a similar purpose. To insure its success, he forbade any student to leave his realm of Sicily and enjoined those already studying abroad to return. He, too, seems to have planned the payment of salaries to his carefully

[3] H. Denifle, *Die Entstehung der Universitäten des Mittelalters bis 1400,* (Berlin, 1885), pp. 298, 424 and 277; and Hastings Rashdall, *The Universities of Europe in the Middle Ages* (Oxford, 1895), II:I, 7, 8 and 10.

[4] There is a contract for a migration from Padua to Vercelli in 1228, carrying such a clause—Rashdall, II:I, 12. Salaries for professors in Italy seem to have been quite commonly provided by municipalities, for there are numerous contracts of somewhat later date, for example at Reggio—*ibid.,* 7; Padua, *ibid.,* 17; Sienna, *ibid.,* 32; Perugia, *ibid.,* 40; and Treviso,

selected group of masters.[5] Thus, within the two decades immediately preceding the appearance of the *studium* at Toulouse in 1229, precedents can be found for the actual conditions of its foundation.

Although the idea cannot be considered as original with him, Romano Bonaventura, who had been raised to the cardinalate in 1216 not long before the death of Innocent III, was indeed the moving power behind the university. The legate was probably a Roman, but nothing can be ascertained about the place or type of his early training. During the early years of the pontificate of Honorius III, he was apparently occupied in duties that required his presence in the Curia, judging from the frequency with which his subscription is encountered on papal privileges.[6] Being thus closely connected with the court of Honorius, Romano was no doubt familiar with the attempts of that pope to re-establish orthodoxy in Languedoc. On being sent to France in 1225, he was almost immediately engaged in endeavors to settle disputes that had arisen at Paris between the chancellor and the university. When the legate had ordered the seal of the arts faculty broken, it so infuriated the masters and students that his house was attacked by a mob, and was saved only by the intervention of the king.[7] Two years later in arranging a peace with the city of Avignon for having opposed the crusaders in their march to the south the preceding summer, Romano had included among other clauses provisions for pay-

ibid., 43. See also his discussion of municipal schools in general, ibid., 35-36.

[5] For Palencia, see Rashdall, II:I, 65-67. For Naples, consult ibid., 22; and Jean Louis Alphonse Huillard-Bréholles, Historia diplomatica Friderici secundi (Paris, 1855), II:I, 450. "Conditiones disponimus, magistros investigamus, bona promittimus, et eis quos dignos viderimus donaria conferemus."

[6] Ulysse Chevalier, Biobibliographie (Paris, 1907), II, col. 4061; and Eubel, Hierarchia catholica medii aevi (Munster, 1913), I, 4. L. de Mas Latrie, Trésor de chronologie d'histoire et de géographie pour l'étude et l'emploi des documents du moyen âge (Paris, 1889), col. 1180, has assigned Romano to the promotion of 1212, but the earliest document to which he subscribed as cardinal deacon of San Angelo dates from April 13, 1216—Potthast, Regesta, I, no. 5100. There is a letter of a register of Innocent III addressed to "Romano archipresbytero et clericis sanctorum martyrum Sergii et Bacchi" for June 26, 1199. This may possibly be the future cardinal of San Angelo, Migne, CCXIV, epistola cii, cols. 651-653.

[7] Rashdall, I, 319; Aubri des trois Fontaines in Monumenta Germaniae historica, XXIII, 917; H. Denifle and E. Chatelain, Chartularium universitatis parisiensis (Paris, 1889-1897), I, no. 58, p. 113, and no. 165, p. 194. The passage from the Chronicon turonense describing the riots may be found in Mansi, XXII, col. 1215.

ment and apportionment of the tithes of the city. Eighty pounds *tournois* were to be assigned in benefice annually to a master of theology, and the bishop, from his portion of the remainder, was to provide for twelve poor students in the same faculty. It would thus appear that the endowment plan for Toulouse may well have been the suggestion of the legate. In 1229 he was again embroiled in academic squabbles at Paris, so his experience in such matters was not inconsiderable.[8]

The actual details of organization, however, appear to have been delegated to other hands. Hélie Guerin, abbot of Grand-selve, was evidently a figure of some importance in the eyes of both Romano and the count of Toulouse. The Cistercian house of Grandselve had received numerous privileges from the counts of this line since its origin in the twelfth century,[9] and the young Raymond had renewed the promise of protection in its favor even before the death of his father, while the war with the French was still in progress. Although the abbey had suffered from the prolonged hostilities and was beneficiary to an amende of 1,000 marks on the part of Raymond by the treaty of 1229, still Hélie, who had become abbot in 1224 after the bitterest part of the war was over, was a party more or less agreeable to both sides.[10] Romano had chosen him as bearer for the project of peace in 1228, and Raymond in turn had named him his procurator for the meeting at Meaux in January. Being the abbot of the nearest Cistercian house to Toulouse, he may have been suggested for this service by Folques who, before reaching episcopal rank, had been monk and then abbot in that order. At any rate it was upon Hélie that the choice of masters finally devolved.[11]

The idea of choosing teachers from Paris, the recognized center of all theological studies, to direct instruction in distant

---

[8] Fournier, *Statuts*, II, no. 1236, p. 301, dated January 4, 1227. John of Garland dedicated to him his *Epithalamium*. I owe this reference to the kindness of my master, the late Louis John Paetow of the University of California.

[9] *Histoire générale de Languedoc*, VIII, Inventaire de l'abbaye de Grand-selve, no. vii, col. 1756; no. ccxxxi, col. 1783; nos. cccxl-cccxli, col. 1797; no. dlxxxii, col. 1828; no. dxcviii and no. dci, col. 1831; no. dcli, col. 1838; no. dcxciii and no. dcxciv, col. 1843; no. dccxxx, col. 1848; no. dccxxxiv, col. 1849; and no. dcclvi, col. 1852.

[10] *Ibid.*, no. dcclxxvi, col. 1855; and *Gallia christiana* (1874), XIII, col. 134.

[11] John of Garland, *De triumphis ecclesiae* (Wright), p. 73.
  "Sed Grandis Silve pius abbas dictus Helyas,
    Sub duce legato, proximo frena capit.
  Parisius doctos abbas elegit . . . ."
    (Printed in Fournier, *Statuts*, I, no. 508, p. 442.)

and somewhat suspect regions was hardly a new one. Himself
a product of Paris and Bologna, Pope Innocent III had directed a
letter, after the foundation of the Latin Empire at Constantinople
in 1205, to the masters and scholars of Paris, urging that some of
them set out for Greece where they could render great aid in
reforming "the *studium* of letters."[12] In imitation of his predecessor, Honorius III had in 1217 requested masters and scholars
of the same *studium* to proceed to Toulouse — newly won back
from heresy — to lecture, preach, and exhort the people in order
that they might not return to their former errors. It is doubtful
whether more was intended by this letter than mere missionary
expeditions, since there was no hint of permanent organization
of any kind, and nothing other than an accumulation of re-
wards in heaven was offered to those who should go. Honorius
wrote just one week later in the same vein to the "prior and
brother preachers of Saint Romain" at Toulouse — the then
recently organized Dominicans — urging them to evangelize op-
portunely and inopportunely. "If you should suffer for this," he
continued, "you will accept it with equanimity, and take glory
with the apostles that you were held worthy to suffer in the
name of Jesus." Quite obviously this was all part of the same
plan.[13]

Just at the epoch when Hélie must have been searching for
candidates to fill the newly arranged masterships, conditions in
the Parisian schools tended to make his commission the easier.
In the suburb of Saint Marcel, a riot had taken place when
certain students had retired to its more open fields for the
customary games that marked the pre-Lenten holidays. Because
of the injury done his men, the prior of Saint Marcel had complained bitterly to the legate and to the bishop of Paris, and

---

[12] *Gesta Innocentii PP. III,* (edited by Baluze) in Migne, CCXIV, col. xvii.
The letter of the pope to Paris is found in *ibid.,* CCXV, *epistola* lxxi,
cols. 637-638; and Denifle, *Chartularium,* I, no. 3, p. 62.

[13] The letter of Honorius to Paris is to be found in Denifle, *Chartularium,*
I, no. 25, p. 83; and Fournier, *Statuts,* I, no. 502, p. 437. Saint Dominic
founded a house for women converts at Prouille in 1207—*Histoire générale de Languedoc,* VIII, no. 137-LXXXVI, cols. 552-553. Folques of
Toulouse made several gifts to Dominic and his canons in 1211 and 1212
—*ibid.,* cols. 553-557; and in 1215 donated a hospice near one of the
gates of Toulouse to them—*ibid.,* no. 184-CXVIII, vi, col. 676. The quotation from the bull of Honorius III is found in a register of that Pope
in the Bibliothèque, Nationale, MS. lat. 3934, f°49. The same is cata-
logued in Potthast, *Regesta,* I, no. 5434, p. 479. "Datum Laterani, vii
kal. Februarii, pontif. nostri anno primo." The Dominican order had been
confirmed by Honorius in a bull of December 22, 1216—*ibid.,* no. 5402
and no. 5403, p. 476.

they had turned the matter over to Queen Blanche for adjudication. She had immediately ordered her provost to punish the culpable, and her commands had been followed with more than justifiable rigor, for a group of innocent students engaged in games outside the walls of the city had been set upon by the royal officers. In the fracas some had been killed and many wounded, and others thrown into the Seine.[14] The masters of the university, horrified at this action, immediately complained on their part to the queen and legate, demanding satisfaction which was not forthcoming. The quarrel between the university and the townspeople grew daily more heated so no settlement could be reached. At last, toward the end of March, the university issued an ultimatum threatening a six year cessation unless their grievances were redressed within a month after Easter.[15] Their efforts still unavailing, the masters and students began to disperse. At the invitation of Henry III some of them fled to England; others sought refuge in places nearer at hand, such as Orléans and Angers; a few set out for Rome to gain the intercession of the pope.[16] The fact that the legate himself was *persona non grata* to the party of the university perhaps accounts for the choice of the abbot of Grandselve as commissioner for the selection of masters for Toulouse. How successful he was cannot be definitely determined, for the only master whose name is known, John of Garland, is the source of this information itself.[17]

Nor is the epoch of the departure of the masters for Toulouse any more certain. If the statement in the *De triumphis ecclesiae*, John's epic poem, that they accompanied the legate southward is to be taken literally, then it could not have been before autumn of 1229.[18] On the other hand the legate's assistant,

---

[14] This is described by Matthew Paris in his *Chronica majora* (edited by Luard in the Rolls Series, 1876), III, 166-169; and in the *Historia Anglorum* (edited by Frederic Madden in the Rolls Series, 1866-1869), II, 308.

[15] Decree of the twenty-one provisors, dated March 27, in Denifle, *Chartularium*, I, no. 62, p. 118.

[16] Denifle, *Chartularium*, I, no. 64, p. 119; Matthew Paris, *Chronica majora*, III, 168; and *Historia Anglorum*, II, 309; and Denifle, *Chartularium*, I, no. 89, p. 144. Also Aubri des Trois Fontaines, (*Monumenta Germaniae historica*, XXIII, 923).

[17] Romano was subject of a scurrilous epigram in this connection, *Chronica majora*, III, 168, where the scholars are reported leaving Paris, "legatum Romanum execrantes." The verses are also cited by Madden from marginal glosses on the Matthew Paris manuscripts, opposite the account of the cessation, *Historia Anglorum*, II, 309, footnote 1.

[18] "Parisius doctos abbas elegit, at illos
    Duxit legatus munera larga pluens."   *De triumphis* (Wright), 73.

Pierre de Colmieu, left almost immediately after Easter to negotiate for the submission of the count of Foix. It is quite possible
that they could have accompanied him, to Toulouse at that time,
but the ultimatum of the Parisian masters was not to take effect
until after the fifteenth of May, so it is rather to be presumed
that John and his colleagues would wait that event. However,
a cessation of lectures had been in force from the beginning, so
perhaps the gifts of the legate and prospects of pay for a summer term might have counted heavily with teachers whose living
depended entirely on the salaries they received from their students.[19] There is nothing to date the matter more precisely,
although a modern writer has set the opening exercises for the
feast of the Ascension of that year (May 24), basing his conclusions upon an undated sermon, attributed to the Cistercian
monk Hélinand, which bears the rubic, "In ascensione Domini
II. Tolosae habitus ad clericos scholares in ecclesia B. Jacobi."
There is nothing to indicate that the sermon was preached in
this year, and in fact it might apply equally well to 1230 or 1231.
That another sermon of the same collection is headed, "In
synodo Tolosana, in ecclesia S. Jacobi habitus," — presumably
referring to the council of November, 1229 — does not attach
the former to that year rather than to the succeeding. It is thus
impossible to come any closer to the exact date of the opening
of the new schools than sometime in 1229, perhaps at the beginning of the autumn term.[20]

There is a letter of Romano dated at Moret (Seine-et-Marne), for June,
1229, Teulet, II, no. 2009, pp. 158-159. On June 5 of the same year he
was at Melun. A letter of that date is quoted in a bull of Gregory IX,
Auvray, I, no. 445, p. 279. Guillaume de Puylaurens has him follow
Raymond south sometime after Pentecost, holding a council at Toulouse
"post aestatem," in Bouquet, XIX, 224. Mansi, XXIII, cols. 191-204 publishes the canons of this assembly dated "mense Novembri."
[19] A letter of Raymond to the count of Foix, dated at Paris, April 25, 1229,
mentions that Romano had already sent Pierre to the South, "maxime
pro facto vestro," Teulet, II, no. 1998, p. 154. By June he had arranged
a treaty with the Count—ibid., no. 2004, p. 157. In the same month
Pierre reconciled the people of Toulouse also—Guillaume de Puylaurens,
chap. xl (Bouquet, XIX, 224). Matthew Paris records the cessation at
Paris—Historia, II, 308.
[20] Adolphe Félix Gatien-Arnoult, in Mémoires de l'académie des sciences,
inscriptions et belles-lettres de Toulouse, (1877), G. IX, 463 ff. The
sermons of Hélinand are found in Migne, CCXII, sermo xv, cols. 595-611,
and sermo xxvi, cols. 692-700. There is no record for a synod at Toulouse during the early thirteenth century, save in 1229. Mansi places
one there in 1219 for which he gives four canons—XXII, cols. 1135-1136.
Of these, no. i is identical with nos. xvii and xviii, and nos. ii-v with nos.
xxv-xxvii of the Council of Toulouse of 1229—ibid., XXIII, cols. 191-204.
This is evidently from a fragmentary source and misdated. At any rate

The question of just what scholastic background Toulouse had before the founding of the University is a difficult one to answer. In the remote past she had been the seat of a Roman school, as Ausonius bore witness; but during the early Middle Ages the educational facilities of the city must have declined, for little can be learned of the presence of either schools or scholars. In Carolingian times there may have been lay schools of some sort, as well as the better known monastic establishments. Lawsuits of the epoch — even in the period of imperial decline — give evidence of the complicated personal juridical system that required experts in three different laws sitting in the same court, while the *formulae* of the various legal acts of the ninth, tenth, and eleventh centuries offer even further proof of their writers' acquaintance with both Roman and Barbarian codes. Occasionally even the citation by book, section, and chapter is given with a paraphrase of the text itself.[21]

The writers of these documents appear in most instances to have been ecclesiastics so there is no indication that calligraphy was a widespread accomplishment. The record for a church council held at Narbonne in 778 is subscribed by the hand of a chancellor, who was also its redactor. An act of 859 confirmed by the bishop of Toulouse in the first person was written by

1219 is impossible as the city was in the hands of Raymond all year, and if these canons had been made during the royal siege, they surely would have had more to say about heresy and heretics. The continuators of Mansi, XXVIa, p. 150, list a council for 1226, "sub Fulcone episcopo," but give no reference to their source. It probably refers to the one held at Pamiers in the Diocese of Toulouse in that year, at which Folques was present; but as his metropolitan and the legate were also present, he could hardly have presided. As the date for the death of Hélinand is unknown, nothing can be adduced therefrom. See on the latter the article by Dom Michel Jean Joseph Brial in the *Histoire littéraire*, XVIII, 87-103.

[21] At a plea heard at Alzonne in the Diocese of Carcasonne in 918 before the bishop of Toulouse and the count's representative, among the *scabins* and *regimbourgs* that composed the court were representatives of the Goths and Romans as well as of the Salian Franks—*Histoire générale de Languedoc*, V, no. 43-XLII, cols. 137-140. A court at Narbonne in 933 had similar composition, *ibid.*, no. 57-LVI, cols. 160-161. References to various laws are frequently found. "Priscarum legum et imperatorum et consulum decrevit auctoritas," reads a foundation charter for the abbey of Vabres by Count Raymond in 862—*ibid.*, no. 160-LXXXVII, cols. 329-331; and again in a charter of his countess just three years later, 874, *ibid.*, no. 186-C, cols. 376-378. "Lege Gotorum" is found in a document of the same year—*ibid.*, no. 185, cols. 373-375. "Multum declarat sive docet lex Romana vel Salica," in a document of 1015—*ibid.*, no. 173-CXLVIII, ii, cols. 363-364. A donation of 1070 gives even fuller citation, "Lex Gothorum praecipit in libro v. ejusdem legis, titulo ii, capitulo vi, ut res donatae, si in praesenti traditae sint, nullo modo repetantur a donatore"—*ibid.*, no. 295-CCXLIX, cols. 579-580.

Benedict, a priest. The prelate of this see quite generally through the middle ages employed a chaplain for his documents, as there is no record of his having had a chancellor.[22] The count, too, occasionally made use of his chaplain for the writing of letters and deeds of gift; for his priest, Ermenricus, has subscribed two for the mid-ninth century. In the tenth century the earliest references to notaries begin to appear, for two documents dated at Narbonne in 955 and 978 mention such an official.[23] There is an act of gift for 1071 confirmed by the hand of the donor himself, who was apparently a layman, proving that at times even such persons could write; but the vast majority of all documents for these centuries are concluded with a signature followed by the familiar qualifications — *monachus, presbyter,* or *levita scripsit.*[24]

As to the actual schools of the Midi, there is very little evidence. In the Carolingian epoch many of the monasteries maintained *scholae* for the instruction of their novices and these no doubt continued, but references to them or their teachers are not frequently encountered. In 977 "Bernard, grammarian, nephew of the defunct archbishop" of Narbonne, is named among the executors of his testament. There was another of this same profession appointed by the archbishop of Auch, about this same epoch, to a prebend in his church "for preaching throughout Aquitaine and Gothia."[25] Slightly earlier, a document to which the bishop of Albi placed his name as witness, is further subscribed by an Amelius *capriscolis;* and in 1072 during a reform in the chapter of Albi there is again reference to this office. The collegiate church of Saint Salvi in the same city likewise had a *cabiscol* in 1035. These appelations are merely corrupted spellings of *capiscolis,* meaning head of the school, an office which is also found in medieval documents under the designation, *caput scholae.*[26] This term was applied

---

22 *Histoire générale de Languedoc,* II, no. 9-VI, cols. 54-57; and no. 152-LXXXIII, ii, cols. 312-313. A document confirmed by the bishop in 1075, has "Raimundus capellanus scripsit"—*ibid.,* V, no. 314, cols. 612-613.

23 *Ibid.,* II, no. 160-LXXXVII, cols, 329-331, and no. 164-XC, cols. 339-340; and *ibid.,* V, no. 98-LXXXV, cols, 222-223, and no. 130-CXIV, cols. 284-288.

24 *Gallia christiana,* XIII, *Instrumenta* (Toulouse), no. vii, cols. 6-7.

25 *Histoire générale de Languedoc,* V, no. 127-CXII, cols. 280-282; and *Gallia christiana,* I, *Instrumenta* (Auch), no. ii, p. 160, dated between 1020 and 1030.

26 The first of these documents, dated *circiter* 941, is to be found in *Gallia christiana,* I, *Instrumenta* (Albi), no. ii, p. 3. The second reads "cabis-

to the canon or monk who directed the choir and occupied a position similar to the *scholasticus* of the northern cathedral and collegial churches. It is not always certain from the context whether this dignitary was actually charged with instruction, other than that necessary to the chanting of the divine office, but it is presumable that what little was done should come through him. In 1209 on the occasion of the founding of a priory for the monastery of Saint Guilhem-le-Desert at Sauve in the diocese of Nîmes, the cellarer, Benedict, was to direct the *caput scholae* of the new institution, while the document recording the actual foundation was witnessed by Aimarius *caput scholae* of the mother house.[27] The cathedrals of Elne, Agde, and Arles and the abbeys of Saint Polycarpe near Limoux and Saint Aphrodise de Béziers also possessed such officials in the eleventh century. At Toulouse, too, the *caput scholae* is early encountered in charters of 1061 and 1098, while with the establishment of regular canons in the cathedral church toward 1077, this officer is listed after the provost, dean, and archdeacons, but before the sacristan.[28] By the twelfth century the terminology grows very uncertain, for a family at Toulouse appears with Capiscolis as surname — one Raimundus even achieving the *capitoulate* in 1180. It is to his home, no doubt, that the statutes regulating the drainage within the city refer, and not to the quarters of the canonical officer, despite the allusion to the cloister of Saint Etienne in the same sentence.[29] In a bull of Alexander III, confirming the privileges of the church of Saint Etienne in 1162, there is mention of a *magister scholae,* and Narbonne also appears to have had a school in the monastery of Saint Paul in 1127. Regulations drawn up in that

colarum honorem" and is found in *ibid.,* no. x, pp. 5-6. The third is in *ibid.,* no. vi, p. 4. See Du Cange, *Glossarium mediae et infimae latinitatis,* II, under *caput.*

[27] *Histoire générale de Languedoc,* V, no. 191-CLXIV, cols. 388-393.

[28] See *ibid.,* no. 158, cols. 337-339, and no. CXV, col. 1518 for Elna; no. 371, cols. 706-707 for Agde; *Gallia christiana,* VI, *Instrumenta* (Nîmes), no. xxi, cols. 188-189 for Arles; the *Histoire générale de Languedoc,* V, no. 352, cols. 675-677 for St. Polycarpe; and *Gallia christiana,* VI, *Instrumenta* (Béziers), no. vii, cols. 132-133 for St. Aphrodise. For the same office at Toulouse, see the *Histoire générale de Languedoc,* V, no. 260-CCXVII, col. 516; no. 400-CCCXXII, col. 755; and no. 325-CCLXVIII, cols. 626-631.

[29] *Histoire générale de Languedoc,* VIII, no. 41, col. 356. There is another reference for 1155, where it cannot be determined whether "Guillelmus capiscol" refers to surname or office, *ibid.,* V, no. 607, cols. 1185-1187, although the document is a capitular one and is closed with "Guillelmus scripsit." For the same name in the drainage regulation, see *ibid.,* VIII, no. 41, cols. 356-358.

year in regard to the special allotments of food for certain of the great feast days, stipulate that all persons from the greatest to the least should be included, "with the entire school."[30] Statutes for the chapter of Maguelonne in 1169 strictly forbade that "any strange canon of whatsoever congregation for any reason should be admitted to the secrets of our chapter, or to the *studium* of our cloisters or to the quiet of our dormitory." These in brief are the only evidences of Languedocian interest in education.[31]

However, there must have been schools of some sort which do not appear in the sources, for the numerous lawyers, physicians, scribes, and notaries who appear in the documents of the twelfth century certainly bear witness to the growing numbers of educated laymen. The chancery of the counts of Toulouse by the end of the century had long outgrown the supervision of their chaplains and had become an elaborately organized department. A charter of Count Alphonse in 1127 still concludes with "Petrus capellanus et cancellarius meus scripsit," but at Saint Gilles in 1139, he apparently employed a public scribe.[32] Raymond V in 1164 made use of a notary for one of his legal documents, and by 1176 there was even a special notary attached to his court. Pierre Fulcod, judge and chancellor, and Bermond, the same notary mentioned above, signed one of his documents as witnesses in 1187.[33] A document of Raymond VI in 1202 includes even more members of his chancery. Raimundus Guillelmus, "judge and chancellor of the lord count" affixed the latter's seal and subscribed, Hugo, "notary of the count of

---

[30] For this officer at Toulouse, see the *Histoire générale de Languedoc*, V, no. 644-DXXXI, ii, cols. 1249-1251. For Narbonne, consult *Gallia christiana*, VI, *Instrumenta*, (Narbonne), no. xxxvii, col. 33. "Procurent illos honorifice, sicut est consuetudo, a majori usque ad minorem, cum universa scola." A Rotgerius signs himself as *caput scholae* in a document of 1145—no. xliii, cols. 37-38.

[31] *Gallia christiana*, VI, *Instrumenta* (Maguelonne), no. xxv, col. 361.

[32] *Histoire générale de Languedoc*, V, no. 495-CCCCV, cols. 944-945; and *ibid.*, no. 543-CCCCXLVII, col. 1035. In 1131 and 1138 there are charters of his with simply "Petrus scripsit" at the close—*ibid.*, no. 515-CCCCXXII, cols. 975-977, and no. 537-CCCCXXXIX, col. 1025. Raymond, count of Tripoli, was using his chaplain in a similar office in 1145, *ibid.*, no. 551-CCCCLIII, ii, col. 1056. In charters of Alphonse in 1147, *ibid.*, no. 571-CCCCLXXII, cols. 1096-1097, and of Raymond V in 1158, *ibid.*, no. 624-DXI, cols. 1218-1220, the "Pontius Vitalis scripsit" of both documents would indicate a permanent chancery of some sort.

[33] *Histoire générale de Languedoc*, V, no. 659-DXLIV, cols. 1285-1286; and no. 658-DXLIII, vii, cols. 1283-1284. "Bermundo domini Tolosani comitis notario qui utrorumque mandate hoc instrumentum fecit et composuit." See also *Gallia christiana*, VI, *Instrumenta* (Nîmes), no. xxvi, col. 197.

Toulouse" wrote the document itself, and "Petrus, chamberlain and Giremundus, scribes of the lord count" were present as witnesses.[34] Other nobles and prelates of the region also had their official scribes or notaries, as documents prove for the viscount of Béziers, the counts of Barcelona and Melgueil, the archbishop of Narbonne, and the bishops of Lascour, Béziers and Nîmes.[35]

Causidici and *jurisperiti,* the lawyers of the time, were apparently not uncommon in the twelfth century. The origins of the law schools at Montpellier — save for the reference to the presence of Placentinus of Bologna in that city toward 1160 — are almost unknown.[36] The frequency, however, with which legal experts are encountered in documents of the immediately surrounding region clearly indicates that instruction in Roman law must have been possible there as early as the beginning of the century. Adelbertus *legisperitus* assisted as judge with the archbishops of Narbonne and Arles and the bishops of Béziers and Agde at a session about the year 1117.[37] Among the witnesses for a document of the abbey of Saint Gilles in 1151 are found Raimundus de Arenis, *jurisperitus,* and Radulphus, *legiferrus.* Radulphus is also mentioned with the designation *causidicus* in 1156, and then became chancellor for Raymond of Toulouse.[38] The count appears to have employed several others

---

[34] *Gallia christiana,* VI, *Instrumenta* (Uzès), no. ix, cols. 301-302.
[35] *Histoire générale de Languedoc,* V, no. 668-DLII, ii, cols. 1303-1304; and *ibid.,* VIII, no. 23, cols. 313-315 are documents of the viscount of Béziers for 1166 and 1175 respectively. *Ibid.,* V, no. 550-CCCCLII, cols. 1053-1054; and no. 621-DX, cols. 1213-1214 are of the count of Barcelona, dated 1152 and 1158. *Ibid.,* VIII, no. 10-X, i, cols. 279-280 is of the count of Melgueil and dated 1171. The archbishop's document dates from 1225, *Gallia christiana,* VI, *Instrumenta* (Narbonne), no. lxiii, cols. 58-59. The same prelate made use of a public notary of Béziers for this purpose in 1238, *ibid.,* no. lxvii, cols. 62-64. The three bishops' documents are found in *ibid.,* I, *Instrumenta* (Lascour), no. ii, col. 198; *ibid.,* VI, *Instrumenta* (Béziers), no. xii, col. 137; and *ibid.,* VI, *Instrumenta* (Nîmes), no. xxx, cols. 201-202.
[36] Denifle, *Die Entstehung,* p. 343 ff., and Rashdall, II:I, 124 ff.
[37] *Gallia christiana,* VI, *Instrumenta* (Agde), no. vi, cols. 317-318.
[38] *Histoire générale de Languedoc,* V, no. 589-CCCCLXXXVI, cols. 1145-1147. The former is later encountered as Cardinal Deacon of Santa Maria in Via Lata under Alexander III. He subscribed a bull in 1162 at Montpellier, *ibid.,* no. 644-DXXXI, i, col. 1249; and confirmed two documents for the countess of Melgueil in 1176, Teulet, I, no. 238, pp. 102-104 and no. 268, pp. 110-111. Other documents where Radulphus is mentioned are to be found in *Gallia christiana,* VI, *Instrumenta* (Arles), no. xxvi, col. 194; *Histoire générale de Languedoc,* VIII, no. 7-VII, cols. 276-277; Teulet, I, no. 238, pp. 102-104; no. 265, p. 110; no. 268, pp. 110-111; and *Histoire générale de Languedoc,* VIII, no. 90-LXV, ii, cols. 435-436.

as well in the capacity of legal advisers, for Bertrandus Radulph-us, *causidicus*, and Gui Cap de Porc, whom the author of the *Chanson* hails as the best legist in Christendom, frequently witnessed his documents. Petrus Rogerius and Arnaldus, *causi-dici*, subscribed documents at Toulouse itself in the early thir-teenth century, and the *Chanson* details the harangue delivered to the people of that city in 1216 by Master Robert, a wise legist.[39] In 1228 the abbot of Saint Antonin in conferring privi-leges on the city of Pamiers promised that neither legist nor decretist should be permitted as advocates in any lawsuit. The *formulae*, with references to the "authority of Roman law," that occur in documents of Nîmes even as early as 1152 and 1178 would also indicate that the study of that subject was prevalent in the locality.[40]

Physicians likewise are occasionally found as witnesses to documents in the Midi. Rotgerius *medicus* subscribed to one at Brive in 1161, Petrus de Margaritis *medicus*, to one for the monastery of Francvaux in 1174, and Johannes *medicus* at Béziers in 1180. This is not astonishing, for the medical schools at Montpellier were notable quite early in the twelfth century.[41] At the same time public notaries became extremely common in the whole southern region. Masters of grammar, however, are encountered but rarely. Pontius, grammarian, witnessed a gift of the abbot of Saint Gilles in 1157, and Pontius and Guillelmus, grammarians, are found in documents of 1172 and 1176, where both the count of Toulouse and countess of Melgueil were con-cerned. Guischardus Willelmus, *grammaticus*, witnessed the testa-ment of the countess in the same year.[42]

[39] For Bertrandus Radulphi, see the *Histoire générale de Languedoc*, VIII, no. 86, cols. 427-429; no. 128-LXXX, cols. 518-522; and no. 152-XCVIII, cols. 591-592. For Gui Cap de Porc, consult the *Chanson*, canto LVIII, 11. 1325-1328 (Meyer edition, I, 61, and II, 72-73); the *Histoire géné-rale de Languedoc*, VIII, no. 128, cols. 518-522; no. 157-CI, cols. 604-608; Teulet, I, no. 756, pp. 286-288; no. 930, pp. 352-353; and the *His-toire générale de Languedoc*, VIII, no. 162-CVI, cols. 619-620. For Petrus and Arnaldus, see Teulet, I, no. 623, p. 230; and no. 858, p. 327. Master Robert is cited in the *Chanson*, canto CLXXIV, 11. 5222 ff. (Meyer edition, I, 224 and II, 271).

[40] "Item nec legista sive decretista in aliqua causa Appanie advocatus erit," *Histoire générale de Languedoc*, VII, no. 268, cols. 870-876. "Constitu-tum est in lege Romanam (sic)," Teulet, I, no. 111, p. 66; "juxta Romane legis auctoritatem," *ibid.*, no. 123, p. 69; and no. 289, p. 119.

[41] *Gallia christiana*, II, *Instrumenta* (Saint Flour), no. viii, col. 134; *ibid.*, VI, *Instrumenta* (Nîmes), no. xxvi, col. 195; and the *Histoire générale de Languedoc*, VIII, no. 40-XXXIII, i, col. 350. For the schools at Mont-pellier, see Fournier, *Statuts*, II, 1 ff.

[42] References to notaries, aside from those already mentioned, are to be

Yet other evidences of the popularity of these secular studies can be cited in the often repeated prohibitions to the canons of Maguelonne against occupying themselves with civil law or worldly business. The clergy of Languedoc had never been famed for its intellectual efforts; and as the twelfth century advanced, its interests seem to have been directed entirely towards the augmenting of property rights.[43] Consequently the references to monastic and capitular schools and their masters grew less and less frequent. By the opening of the thirteenth century, the office of *cabiscol* had disappeared entirely from the chapter of Saint Etienne at Toulouse, for there are sufficient documents for this period to prove its existence had the office continued. Another way in which an estimate can be made of the weakness of ecclesiastical education in the Midi in comparison with that of northern France, Germany, or Spain, is by paging through the *regesta* of papal letters for the twelfth and early thirteenth centuries. Not once is a *cancellarius, scholasticus, magister scholarum,* or other clergyman having anything to do with schools, addressed or even mentioned for this region. For northern France, the Netherlands, and Germany such persons are addressed with great frequency during the same period, although for Portugal, Spain, and Italy they occur less often. Aside from the references already given, the only further citations of schools in Languedoc in the later twelfth and early thirteenth centuries, are a school of the Jews at Toulouse in 1180, and schools of heresy in an abjuration of 1210.[44] In answer

found in the *Histoire générale de Languedoc,* V, no. 207-CLXXVI, col. 417; no. 592-CCCCXC, cols. 1156-1157; and *Gallia christiana,* VI, *Instrumenta* (Nîmes), no. xxvi, 195. The *tabellionat* of the city of Béziers was in the conferral of its bishop in 1180. *Histoire générale de Languedoc,* V, Catalogue de Béziers, nos. lxxviii-lxxix, col. 1429. St. Sever near Agde, Villemagne and Aniane had public notaries in 1187, 1197 and 1201 respectively—*Gallia christiana,* VI, *Instrumenta* (Agde), no. xxi, cols. 331-332; *ibid.,* (Béziers), no. xx, cols. 144-147; and *ibid.,* (Nîmes), no. xxviii, cols. 199-200. References to the grammarians are to be found in the *Histoire générale de Languedoc,* V, no. 620, cols. 1211-1213; Teulet, I, no. 238, pp. 102-104; and no. 268, pp. 110-111.
[43] Potthast, *Regesta,* no. 15818, p. 516; no. 16130, p. 539; and no. 16218, p. 554. See also Emile Molinier, "Etude sur l'organization de l'université de Toulouse au quatorzième et au quinzième siècle," in the *Histoire générale de Languedoc,* VII, note LX, p. 372.
[44] *Histoire générale de Languedoc,* VIII, no. 41, col. 357. "Et alie aque de Judaicis currant ante scolam Judeorum et dehinc versus Sporterlam." Abjuration of Etienne de Servian in *ibid.,* no. 150-XCVI, col. 584. "Confiteor me graviter arrasse . . . eo quod hereticos et etiam heresiarchas, . . . in castris meis recepi, defendi, fovi et permisi tenere scholas de heresi et publice predicare et publice disputare."

to the request of Honorius in 1217, there may have been some attempt at instruction in theology at Toulouse. Indeed there is a Master Alexander Savensby, an Englishman, who is credited with having taught there, and under whom Dominic and six companions are said to have studied.[45] This ecclesiastic — later master and clerk of the apostolic camera — was consecrated bishop of Coventry by the pope himself, Easter Sunday, 1224, so his sojourn at Toulouse must have occurred before the Montforts were driven from the city.[46] In 1233 the ignorance of the local monastic clergy was such that a canon of the Council of Béziers had to issue orders to all abbots, priors, and conventual provosts to maintain within their monasteries a master of their order or a secular clerk who should teach grammar to the young and other uneducated members of their institutions. Thus it can be seen that the establishment of a university in such a region was really quite a radical departure.[47]

Among the active patrons of the infant *studium* when it was finally established at Toulouse was its zealously orthodox bishop only recently returned from an exile of over ten years.[48] Folques had been a staunch partisan of the Count de Montfort and the crusaders, and had many times raised forces in the north to fight against his own city. His early struggle to restore the bishopric to its former position had not made him loyal to his adoptive city, and his long periods of exile among their enemies certainly did not render him popular with the natives of Toulouse. He appears to have been sincere in his partisanship,

[45] Denifle, *Die Entstehung*, p. 325, citing Mamachi, *Annales ordinis praedicatorum*, I, appendix p. 283; and Gatien-Arnoult, in the *Mémoires de l'académie des sciences, inscriptions, et belles-lettres de Toulouse* (1877), G., IX, 472, citing Percin, *Monumenta*, pars I, 19. Baluze, at folio 11 of Bibliothèque Nationale MS. lat. no. 4222, refers to "Franciscus Godwinus in catalogo episcoporum Coventrensium numero 44, pag. 370" as source for this information. Francis Godwin, *De praesulibus Angliae commentarius* was published in two parts at London in 1616, and reedited by William Richardson in two volumes at Cambridge in 1743. (Charles Gross, *The sources and literature of English history from the earliest times to about 1485*, 2nd edition, 1915, no. 803, p. 148).

[46] Potthast, I, no. 7223, citing Matthew Paris, *Historia Anglorum, ad an. 1224;* and *Annales de Waverleia* in *Annales monastici* II, 299. For further references consult Eubel, *Hierarchia catholica*, I, 207, and William Stubbs, *Registrum sacrum Anglicarum* (Oxford, 1897), p. 56.

[47] Mansi, XXIII, Concilium Biterrense, cols. 269 ff. This canon is also found in Guillaume Catel, *Histoire des comtes de Tolose* (Toulouse, 1623), p. 351, without precision as to the council.

[48] John ot Garland, *De triumphis ecclesiae* (edited by Wright), p. 73, quoted in Fournier, *Statuts*, no. 508, p. 442.
"Multa novo studio dedit hic solatia, postquam
Romanus studium sanxit in urbe novum."

however, and — unlike Arnaud of Cîteaux, who, when rewarded
with the see of Narbonne, supported the citizens of that city
in their pleas to save their walls — never compromised with the
party of Languedoc, whom he considered abettors of heresy.
In no sense of the word, however, was he a mere despoiler of
the Midi for the benefit of the northerners. During the period
of his first return from exile, he had been actively engaged in
launching the new Dominican order, for the recognition of
which he had pleaded at Rome in 1215. In the following year
with the consent of his chapter he had given to Dominic and
his brother preachers the church of Saint Romain at Toulouse.[49]
Evidently by the end of the year Folques had grown so dis-
couraged at the results of his labors that he had petitioned
Honorius to be relieved of his see or at least to have his diocese
divided, for he received a response early in 1217 urging him to
continue his duties and to strive to regain his people from their
sins.[50]

Affairs within the city itself were far from normal during
the early years of the new university. The *capitouls* of Toulouse
had been obliged to bargain for peace and forgiveness at the
same time that their count was so engaged. Several of them
had accompanied him to the North in 1229, and some twenty
of them had remained as hostages in the charge of the count of
Champagne. Among the safeguarding clauses that had preceded
the ultimate treaty was one promising the destruction of the
walls and the leveling of the ditches around thirty cities of upper
Languedoc. To these, the final draft added the city of Toulouse
itself, and it was agreed that its hostages should remain at
Meaux until at least five hundred sections of the wall had been
destroyed and a like portion of the ditches leveled.[51] Their
count himself did not return south until all the provisions of
the treaty were in the process of fulfillment, preferring to remain

---

[49] Bernard Gui, "Libellus de magistris ordinis praedicatorum" in Edmund Martène and Ursin Duran, *Veterum scriptorum et monumentorum
historicum dogmaticorum moralium amplissima collectio* (Paris, 1724-
1733), VI, 400. The foundation charter is to be found in *Gallia christiana*, XIII, *Instrumenta* (Toulouse) no. xlii, col. 28.

[50] Bull found in Bibliothèque Nationale MS. lat. 3934, f°61. "Datum
Laterani, v kal. Februarii, pontif. nostri anno primo" (January 28, 1217).
The fact is referred to in *Gallia christiana*, XII, 23-24, without citation.
Potthast does not list it.

[51] Letter of Raymond to Thibaud in Teulet, II, no. 1994, pp. 152-153; the
preliminary draft of the treaty in *Histoire générale de Languedoc*, VIII,
no. 270-CLXXXIII, ii. cols. 879-883; and the final draft in *ibid.*, no. 271-
CLXXXIV, cols. 883-892.

in the north in voluntary exile. The vice-regent for the legate, Pierre de Colmieu, and the king's lieutenant started for Languedoc soon after the treaty had been ratified; and after arranging a peace with the count of Foix, Pierre had reconciled Toulouse in July.[52] In the autumn Romano appeared and a council was held at which measures for searching out heretics were originated. By the Treaty of Paris, the war against the abettors of heresy had officially ended in what amounted to the complete surrender to the church and royal power, but the unrelenting war upon heretics themselves was yet to begin. During the two long decades of the crusades, the interests of all had been primarily directed towards crushing the local nobility who had persistently refused to regard heresy as a serious matter and who had with equal persistence pillaged and seized the property of the church. With them effectively humbled and reduced to a state where they could no longer offer resistance to royal or papal dictates, attention could once more be turned to the original purpose of the crusade, the extermination of heresy. Reconstruction after the ravages of a long war is always difficult. This is rendered even more so when the region is placed under the tutelage of forces of occupation. The conditions at Toulouse, where to these was added the necessity of assisting in the search for heretics among compatriots and neighbors, can readily be imagined.

By the treaty of 1229 Raymond had promised to expel the heretics from his own land and even from such regions as were to be held temporarily by the king, not sparing relatives, vassals, or friends. He was to assist in seeking out their believers and abettors by means of his bailiffs and was to offer a bounty of two marks of silver for a period of two years, and one thereafter, to anyone who should capture a heretic. When the legate arrived at Toulouse in November, a council was assembled at which the archbishops of Bordeaux, Narbonne and Auch and many of their suffragans were present. The counts of Toulouse and Foix, and the royal seneschal of Carcasonne with other barons and two *capitouls* of Toulouse were likewise admitted to the proceedings, in order that they might approve and swear to observe all the arrangements therein enacted.[53] Here the

[52] Guillaume de Puylaurens, chap. xl (Bouquet, XIX, 224). The letter of Louis announcing these facts is listed by Auvray, II, no. 4798, col. 1288.
[53] *Histoire générale de Languedoc*, VIII, no. 271-CLXXXIV, cols. 883-893; and the similar orders issued by Louis IX to his bailiffs in the Diocese of

matter of suppression of heresy was considered, and eighteen canons of most rigorous nature were drawn up to regulate the details. By means of these it was hoped to restore to the fold a region long given to indifference and heterodoxy. An inquest was at once organized to which the faithful were first called to render evidence. Later the suspects were summoned. Those who came immediately and submitted to the legate found mercy at his hands; others who delayed until they were compelled to appear received harsher penalties; and the few who, denying the accusations, demanded to know the names of their accusers, were finally circumvented and compelled to submit to the legate at Montpellier, when he published a complete list of all accusers from which they were asked to choose the names of their enemies. Moving again eastward to Orange on the Rhone, Romano dictated letters of penance for the suspects who had been found at Toulouse and sent these letters to Folques, who published them in the church of Saint Jacques.[54] That this inquest had only rendered the peace imposed upon the south still more precarious is amply confirmed in the chronicle of Raymond's chaplain, Guillaume de Puylaurens. The legate had forseen the disorders that would follow his departure for Rome, so had carried the records of his inquests with him lest the names of the witnesses who had testified against the heretics be published broadcast, and they should suffer for it. In spite of his precautions this was exactly what did happen. On mere suspicion of having borne witness against their neighbors, such persons were killed, while open persecutors of heretics and even the royal seneschal were in danger of assassination. This naturally placed the count in extreme disfavor both at Paris and Rome, and many of his vassals returned to their accustomed rapine, seizing the tithes of the bishop, persecuting his clerks, and raiding his domain at Verfeuille. The latter had been very bountiful in his largess — from the few tithes he was able to collect during that summer — to the prelates and pilgrims who had honored him during his long exiles.[55] This was, of course, only an added grievance to his already exasperated diocesans, so the welcome for the Parisian masters who clung to him for guidance and protection must have been a cold one.

Narbonne, Mansi, XXIII, cols. 185-188. See also Guillaume de Puylaurens, chap. xl (Bouquet, XIX, 224).

[54] Mansi, XXIII, cols. 191-204; and the letters of Romano in the *Histoire générale de Languedoc,* VIII, no. 283-CXCVI, cols. 916-919.

[55] *Loc. cit.,* chap. xl (Bouquet, XIX, 224).

During the early years students and masters could hardly have been very numerous at Toulouse. John of Garland was one of the first to arrive; and the only colleague whom he deigns to mention is Roland of Cremona, who did not appear until sometime in 1230. An elaborate prospectus, extolling the advantages of the new *studium,* conserved in John's long epic poem, the *De triumphis ecclesiae,* although perhaps for the most part a mere rhetorical exercise, still probably reflects accurately enough the state of the *studium* during its infancy.[56] There it is learned that Romano had offered a plenary indulgence to all masters and students who would seek out Toulouse; and although many were reported to have already so availed themselves, still it was hoped that the legate would send more theologians and decretists, a detail bespeaking perhaps the paucity of actual numbers. What is still more enlightening as to the attitude of those upon the scene is the subsequent clause, wherein it is confidently hoped that the legate would set a term to the time they would have to remain to gain full benefit of the indulgences granted. In spite of the glowing periods heaped upon city and region, "another promised land, flowing in milk and honey, where prolific herds flourish, where fruit trees bud, where Bacchus reigns over vineyards, where Ceres rules over the fields," John of Garland — for the author of this flowery appeal with its classical allusions could be none other — betrays the secret of his own interest in the struggling *studium.* One is even inclined to credit him with the specious vein of the eloquent advertiser. There, he says, theologians expound in schools and at crossroads; logicians guide Aristotelian tyros through the liberal arts; grammarians cultivate the babbling tongues; musicians soothe the popular ear "with the mellow organ of the throat"; while decretists extol Justinian, and physicians sing the praises of Galen. Even the books on natural philosophy prohibited at Paris were available there for those who would scrutinize the very depths of nature. When it came to enumerating the more material advantages, deflection was even greater from the norm of prosaic truth:

"Wine, for a little, bread for a little, is to be had;
    Meat, for a little, fish for a little, is to be bought."

[56] *Loc. cit.,* (Wright edition), 96; also published as a document in Denifle, *Chartularium,* I, no. 72, p. 130, and in Fournier, *Statuts,* I, no. 504, p. 439. For John's biography see Louis John Paetow, *Morale scolarium of John of Garland* in *Two medieval satires on the university of Paris* (Berkeley, 1927), 90. For Roland, consult Guillaume de Pelisse, *Chronicon*

John himself tells that in that very year there was a famine at Toulouse, which is only to be expected after the ravaging and devastation of the crusaders.[57] He boasts also of the courtesy of the people, the liberality of the count in promising salaries, and the security against maltreatment and the satisfaction guaranteed by the *capitouls* of Toulouse; but within three years, he himself was fleeing these same hosts. Guillaume de Pelisse corroborates quite graphically the actual state of affairs, for in describing the Dominican efforts of this year, he remarks: "Nor indeed did this avail in extirpating heresy, for the heretical men seeing them adversely, and hearing unaccustomed things, frequently derided them." It would thus seem that on more than one count, John stands convicted of idle verbiage.[58]

Those who did seek the south must have been for the most part masters and students from the disbanded schools at Paris. In August, 1229, Louis IX had issued a confirmation of the royal privileges conferred by his grandfather on the scholars at Paris as a peace offering to the distraught *studium*, but it was evidently to no avail. In November, Gregory IX himself took matters in hand, writing to the bishop of Paris to chide him for his tactlessness in handling the affair and appointing papal judges to arrange an agreement. Louis and his mother were also warned to render due satisfaction to the injured university. The following spring the case was still dragging on, for Gregory, on receiving messengers from the king, wrote also to the masters that he might hear their side of the matter.[59] This letter he directed to both Paris and Angers, which is sufficiently indicative of where most of the dispersed masters were dwelling. Among the few chroniclers who record Toulouse as a haven for the exiled Parisian masters and scholars, Guillaume de Pelisse, a Dominican friar, was the only one, aside from John of Garland, actually upon the scene and contemporary to the facts he recorded.[60] The breach between the masters and king and

edited by Douais, Paris, 1881), p. 86, *ad an.* 1230. "Legebat ibi tunce temporis theologiam magister Rotlandus, qui venerat de Parisius ubi fuerat factus magister in theologia cathedralis," cited by Denifle, *Die Entstehung*, 327, footnote 443.

[57] "Tholosam ferit ista fames, sed Fulco beatus
    Pauperibus vitam prorogat ere, cibo."
    —*De triumphis*, p. 99.

[58] Cited by Denifle, *Die Entstehung*, p. 329, footnote 451.

[59] Denifle, *Chartularium*, I, no. 66, p. 120; nos. 69-71, pp. 125-129; and nos. 74-75, pp. 132-133.

[60] The *Annales de Dunstaplia* (edited by Luard, Rolls Series, 1866) in the *Annales monastici*, III, 117, under the year 1229 record the flight to

bishop at Paris was not entirely healed until the spring of 1231. It is presumably just one year later that John fled from Toulouse, and although the reason proffered for this hasty departure was the failure in the payment of the promised salaries, still it is entirely possible that the lure of the newly reopened schools in the *rue du Fouarre* was a strong one, for he continues:

"The crowd from the flourishing *studium* gradually receded; I, who write all this am first to recede."[61]

Of the two scholars certainly connected with the university in its first years, John of Garland is by far the better known. Born in England, where he completed his early studies under the guidance of John of London, he soon transferred to Paris, which he seems to have considered his "foster-mother." There he began teaching the rudiments of Latin to the scholars of the *Clos de Garlande*, where he remained until the unfortunate riots of 1229 and the offers of the legate gave him opportunity for a visit to the south. From the works of this scholar it can be seen that his sojourn in the Midi made a great impression on him. One whole book of his long epic poem is devoted to the Albigensian crusade and the author's own observations in the region. A paragraph on engines of war in his *Dictionarius* enumerates in detail those he had seen before the walls of Toulouse. John also refers to a *Conductum de Tholosa* or guide book for the city, which he said he had written. Aside from the fact that he re-

---

Angers with the statement that few remained in Paris. Guillaume de Pelisse has been edited both by Douais in *Sources de l'histoire de l'inquisition dans le Midi de France* (Paris, 1882) and by Charles Molinier, *De fratre Guillelmo Pelisso veterrimo inquisitionis historico* (Paris, 1880). "Missi etiam fuerunt tunc Tholosam quam plurimi magistri de Parisius et scholares, ut studium generale ibi fieret et fides doceretur ibidem et omnes scientie liberales," p. 84 of Douais edition. Bernard Gui, another chronicler native of the region but who wrote nearly a century later, seems to merely have made use of the work of Guillaume, his predecessor in the office of inquisitor, for he adds nothing to the evidence of John and Guillaume and uses the identical words of the Chronicon of Gerard d'Auvergne. "Alii quidem Remis, alii Andegavis, alii vero in Angliam, et alii in Italiam vel in Hispaniam, sive in alias provincias mundi, causa studii sunt profecti," (Bouquet, XXI, 214). To these Bernard has added, "Multi quoque magistri et scholares Tholosam venerunt et rexerunt ibidem," *Flores chronicorum* (Bouquet, XXI, 695). For the dating of these French chroniclers, consult Molinier, *Sources,* III, no. 2475, p. 74; no. 2791, p. 173; and no. 2844, pp. 184-187.

[61] Documents in Denifle, *Chartularium,* I, nos. 79-82 and 84-85, pp. 136-142; and *De triumphis* (Wright) p. 100. "Illic exegi spacio studiosa trienni Tempora, Romano sub duce lector ibi."
"Doctorum primo sunt certa salaria, donec
    Cuncta negans livor cepit habere locum.
Florentis studii paulatim turba recedit;
    Hec ego qui scribo cuncta recedo prius." *Ibid.,* p. 105.

mained there about three years, he tells little of his work in Toulouse, although one brief passage does ridicule the ignorance of his students to whom a rule for computing Easter had to be given. Into his lectures on grammar, he tells us he incorporated edifying material from theological works and the lives of the saints.[62]

His colleague, Roland of Cremona, an Italian Dominican, had entered the order at Bologna in 1218, where he had been teaching philosophy. Going soon after to Paris to study, he was among the first of the friars to receive the license in theology.[63] On arriving at Toulouse in 1230, he was soon deeply engrossed in the baiting of heretics. John of Garland has hailed him as even greater than his valiant namesake, for whereas the knight had "strewn bodies," the theologian had crushed heretical depravity. This zealot has also been credited with a *summa* of theology and philosophy, of which no trace has been found, so it cannot be determined whether the work was a product of his

[62] For the biography of John of Garland, see Paetow, *Two Medieval Satires*, and Gatien-Arnoult in the *Mémoires de l'académie des sciences, inscriptions, et belles-lettres de Toulouse* (1857) E, 1, 207 ff.; and in the *Revue de Toulouse* (1866), 117 ff. "In civitate Tolosae, nondum sedato tumultu belli, vidi antemuralia, liceas et superfossata profunda, turres et propugnacula tabula . . . et perrarias sive tormenta (quarum una Simonem comitem Montis-Fortis pessundebat)"—*Dictionarius* (edited by Scheler, "Trois traités de lexicographie latine du XIIe et du XIIIe siècle" in *Jahrbuch für romanische und englische Literatur*, VI, 153, paragraph 49. "Tunic ibi de Pascha fuit ignorancia multis," *De triumphis* (Wright), p. 87. "De spe deque fide suevi recincre libellum, hinc et apostoliaca gesta ligata tuli"—*ibid.*, p. 101.

[63] "Inter quos Bononiae fuerunt magister Rolandus Cremonensis, summus philosophus, qui primus Parisius ex fratribus in theologia rexit"— *Brevissima chronica reverendorum magistrorum generalium ordinis praedicatorum*, in Martène, *Amplissima collectio*, VI, 349, *ad an.* 1218. "Italus huc veniens ad robora nostra magister Rolandus," *De triumphis* (Wright), p. 78. Denifle refers to a passage in a manuscript of Stephen de Salanhaco, where he is called *primus licentiatus*, *Die Entstehung*, p. 327, note 444. "Rotlandus, qui venerat de Parisius, ubi fuerat factus magister in theologia cathedralis," Guillaume de Pelisse, *Chronicon* (Douais, p. 86), also cited by Denifle, *Die Entstehung*, p. 327, note 443. See also Denifle, *Chartularium*, I, no. 34, note, p. 94. The first Dominican master at Paris was created after the dispersion of 1229—*ibid.*, no. 230, pp. 252-258. Rashdall, *Universities*, I, 370-372, refers to Roland's inception under John of Saint Gilles but finds inconsistency in the chronology. Perhaps the inception referred to was one as *sententiarius*, rather than as master? In the list of lectors Roland would appear quite naturally first, as he surely read in his own convent before the entrance of John into the order in 1228, so the latter would be thus the second lector, in spite of his being a full-fledged master before taking the Dominican habit. The occasion of Roland's transfer to Toulouse was presumably twofold, to aid the new *studium*, and to make room for other Dominican masters at Paris. John of Saint Gilles, on the authority of Denifle, followed his student on the chair at Toulouse, *Die Entstehung*, p. 330, and note 457.

stay at Toulouse or of his later activities in Italy. On leaving this city, Roland went to Italy where, in preaching to a crowd assembled before the cathedral of Piacenza in October, 1233, he was stoned and wounded by some heretics and their abettors. The friar recovered from his wounds, however, for in November of 1234 he was ordered by the pope to take action against some heretical Florentine merchants.[64]

About this epoch the renowned Cistercian monk and preacher, Hélinand, is known to have been in Toulouse. In his collected sermons two are found which he preached in the city, but the exact date of his sojourn is very uncertain. It is presumable that perhaps he too came south at the request of the abbot, Hélie, to assist by his sermons in restoring Toulouse to orthodoxy. The abbey of Grandselve had a house there as early as 1178, where Hélinand could have remained during the period of his labors. It is doubtful, however, that he was more than an occasional preacher before the assembled masters and students, for the Cistercians had not yet entered actively into the educational field.[65] From the opening words of his sermon to the scholars on the feast of the Ascension, it would appear that he had been forced against his will to officiate that day before a distinguished audience without having had proper time for preparation; he complains that it was the third occasion in a single week on which he had been obliged to preach.[66] His only other reference

---

[64] "Forti Rolando major, quia corpora stravit ille, sed hereticum contudit ille nephas," De triumphis (Wright), p. 78. For other references to Roland, see Tiraboschi, Storia della letteratura italiana (Milan, 1823), IV, 201; and the articles of Gatien-Arnoult in the Mémoires de l'académie des sciences, inscriptions, et belles-lettres de Toulouse (1857), E, I, 207, and (1877-1882), G, IX, 476 ff.; and in the 1866 volume of the short-lived Revue de Toulouse another article by the same author, "Trois maîtres de théologie à l'université de Toulouse." The exact date of Roland's departure from Toulouse is uncertain. For his career in Italy, consult Johannes de Mussis, Chronicon Placentinum in Lodovico Antonio Muratori, Rerum italicarum scriptores (Milan, 1723-1751), XVI, 461; and the bulls of Gregory IX in Auvray, I, no. 1560, col. 858; no. 1569, col. 862; nos. 1606-1607, cols. 883-884; and nos. 2065-2066, col. 1118. For the affair of the Florentine merchants, see ibid., no. 2216, p. 1189.

[65] Histoire générale de Languedoc, VIII, Catalogue de Grandselve, no. dxx, col. 1820. The document refers to a rent in grain to be delivered at the house in Toulouse. Their house for student-monks at Paris dates only from 1227, Denifle, Chartularium, I, no. 53, p. 109.

[66] "Ter in ista hebdomada sermonem facere coactus sum, tam justae reprehensioni expositum, quam praemeditatione legitima non exsculptum," quoted from a manuscript source by Richard Albert Lecoy de la Marche, La chaire française au moyen âge (Paris, 1886), p. 166, footnote 1. The sermon as printed in Migne, CCXII, sermo xv, cols. 595 ff., reads, "Cum sermonum hunc facere coactus sum," etc. The former work gives an excellent evaluation of Hélinand's literary ability, pp. 157-169.

to things scholastic, a bit of local interest towards the middle of his lengthy discourse, perhaps to recall the flagging attention of his hearers, is the oft-quoted passage wherein he bemoans the plight of virtue. "Lo, the clerks at Paris quest the liberal arts, at Orléans, authors; at Bologna, codices; at Salerno, mortars; at Toledo, demons, but nowhere morals."[67] That such a noted pulpit orator as Hélinand should come from the north at this time is proof of the enormous importance placed upon the reconversion of the Midi. His sermons at Toulouse were no doubt pleasing to John of Garland, for they have a sufficiently pompous flow and are generously interpolated with selections from both pagan and Christian classics — an eminently profitable exercise for the uncultured ears of grammatical students.

[67] For Hélinand see the articles by Gatien-Arnoult in the *Mémoires de l'académie des sciences, inscriptions, et belles-lettres de Toulouse* (1857); E, I, 207; and in the *Revue de Toulouse* (1866), avril-mai; and by Dom Brial in the *Histoire littéraire*, XVIII, 87-103.

CHAPTER 3

GROWTH OF THE UNIVERSITY DURING THE FIRST CENTURY OF ITS EXISTENCE

I N the supercharged atmosphere of its early years, the *studium* began to decline. When the Dominicans were requested by the *capitouls* to refrain from their over-zealous activities, Roland took particular offense and preached the more boldly. Disinterments and burnings of the bodies of deceased heretics followed. It is evident that feeling was soon running so high that neither the theologian nor his colleagues in other faculties could long withstand it. This is corroborated by the testimony of John of Garland, who, fearing insidious men, took passage from Toulouse on a swift boat. Once embarked, however, he discovered in the boatman a bandit lying in wait for booty and only saved himself from an impious mob at Castelsarrasin by employing a clever ruse.[1] Except, then, for the school in the Dominican cloister, the *studium* could hardly have survived the year. Another blow to the orthodox cause was the death of the ever-active Folques in December of 1231, after nearly twenty-six years of episcopal labors. His successor was Raymond de Miramont, who as provincial prior of the Dominicans had aided greatly in establishing them in their new convent at Toulouse. Persecutions continued throughout this year. Guillaume de Puylaurens especially mentions a joint expedition of bishop and count into the mountains where nineteen heretics were captured. It is this, no doubt, that lay behind the precipitate flight of John and the dissolution of the university.[2]

Even as early as 1230, Count Raymond was having difficulties in meeting the enormous financial obligations of the Treaty of

[1] Percin, *pars* II, 199, cited by Gatien-Arnoult, *Mémoires de l'académie des sciences, inscriptions et belles-lettres de Toulouse* (1877), G, IX, 475 ff.; and the *De triumphis* (Wright), p. 105.

[2] According to Folques' instructions his body was buried at Grandselve near the high altar of the abbey-church, where, as late as the seventeenth century his tomb could be seen—Guillaume de Puylaurens, chap. xli, Bouquet, XX, 765); and Catel, *Histoire des comtes de Tolose*, p. 346. For Raymond de Miramont, see Bernard Gui, *Fundatio conventuum praedicatorum*, in Martène, *Amplissima collectio*, VI, 460.

Paris. A letter of Gregory in July informed the count that Pierre de Colmieu had been directed to investigate his ability to pay the 10,000 marks and to make the pilgrimage to the Holy Land; and if matters were as he claimed, an extension of time would be granted. By the Treaty of Paris this pilgrimage had been promised for a date before August, 1230, but in a succeeding agreement with Romano the term for its fulfillment had been extended to Easter of 1231. In the preceding September the pope had authorized Raymond to tax the clergy as well as the laity of his domains in order to raise the required sum. In 1231 Raymond was obliged to mortgage Marmande to the abbot of Cîteaux for 200 marks of silver annually against the amount still owing to that monastery.[3] His obligations toward his king, too, seem to have been no more easily satisfied, for the Languedocian bishops were summoned to Melun in 1233 to confer with Louis upon the articles of the peace that had not been met; and Raymond himself was persuaded to issue new and more stringent statutes against heresy in April. Gregory, too, kept urging continued activity in his letters to the king, bishops and count. In July the archbishop of Vienne was named to replace the bishop of Tournai as legate and was armed with all the necessary powers for further repression. It was also in this year that the first Dominican inquisitors were appointed for Toulouse. It is no wonder, then, that under these circumstances the salaries of the masters remained unpaid.[4]

There was evidently someone to look after the cause of the declining *studium* even during this gloomiest of epochs, for in the early spring of 1233 several bulls and letters were issued from Rome with the evident purpose of reënforcing its position.[5] On April 27 a letter was directed to the "university of masters

[3] Auvray, I, no. 477, cols. 309-310; *ibid.*, II, no. 4791, col. 1289; Teulet, II, no. 2075, pp. 184-185; nos. 2164-2165, pp. 226-227; and no. 2168, p. 228.

[4] Guillaume de Puylaurens, chaps. xli and xliii (Bouquet, XX, 765 and 766). For the conference with Louis, see the *Histoire générale de Languedoc*, VIII, no. 300, cols. 963-969; and Teulet, II, no. 2254, pp. 248-250; both of which read "xii kalendas maii." The same document in Mansi, XXIII, cols. 265-268 gives "xii kalendas martii." For the papal letters, see Auvray, I, no. 1165, col. 662, dated March 7, 1233; *ibid.*, no. 1166 and no. 1170, cols. 662-663, of March 8 and 15 respectively; the *Histoire générale de Languedoc*, VIII, no. 301-CCIX, cols. 969-970, dated May 2. The letter to Raymond himself is dated May 26, 1233, Teulet, II, no. 2241, pp. 252-253. See also Auvray, I, nos. 1472-1473, nos. 1481-1484 and no. 1486, cols. 819-821.

[5] This was perhaps the legate, the bishop of Tournai, who was recalled to Rome by a letter dated February 19, 1233—Auvray, I, no. 1104, col. 635.

and scholars at Toulouse," in which the pope, recalling the foundation of the *studium* by Romano and confirming the actions then taken by the legate, conceded to the new *studium* all the liberties enjoyed at Paris. At this the northern *studium* took offense and had to be reassured the following year that the favor would not derogate their ancient customs and that examinations could be observed as in the past.[6] By this same bull the pope also granted to Toulouse the privilege of a committee of clerks and townsmen for arranging prices for student lodgings; ordered that students of theology residing in the city should be able to receive the fruits of their benefices although not present in person; extended the right of ecclesiastical jurisdiction to all masters, students, and their servants, and conferred the right of universal recognition without further examination on all its graduates. The count and his bailiffs were to be compelled to give them protection, and the promised salaries were to be paid. Almost identical letters were addressed to the archbishop of Narbonne and the bishops of Toulouse and Carcasonne the following day and on the thirteenth to Count Raymond himself.[7] On the twenty-eighth of the same month the count, *capitouls* and people of Toulouse had been forbidden to withdraw foodstuffs from the city by boat in time of scarcity, lest the *studium* should suffer, although this prohibition was directly contrary to municipal statutes of 1202.[8] Later in the same year the pope granted a special indulgence to all who should give alms to the Hospital of Saint Raymond, a foundation which the abbot and convent of Saint Sernin at Toulouse had assigned for the reception of "scholars and other paupers," because such a great multitude had gathered there that they were unable to provide them with beds and other necessaries. Whether or not these indigents were for the most part students, there is no way of telling; but at any rate it gives proof that some provision was being made for the welfare of university members.[9]

In 1234 as Raymond again showed an inclination to conform to the provisions of the peace, letters were sent from Rome ad-

---

[6] Auvray, I, no. 1273, col. 714; and Fournier, *Statuts,* I, no. 509, p. 442. The latter document dates from April 3, 1234.

[7] *Histoire générale de Languedoc,* VII, 433-434; Fournier, *Statuts,* I, no. 506, p. 441; and Du Boulay, III, 150.

[8] Fournier, *Statuts,* I, no. 507, p. 442; and Auvray, I, no. 1267, col. 713. For the municipal stautes on this matter see Catel, *Histoire des comtes de Tolose,* p. 228; and the *Histoire générale de Languedoc,* VIII, no. 108, cols. 475-476.

[9] Auvray, I, no. 1673, p. 922, dated December 22, 1233.

monishing the legates and prelates to act a little more favorably
toward him and not to be so prone to excommunicate him on the
slightest pretexts. His recently edited statutes against heresy
were confirmed at the same time.[10] In April the legate was
urged to renewed activities, but by November he was again
warned to proceed with discretion in the matter of heresy and
to treat the count "benignly."[11] The persecution of heretics was
nevertheless continued. A priest in the diocese of Cahors had to
be provided with a suitable benefice in another region because
he had rendered himself odious to his parishioners by his persecuting zeal. About this same time the bishop of Albi and abbot
of Grandselve were ordered to investigate charges against one
of Raymond's bailiffs. The count himself was urged to continue
his efforts, but by August he was again excommunicated for
despoiling a church in the Agenais.[12]

The year 1235 was another dark one for the fortunes of the
studium. Brother Guillaume Arnaut, the Dominican inquisitor,
was expelled from Toulouse by the vicar of the count and the
capitouls for his activities against heretics. The prior of Saint
Etienne and the parish priests who had read the citations of the
friar were also driven out. When the Dominicans in turn en-
deavored to publish the inquisitorial summons, they were besieged in their cloisters while the *capitouls* forbade anyone the
giving or selling of anything to the convent. The Dominican
bishop and his canons also suffered their share of the wrath of
the townspeople. Even the episcopal mansion in which the
bishop lay sick was invaded, and his horses and other valuables carried off, while in his church some of the canons were
wounded. The bishop and chapter were compelled forthwith
to leave the city, and the Dominicans were ejected with violence. In November, Guillaume Arnaut excommunicated the
capitouls with the consent of the bishops of Toulouse and Carcasonne; and later the two bishops and their metropolitan of
Narbonne likewise fulminated similar penalties. The Franciscans
who published the sentences were immediately evicted, and

---

[10] Auvray, I, no. 1711, cols. 943-944; and no. 1719, col. 946.
[11] Not only did the legate receive instructions in the spring, *ibid.*, nos. 1917-
1918, col. 1049; and no. 1923, col. 1051, but the kings, prelates, and
nobles of the surrounding regions were also asked to assist, *ibid.*, nos.
1914-1916, col. 1048; and nos. 1919-1920, cols. 1050-1051. The letters
to the legate in the autumn are in *ibid.*, no. 2218, col. 1192; and no.
2284, col. 1199.
[12] *Ibid.*, no. 2155, col. 1152; no. 2220, col. 1194; no. 2283, col. 1199; and
ibid., II, no. 2732, col. 142.

in the disorder the *studium* itself could hardly do else than dissolve.[13]

The following April saw the matter still unsettled, for Gregory IX commanded the archbishop of Vienne to publish the sentences every Sunday and feast day in every church of the district to which he was accredited as legate.[14] The count himself was again addressed in letters of the same date and urged to amend his ways. After enumerating the details of the ejection of the inquisitors, the pope ordered Raymond to fulfill his crusading vow by embarking for the Holy Land with the coming of the following March, there to remain for the space of five years.[15] For this reason Louis IX was asked to send his brother, Alphonse, as regent to the south, and all the converted heretics whose penance had been imposed in the form of this pilgrimage were warned to make ready to accompany Raymond. The king and count were also exhorted to observe the provisions of the treaty of 1229, especially in regard to the expelling of heretics, and Raymond was reminded of the sum of 10,000 marks still owing in his reparation payments.[16] As the month approached for departure for the Holy Land, Raymond began to seek its deferment to a year from the subsequent feast of Saint John. He complained bitterly of the inquisitors and even had Louis IX write to the pope on his behalf. The pope replied that his legate should investigate the former plea but that he would not remove his inquisitors, the friars Guillaume and Bernard, as the count had produced no reasonable charges against them.[17]

Meanwhile Raymond had embroiled himself with the count of Provence by aiding the rebellious citizens of Marseille. In complaining of this matter to Louis and Raymond, the pope

---

[13] *Fundatio conventuum praedicatorum*, in Martène, *Amplissima collectio*, VI, 460; and Martène, *Thesaurus novus anecdotarum*, I, 992.

[14] Dated April 28, 1236, in Fournier, *Statuts*, I, no. 510, p. 443 ff., but incorrectly addressed to Romano in the heading. The text reads correctly—"venerabili fratri Vienensi archiepiscopo."

[15] Auvray, II, no. 3126, cols. 375-378. The King of France, the *capitouls* of Toulouse and Pierre de Colmieu were addressed in almost the same fashion in letters of the same date—*ibid.*, nos. 3128-3129, col. 379. Deniflle, *Die Entstehung*, 331, footnote 460, cites these bulls; as does also Fournier, *Statuts*, I, no. 510, p. 443, footnote 1, in which he unwittingly gives a resumé of the bull he has published in full as well as those addressed to King, *capitouls* etc.

[16] Auvray, II, no. 3138, col. 382; nos. 3188-3189, cols. 407-408; no. 3191, col. 409; and no. 3199 and no. 3201, col. 415.

[17] *Ibid.*, no. 3498, col. 558; and a letter to the legate in the same vein, *ibid.*, no. 3501, col. 560.

took the opportunity of drawing attention to the fact that the promised salaries of the masters had not been paid and that as a result the *studium* at Toulouse was "irreparably dissipated."[18] Soon after, Raymond tried again to come to an agreement. The archbishop of Vienne in his capacity of legate was admonished to permit the count to send messengers to Rome, while the count was exhorted to observe the peace of 1229 as he had promised. Matters seem to have come to a standstill during the rest of the year, neither the count nor the pope taking further action save for a papal bull permitting the local prelates to absolve paupers from vows of pilgrimage to the Holy Land.[19]

When the count's messengers arrived at Rome they presented a long series of pleas. In the first place, Raymond asked to be absolved from the sentence of excommunication laid against him for not embarking for the Holy Land and for not paying the sum of 10,000 marks still owing. This he was unable to pay and still meet the expenses of a crusade, which he promised to make voluntarily with the other barons, if absolved. He likewise asked that he might lead the repentant heretical barons with him on the same passage and that the inquisitorial powers be removed from the Dominicans and returned to the bishops or other non-suspect prelates. Petitioning for absolution from other sentences incurred in his quarrels with ecclesiastics both in the dioceses of Agen and of Vaison, he also sought the rehabilitation and burial of his father. From the same plea it is learned that Toulouse had recalled the expelled inquisitors, but had not yet been absolved, and that the count himself had come to an agreement with the masters and was prepared to pay them the stipulated salaries. Of these requests a number were denied at the Curia, including those for the discontinuance of the Dominican inquisitors and for the absolution of the count on the matter of salaries.[20]

---

[18] *Ibid.*, no. 3699, col. 662, is directed to Louis; and *ibid.*, no. 3704, col. 665, to Raymond. The text of the former is also printed in Fournier, *Statuts*, I, no. 512, p. 445, with the incorrect date, "1233, 20 juillet." The text of the latter is edited also in Teulet, II, no. 2514, col. 339. Similar letters were sent to queen Blanche, Auvray, II, no. 3700, col. 664; to the bishop of Senlis, no. 3701, col. 665; to the archbishops and bishops of the realm, no. 3702, col. 665; and to the legate, no. 3703, col. 665. These are also cited by Denifle, *Die Entstehung*, 331, footnote 461; and by Fournier, *Statuts*, I, in a footnote to no. 512, p. 445.

[19] Auvray, II, no. 3786, col. 717; and also Fournier, *Statuts*, I, no. 511, p. 445. See also Auvray, II, nos. 3800-3801, cols. 724-725. The letter in regards pauper-pilgrims is given in *ibid.*, no. 3915, col. 818.

[20] Given without date in *ibid.*, no. 4758, cols. 1243-1248. The part con-

In May the cardinal-bishop of Praeneste was appointed as legate for Provence and was invested with sufficient powers to absolve Raymond from the numerous sentences of excommunication that stood against him, should sufficient guarantees be offered for his future good behavior. At the same time the inquisitors were enjoined to cease their activities for the space of three months.[21] This was later extended to six, so it was evident that a definite effort was to be made to pacify the region permanently if such a thing were possible.[22] These plans were slightly disarranged by the inability of the bishop of Praeneste to act; as a consequence, the major part of the same bulls was redirected with modifications of name and date to the bishop of Sorano early in August.[23] There is little to be learned of the legation of this prelate, although in February of 1239 certain masters of the University of Toulouse directed letters to him testifying to the payment of their salaries by the count. As this arrangement had been made by the legate with the consent of the parties concerned at a meeting at Lavaur, they requested that he issue letters patent that his injunctions to Raymond had

cerning the masters is printed also in Fournier, *Statuts*, I, no. 515, p. 447. The former is headed: "Istas petitiones nuntii comitis Tolosani porrexerunt ante quam esset mentio de legato mittendo, et earum quaedam admisse sunt, quaedam vero non." The earliest letters concerning the new legate are dated May 13, 1238, which gives a terminus ante quem for the document. The clauses bearing asterisks in the document as edited by Auvray were refused. Another part of the register contains a repetition of these denied clauses, Auvray, II, no. 4781, col. 1264.

[21] Auvray, II, nos. 4759-4760, cols. 1248-1249. Further instructions to him were forthcoming a little later, *ibid.*, nos. 4771-4774, cols. 1257-1258; nos. 4778-4780, cols. 1262-1263; and no. 4769, col. 1256. Nos. 4398-4399, cols. 1052-1054 in the main portion of the register for the Pope's twelfth year are also addressed to him, dated June 5 and June 3 respectively. The latter is repeated under June 4, in no. 4765, cols. 1253-1254; and printed in full in Fournier, *Statuts*, I, no. 514, p. 447. In the register of Gregory both are cancelled, however. Other documents of the same date are Auvray, II, nos. 4764-4766, cols. 1253-1254. The bull ordering absolution from excommunication for expelling the Dominicans is given in *Statuts*, I, no. 513, p. 446. The King of France, and the archbishops, bishops, counts and barons of the Midi were also informed of the new legation—Auvray, II, nos. 4762-4763, cols. 1251-1252; and nos. 4767-4768, cols. 1254-1255.

[22] Auvray, II, no. 4775, col. 1259.

[23] In the registers of Gregory, the addresses and dates in many instances were merely scraped and modified to suit the change. See Auvray, II, no. 4337, col. 1009; nos. 4347-4349, cols. 1015-1019; nos. 4351-5353, cols. 1019-1021; and no. 4397, col. 1051. No. 4350, col. 1019, was evidently allowed to remain unchanged through error. One of these letters is given in full in Teulet, II, no. 2738, p. 386. The bishop of Praeneste is addressed as papal vicar on matters pertaining to Rome itself in October 1238, Auvray, II, no. 4549, col. 1147, which probably explains his relief from duty as legate.

been fulfilled. The sum received by the masters at this time, 500 pounds *morlanensium,* is designated as the full sum due at the approaching Easter. At the time of the count's transaction with the *studium* in 1238, not all of the masters were present in Toulouse, for the absent had to be represented by procurators. The same thing seems to have been true when the receipt for payment was given in the following year, as three procurators or syndics signed on behalf of the university of masters, and only two additional masters in the university were present. If the procurators were actually masters as well as legal representatives, which is not clearly stated, then only five of the full complement of fourteen could have been in the city at the time, a fact which does not bear witness to a flourishing condition in the *studium.*[24]

In spite of these legations Raymond was unable to make his peace with the church on all the charges upon which he had been excommunicated, although he had come to an agreement with and promised obedience to the legate at Clermont in March of 1241. There he had been requested to join the legate, now again the bishop of Praeneste, in a journey to the Curia, for the latter was to lead the trans-Alpine prelates to the council summoned for that year.[25] Raymond delayed at Montpellier for a meeting with the king of Aragon and thus failed to meet the churchmen who had already embarked. Through this fortunate circumstance he escaped capture at sea by the Pisan and Sicilian fleets in the pay of Frederick II.[26] Returning as far as

[24] Fournier, *Statuts,* I, no. 516, p. 447. Guillaume de Puylaurens, chap. xliii (Bouquet, XX, 766) makes no mention of the activities of this legate, but limits his discussion to the work of the bishop of Praeneste, who was re-announced as legate in a papal letter to Louis and Blanche, dated October 21, 1239—Teulet, II, no. 2835, p. 416; and no. 2836, p. 418. The bulls for the bishop of Sorano as noted above, are cancelled in the register. The last letter to him as legate bears the date, April 15, 1239, Auvray, III, no. 4808, col. 14. The bishop of Praeneste is addressed even earlier by the Pope himself, as one already upon mission in Languedoc, *ibid.,* no. 4934, col. 114, dated October 1, 1239, but the exact date of his appointment is unknown. There are three enigmatic bulls dated September 5 and 12 of the same year, directed to the bishop of Porto as legate, which are probably scribe's errors of *Portuensi* for *Praenestino,* for there is no evidence that Romano was again so commissioned. His very age at this time would surely have precluded such an arduous journey. As these follow in series, only the first one bears the address to the bishop of Porto, Auvray, III, nos. 2924-2929, cols. 103-109. There is reference in the last bull to the bishop of Sorano "tunc in partibus illis . . . legatus."

[25] *Histoire générale de Languedoc,* VIII, no. 336-CCXXXIV, cols. 1052-1053; and Auvray, III, no. 5939, col. 443; and Guillaume de Puylaurens, chapter lxiv (Bouquet, XX, 767).

[26] Guillaume de Puylaurens, *loc. cit.;* and Auvray, III, no. 6030, col. 509.

Montpellier, the count again met the king of Aragon and arranged with him to have his petitions carried to Rome. From these it is learned that Raymond was still under ban of excommunication and that several clauses of the petition of 1238 were still unanswered although not among those denied in the register of Gregory IX. However, the plea from release from excommunication for the unpaid academic salaries is not repeated even though it appeared in 1238 among the denied clauses. When the messengers bearing these letters reached Pisa on their way to Rome, they were greeted with tidings of the death of the pope, so nothing further could be done.[27] In the following year Brother Guillaume Arnaut with several of his assistants was murdered at Avignonet in the diocese of Toulouse, and war almost broke out between the southern nobles under Raymond's banner and the king of France. This was averted, however, through the efforts of the Bishop Raymond and through the news of the perfidy of the count of Foix who had sworn homage directly to the king.[28] In this same year Raymond was again excommunicated by the archbishop of Narbonne for abetting heretics, in spite of his protestations of good faith in their pursuit, dated but two months before. By the next year he had evidently proved his point, for papal letters of cassation and Raymond's letter of summons to the prelates of his domains to exercise the inquisition are both extant.[29]

During the second decade of its existence, the *studium* appears to have settled down to a more peaceful life. It was during this time that the first college was founded in the city by the testament of Vidal Gautier. This wealthy patron gave five adjoining houses and gardens near Saint Pierre des Cuisines for the use of poor scholars who, he stipulated, were to be at

[27] Teulet, II, no. 2920, pp. 450-451; and Guillaume de Puylaurens, chap. xlv (Bouquet, XX, 768).
[28] Two accounts naming the murdered, but varying slightly in details, are given in Catel, *Histoire des comtes de Tolose*, 362-363. Guillaume de Puylaurens, chap. xlv (Bouquet, XX, 769) has another. The letters in connection with this reëstablishment of peace are to be found in Teulet, II, no. 2996, p. 482; no. 3000, p. 484; and no. 3013, p. 488.
[29] For the excommunication and protestations of the Count, see the *Histoire générale de Languedoc*, VIII, no. 350-CCXLV, cols. 1088-1090; and no. 352-CCXLVI, cols. 1090-1091. The letters of absolution are in Teulet, II, no. 3144, pp. 523-524; the summons is printed in the *Histoire générale de Languedoc*, VIII, no. 363-CCLV, cols. 1121-1122; and a letter of the Pope to Raymond himself in *ibid.*, no. 369-CCLX, cols. 1142-1144. The latter is given with full dating phrase in Teulet, II, no. 3184, pp. 534-535, which shows it to be of May 17, 1244 instead of 1243.

least twenty in number; and he further endowed his foundation with the rents of eighteen other houses in the neighborhood. Students might be chosen from any of eleven surrounding dioceses, as well as from that of Toulouse itself. Evidently the *studium* was growing.[30] This is confirmed to some extent by a letter of Innocent IV in 1244. Since scholars of diverse nations gathered for the *studium* of letters in that city, and as they occasionally laid violent hands on one another — incurring pains of excommunication thereby, owing to their clerical statuts — the bishop of Toulouse was granted the privilege of dispensing them from such penalties during a five year period, in case a legate were not present in the city.[31] In the following year the bishop received orders to admit poor students to the hospitals of the city, and the count, *capitouls,* and people of Toulouse were the recipients of letters thanking them for the aid they had given to the university in the past and exhorting them to continue the good work by extending to the masters and students a special protection in the future.[32] At about the same time the *studium* itself was favored by the confirmation of the privileges conferred upon it by Gregory IX in 1233[33] and had its position further reënforced by the application to the schools at Toulouse

[30] Fournier, *Statuts,* I, no. 517, p. 447; and the *Histoire générale de Languedoc,* VIII, no. 360, cols. 1110-1113, give the text of this testament in part and as a whole respectively. They both have dated it "1243 mars 29." Although the day is before Easter, the style of Toulouse was commonly that of the Annunciation until after Alphonse of Poitiers, which would place this document in 1242. See, Giry, *Manuel de diplomatique* (Paris, 1894), p. 122 and footnote 6.

[31] Elie Berger, *Les régistres d'Innocent IV,* (Paris, 1884), I, no. 544, col. 95, dated March 8, 1244.

[32] Fournier, *Statuts,* I, nos. 520-522, p. 450.

[33] *Ibid.,* no. 518, p. 449, the "Olim operante illo"; and no. 519, p. 450, regarding the ban on the removal of food in time of want. Fournier remarks that the former is not quite similar to his no. 506, failing to note that in this case the bull is addressed to the university and not to the count. Save for an "ad instar felicis recordationis Gregorii pape predecessoris nostri," the name of the Pope, and the dating phrase, the document is identical with the one addressed to the same body by Gregory IX in 1233, cf. Du Boulay, III, 149. Percin, *pars* II, 153, mentions this renewal under 1248, but does not quote the dating phrase, for which he cites "Ex codice mss. Carcassonensi." Obviously an "anno iii" had been misread "anno vi." Gadave, no. 19 has listed the confirmation under 1248, citing Percin; and Gatien-Arnoult in the *Mémoires de l'académie des sciences, inscriptions, et belles-lettres de Toulouse* (1878), G., X, p. 20 has likewise followed Percin. This same bull was renewed again by Innocent's successor, Urban IV in 1264—Fournier, *Statuts,* I, no. 524, p. 452. The Bibliothèque Nationale MSS. lat. 4221C, 4221D, and 4354C, and the *Livre rouge* at the Bibliothèque de l'université de Toulouse give the same incorrect date for this second confirmation. They have garbled the dating phrase of Urban's confirmation with that of the original of Gregory IX and also with that of the confirmation by Innocent IV.

of the epoch-making bull, *Parens scientiarum,* originally enacted
by Gregory for Paris. This would in itself indicate that conditions in the university were improving as its provisions were all
of a constitutional nature.[34]

Aside from the few masters mentioned in connection with the
payment of salaries in 1239, the personnel of the *studium* during
the first twenty years remains somewhat of an enigma. John of
Garland, Roland of Cremona, and John of Saint Gilles are the
only masters whose biographies are even tolerably well known.
Laurentius Anglicus, who followed John of Saint Gilles in the
Dominican chair of theology, is little more than a name.[35] The
above-mentioned letter to the legate testifying as to Raymond's
payment of salaries lists the names of two who were undoubtedly
masters—Master Sicardus, a canon of Narbonne, and G. Arnaldus,
archdeacon of Lantarena. However, the syndics who receive prior
mention in the document, Master Luppus, Master P. de Monte-
landerio, and Master G. Xantonensis, can very well have been
regents also, though the wording makes this somewhat uncertain.
Sicardus is encountered again without reference to his mastership in a document of the count of Toulouse dated at Béziers
in 1243, while Lupus Ispanus, a master in medicine, was present
at Penne in the Agenais in March, 1242, on the occasion of the
desperate illness of Raymond VII. Upon his advice and that of
several other physicians present, the count was absolved of
excommunication as one in imminent peril of death.[36] Of the
other masters, nothing further can be learned.

[34] Fournier, *Statuts,* I, no. 523, p. 451. Save for the address, exordium and
dating phrase, the two are identical. Cf. Denifle, *Chartularium,* I, no.
79, p. 136.
[35] John and Laurentius are reported by Guillaume Pelisse (Douais), p. 105;
and cited by Denifle, *Die Entstehung,* p. 330, and footnote 457. Du
Boulay, III, 139; Bertrand, *Gestes des Tolosains,* Nv; and—after the
former—Gatien-Arnoult in the *Mémoires de l'académie des sciences, inscriptions, et belles-lettres de Toulouse* (1877), G., IX, 473, regard Anthony of Padua also as a Franciscan master at Toulouse during this
period. The first mentioned reports the same master later at Paris, although the *Chartularium* has no reference to him. Wadingus, *Scriptores
ordinis minorum* (Rome, 1906), p. 27 tells of Anthony as master at Bologna only. Hilarin Felder, *Geschichte der wissenschaftlichen Studien im
Franziskanorden* (Freiburg im Breisgau, 1904), 147 and 238, asserts that
he was at Toulouse in 1225, citing Surius, *Legenda.* Although there was
a lull in the hostilities during this year, it is rather improbable that anyone could do much teaching at Toulouse.
[36] Fournier, *Statuts,* I, no. 516, p. 447. The index of the *Histoire générale
de Languedoc,* VIII, identifies the Luppus, who heads the list of procurators as Luppus Ispanius, the physician to Raymond VII mentioned
in *ibid.,* 348-CCXLIII, cols. 1084-1087. Sicardus has further mention in
ibid., no. 363-CCLV, col. 1122.

In 1251, after the death of Raymond, Alphonse of Poitiers, then count of Toulouse, called together at Toulouse a group of experts in law to render decision upon the testament of his father-in-law. Among these Guido de Regio, *Doctor Legum,* and Master Gyraldus de Andriano, *Doctor in Decretis,* are found, but there is nothing to prove that they were regents in the *studium.* Among the jurisconsults there mentioned was Guido Fulcod, who later became Pope Clement IV.[37] There are other conjectural masters cited by Percin, Catel, and Gatien-Arnoult, but their importance for Toulouse is as slight as the evidence of their presence in the *studium.* The mere reference to a lawyer or physician at or near Toulouse by no means guarantees that he taught in the university, for such persons were frequently encountered throughout the Midi long before the foundation of that institution.[38]

In the middle of the century, the poor students in the Hospital of Saint Raymond acquired a building of their own. This was due to the combined efforts of the Dominicans and the convent of Saint Sernin. Strangely enough, the inquisition, which had almost been the undoing of the university in its early years, now lent a helping hand. In February, 1250, Guillaume, bishop of Agen, a former Dominican inquisitor for the lands of the count of Toulouse, gave a house to the abbot and convent of Saint Sernin in recognition of their assistance and liberality. This house, which had formerly been used as a prison for heretics, was conveniently close to the Hospital of Saint Raymond "where poor scholars dwell." It was not until May 4, 1256, that the actual conveyance of the building occurred. Then the existing inquisitors for Toulouse added further conditions to the gift before conferring the key on the abbot. These were that the

37 *Histoire générale de Languedoc,* VIII, no. 424, cols. 1292-1294.
38 Gatien-Arnoult in the *Mémoires de l'académie des sciences, inscriptions, et belles-lettres de Toulouse* (1857), E., I, 207; (1898), G., X, 21-30; and (1879), H., I, 8-12. Percin, *Monumenta,* pars II, 196 ff. gives a long list of masters who presided in the Dominican convent of Toulouse. Among those cited by Gatien-Arnoult are Jacques de Toulouse and Elias Bruneti. As examples of lawyers and physicians in the Midi during this period are: Pontius Astraldus, *legista,* encountered as witness for a donation to the count of Toulouse, August 10, 1231, (Bibliothèque Nationale MS. lat. 12853, f.248); Arnaldus Bernardi, *medicus,* found as witness in a document of March 27, 1236 (*ibid.,* f°301), who is also named as procurator for the abbey of Boulbonne in 1234 (Catalogue de Boulbonne, no. cvii, in the *Histoire générale de Languedoc,* VIII, col. 1901); Raymundus Rusticus, *legista,* who witnessed an act of fidelity, September 12, 1243, (Bibliothèque Nationale MS. lat. 12853, f°307). These were certainly practitioners rather than teachers of their respective arts.

house should be sealed on the ground floor and fitted upstairs and down with cells and suitable study rooms, that ingress to the building should be from the hospital by means of an arched stone bridge to be constructed over the street, and that repairs should be made by the abbot and convent. In this can be seen another step in growth of the College of Saint Raymond, for although the collegiates were still under the superintendence of the almoner of Saint Sernin, they had a house and courtyard distinct from the hospital.[39]

During its fourth decade there is yet further proof of augmenting numbers in the university. Clement IV, himself a Frenchman and noted lawyer, was a native of Saint Gilles in Provence. As Gui Fulcod, he had been married and had had children before becoming clerk, and in a legal capacity had been councillor of Louis IX. On the death of his wife he was raised to the see of Le Puy and later transferred to Narbonne. On becoming cardinal of Santa Sabina, he was sent on legation to England and was absent at the time of his election in 1264.[40] In 1266 this pope wrote to the archbishop of Narbonne ordering him to correct matters at Toulouse. Some of the masters and students, misusing their privileges of restricted jurisdiction, had been summoning persons living at great distance and compelling them to come to that city for trial for alleged injuries. Under the burden of this litigation, the unfortunate defendants were often forced, as the pope expressed it, "into damnable pacts." The archbishop was to take measures to stop such scandals by means of ecclesiastical censure to be effective against members of the university unless they could make "full and express mention" of the indult by which they were exempt from suspension, interdict, or excommunication.[41] In this same year, the

---

[39] Letters patent of the bishop and of the two Dominican inquisitors are included in a *vidimus* of 1524, Archives départementales de la Haute-Garonne, fonds Saint Raymond, XV, sac AF, liasse i, titre 8.

[40] Bernard Gui, *Catalogus brevis*, Bibliothèque Nationale MS. lat. 4040.

[41] Fournier, *Statuts*, I, no. 539, p. 464, has misattributed this document to Clement V. The document itself contains the words, "in Narbonensi provincia presertim de, qua originem traximus." Clement V was a native of Gascony and archbishop of Bordeaux before his election, so this document could obviously not be from his chancery—Bernard Gui, *Catalogus brevis*, Bibliothèque Nationale MS. lat. 4040. It is also dated from Perugia, and the latter Pope never left France. This document is correctly given by Molinier in the *Histoire générale de Languedoc*, VII, "Statutus et privilèges de l'université de Toulouse," no. ix, cols. 440-441, and also by Baluze in Bibliothèque Nationale MS. lat. 4222, f°17—"Ex archivo Archiepiscopi Narbonen." Denifle, *Les universités françaises au moyen âge—avis à M. Fournier* (Paris, 1892), 27, has noted this error. The correct date is January 8, 1266.

bishop of Toulouse, unable to cope with the unruly members of the "multitude of clerks" who had collected because of the *studium,* published an *ipso facto* excommunication of all clerks and scholars who should presume in the future to bear arms by day or night, and the same penalty was also threatened against those who supplied such persons with weapons. Desiring to see this statute thoroughly observed both in the city and burg, the bishop authorized the vicar and *capitouls* to arrest all armed clerks or scholars, wherever and whenever found, with the understanding that they were, upon request, to be turned over to him or to his *officialis* for judgment. Some three years later the power of capturing clerks caught at a serious offense was also conceded to the *capitouls* with a similar reservation of jurisdiction.[42]

In 1272 the university must have had some need for protection, for the archbishop of Narbonne, the bishop of Toulouse and the elect of Carcasonne, pleading arduous ecclesiastical business which prevented their assembling for the purpose, delegated to an archdeacon in the church of Narbonne and to the *officialis* of Comminges their duties as conservators of privileges of Toulouse, intrusted to them by Innocent IV.[43] One of these privileges, it will be remembered, forbade the exportation of food from the city in time of want, and the other reiterated the initial grant of academic powers by Gregory IX. Whether the year was a lean one or whether the judicial exemptions of the students had been violated is not made clear, but the delegation of powers in itself is enough to indicate that there must have been at least occasional appeals to these conservators.[44]

[42] Fournier, *Statuts,* I, nos. 526-527, p. 453. Gadave, no. 25, lists for 1266, a letter of the *capitouls* of Toulouse to Count Alphonse, relative to a sum of money due him by the University, citing both manuscript and printed sources. This is merely a misreading of the word *universitas* as applied to the municipal corporation.

[43] Archives départementales de la Haut-Garonne, *Livre blanche de l'archevêché,* f°42. The letters of Innocent IV renewing those of Gregory IX—the "Olim operante illo" bull, and the one forbidding the exportation of food in time of want (Fournier, *Statuts,* I, nos. 518-519, pp. 449-450)—are quoted in full. The bulls as printed in Fournier are not addressed to these prelates; but the copy of the latter sent to Orléans in 1309 by the *officialis* of Toulouse was directed to the bishops of Carcasonne and Toulouse and the elect of Narbonne—Bibliothèque Nationale MS. lat. 4223A, f°13v°. This enclosure is listed by Fournier under Orléans in the *Statuts,* I, no. 25, p. 25.

[44] The archbishop of Narbonne was engaged at that moment in erecting a new cathedral church which no doubt accounts for some of his preoccupation, "Chronique de Saint-Just de Narbonne" in the *Histoire générale de Languedoc,* VIII, no. 5, col. 219.

Upon the death of Count Alphonse in 1271, Philip III had proceeded to annex the county of Toulouse and the Agenais; and the royal seneschal at Carcasonne was ordered to take immediate possession. The changes thereby entailed in local administration threw the whole region into a confusion from which it did not entirely emerge for some years. There were continual complaints from Languedoc to the king over the violations of old customs and old privileges.[45] Among these pleas was that of Bertrand, bishop of Toulouse, against the royal vicar in that city in the matter of jurisdiction over clerks. A first complaint was directed to the *parlement* at All Saints' term in 1282. This document contained a long list of grievances, among them one that the bishop and his *officialis* had been impeded in the capture of clerical malefactors who were taking refuge in the houses of laymen or elsewhere in the royal domain. The judgment handed down in this instance permitted the bishop to take his clerks in the streets and squares, or even in houses, with the consent of the owners.[46] Two years later at the Purifiication session, a more elaborate decision was forthcoming on behalf of the bishop, whereby the vicar was confirmed in his right to proceed against any criminal clerk, unless the accused claimed benefit of clergy and offered proof of his status; but in case of doubt the bishop was to decide in the matter. In regard to clerks engaging in secular business, the vicar had claimed that it had long been the right of the king and of his court at Toulouse to have jurisdiction in cases involving pecuniary penalties only. This the bishop denied, so the judges ordered inquest made as to the truth in the matter. In cases involving corporal penalties, whether the clerks were married or unmarried, or whether they did or did not engage in secular business, the vicar was strictly denied any jurisdiction. In the past when clerks had brought suit against other clerks engaging in business or against laymen in the ecclesiastical court, the vicar had prohibited their responding and had punished them when they did appear. As this, too, was claimed as an ancient usage by the vicar and the contrary alleged by the bishop, an inquest was

---

[45] *Histoire générale de Languedoc*, X, preuves, charte no. 1-I, cols. 79-80. See also the petition of the prelates of the province protesting the military service demanded of them, *ibid.*, no. 10-V, cols. 111-115; and those of the *capitouls* answered by an arrest of *parlement* in 1279, *ibid.*, no. 26, cols. 153-158, and no. 27, cols. 159-165.

[46] Archives départementales de la Haute-Garonne, *Livre blanc de l'archevêché*, f° 56v°.

ordered upon this point also. The prelate had likewise complained that clerks acquitted in his court had been subject to capture by the vicar who had prohibited even parents and friends of the unfortunates to receive them or give them food until an arrangement had been made with him. This was in the future to be denied to the vicar. Other clerks laying aside their clerical garb and going about in variegated garments in order to escape coercion for crimes in the episcopal court had been protected by the vicar. This too, was ordered stopped in cases where at the time of citation the culprits were known to have been in possession of clerical status. There were likewise disputes over the vicar's interference with clerks taken in minor offenses, over his exacting confessions from them before turning them over to ecclesiastical jurisdiction, over his releasing clerks instead of remitting them to the episcopal *officialis,* and over his imprisoning them in the Chateau Narbonnais until they should render satisfaction to merchants for contracts made under the royal seal. From all of this the vicar was ordered to desist in the future. Among these instances cited, there surely can be seen the plights of many an unfortunate scholar, although further details are lacking.[47] Again in 1292 royal letters of Philip IV were necessary in this matter, forbidding the seneschal to interfere with the bishop's right of punishing clerks, even after they had quitted their habits, and prohibiting the *capitouls* to imprison, torture, or throw by night into the Garonne, clerks subject to the bishop's jurisdiction.[48]

Among the masters who taught at Toulouse during this epoch was Jacques de Revigny. This information is supplied in a gloss of Bartolus who quotes his own master, Cynus, on a

[47] The arrest of the *parlement* of Paris rendering decision in this matter is published in the *Histoire générale de Languedoc,* X, no. 18, cols. 133-136, after Bibliothèque Nationale MS. lat. 9993, f°s 25-26, in which the year is missing. The editors have suggested "Vers 1275." The identical document occurs in the *Livre blanc de l'archevêché,* f° 55 ff., with a letter of King Philip directing it to the attention of his seneschal, dated March 22, 1284. The whole was made into a public document at the request of the vicar, May 7, 1284, and with this subscription it appears in the *Livre blanc.* The introductory paragraph as it appears printed in the *Histoire générale de Languedoc,* as well as mentioning the session of the court, also refers to a public document made by Vitalis Aycardi, notary of Toulouse, so the two documents are certainly from the same source. The passages from the *Livre blanc* cited above are the same as those appearing in the printed form.

[48] Fournier, *Statuts,* I, nos. 533-534, pp. 457-458. Scholars are mentioned neither in the manuscript source—the *Livre blanc de l'archevêché,* f^o64— nor in Fournier's heading, although Gadave has included them in both documents in his register, nos. 27 and 28.

legal point recounted to him by Pierre de Belleperche when he visited Bologna in the Jubilee Year of 1300. Belleperche, while a student at Toulouse, recalled hearing Franciscus Accursius the Younger discuss his father's opinion on this matter, to which exception was taken by Jacques de Revigny, a famed master of the *studium*. Accursius himself was not a regent at Toulouse but a dignitary visiting the area as advocate for the king of England in connection with the transfer of the Agenais.[49] Guillaume Durant the Younger has also been claimed as student and professor at Toulouse, but modern scholarship has shown that it was the nephew of that bishop of Mende who taught in this *studium* in the early fourteenth century.[50]

On the whole, the growth of the *studium* to 1300 was slow and, after the death of Count Raymond, comparatively uneventful. Perhaps this in itself best accounts for the paucity of documents dealing with university affairs. Although there is but slight reference to the fortune of the university during the last twenty years of the thirteenth century, some indication of other features of its life may be drawn from local annals. In 1281 on the vigil of the Ascension, when the customary procession was traversing the Old Bridge over the Garonne, a span collapsed, plunging a large number of persons into the water, among them fifteen clerks, "notable and honored persons." The chronicler does not mention whether there were any masters and students among them or among the two hundred others reported

[49] See Gatien-Arnoult in the *Mémoires de l'académie des sciences, inscriptions, et belles-lettres de Toulouse* (1879), H., I, pp. 2-8; and Rodière, "Recherches sur l'enseignement du droit dans l'université de Toulouse," in the *Recueil de l'académie de legislation de Toulouse* (1860), IX, 254-255. Both refer to Savigny, *Geschichte des Römischen Rechts im Mittelalter,* chap. 48. Rodière quotes Bartole: "Quidem ut domini Franc. Acc., cum semel fuerit advocatus pro rege Angliae, in studio Tholosano repetit istam legem et recitavit, et tenuit opi. patris sui prout jacet Do. Jaco. de Rave. qui erat ibi magnus doctor, in forma discipuli surrexit contra eum, et opp. sic . . . Et istud retulit Pet. de Bel. perti dum in anno Jubileo vaniret Roman ad indulgentiam tamquam peregrinus et Bono repetit istam L. Dom Cyno (V. l'édition de Bartole de Lyon 1552) secunda Bartoli super codice." Accursius was among the envoys of Edward I dispatched to the Agenais in 1275. George P. Cuttino, *Le Livre d'Agenais* (Toulouse, 1956), Introduction, ix and xviii, n. 30, citing the *Calendar of Patent Rolls* (London, 1901, 1913), p. 94 and Rymer, *Foedera* (London, 1821), I, 94.

[50] Gatien-Arnoult in the *Mémoires de l'académie des sciences, inscriptions, et belles-lettres de Toulouse* (1879), H., I, 12 ff., for the former view. Paul Violet, "Guillaume Durant le Jeune" in the *Histoire littéraire*, XXXV, 4, has demonstrated the latter. Denifle remarks the lack of foundation for the presence of Arnaud de Villeneuve in Toulouse about this same epoch, *Die Entstehung*, 335, footnote 481.

to have been concerned in the accident, but doubtless the university would have been well represented on such an occasion as a Rogation procession.[51] In 1285 crops were so poor that no Dominican convent could be found in the whole province with sufficient means to support its own brethren, and the logical and arts *studia* could not be held in that year. Such a famine must also have affected the university, although there is no evidence to corroborate this suspicion.[52]

The opening of the fourteenth century marked the beginning of a great epoch in the history of the university. In 1298 Toulouse had been considered important enough as a school of canon law to receive a copy of the officially re-edited *Decretals* issued by Boniface VIII.[53] The *Sextus,* as this work was known, was similarly directed to Paris, Bologna, Oxford, Salamanca, and Orléans in the same year with orders that no older editions were henceforth to be considered legal. A further example of the growing importance of this *studium* is a regulation of the general chapter of Cluny in 1301, whereby monks of that congregation were limited in the study of canon law to Orléans, Toulouse, Montpellier and Avignon.[54] In the matter of summoning a general council for the trial of Boniface VIII, the support of Toulouse was solicited by the king and graciously conceded to him. The memory of the famous quarrel must have long endured at Toulouse, for Guillaume de Montlauzon in his *Lectura super Sexto* recounts how Boniface was held in so little esteem there that it was the custom to omit one of his decretals in the schools out of respect for the Colonna, one of whom had married the daughter of a local noble.[55]

51 *Praeclara Francorum facinora,* edited by Catel, *Histoire des comtes de Tolose,* p. 140.
52 Cited by Célestin Douais, *Essai sur l'organisation des études dans l'erdre des Frères prêcheurs au XIIIe et au XIVe siècle* (Paris and Toulouse, 1884), p. 184, from the proceedings of the provincial chapters.
53 Fournier, *Statuts,* I, no. 538, p. 463, dates this bull correctly from the year of the pontificate, but refers to the mistaken date, 1304, added by the manuscript source—Bibliothèque Mazarine, MS. 461. This manuscript—bearing the present *cote* MS. lat. 1304—is a copy of the *Sextus,* at the end of which the bull of Boniface directed to Toulouse is quoted. Immediately after the dating phrase, which falls on the last page of the volume, the pious scribe has added: "Anno Domini M° CCC° quarto, Deo gratias. Amen."
54 For the *Sextus* see Denifle, *Chartularium,* I, no. 608, p. 81, footnote; and Fournier, *Statuts,* I, no. 16, p. 9, who quotes the document for Orléans, dated September 23. For the Cluniac regulation, consult Fournier, *Statuts,* III, no. 1870, p. 449; and Denifle, *Chartularium,* II, no. 1186, p. 687, note.
55 Denifle, *Chartularium,* II, no. 634, p. 101; and Fournier, *Statuts,* I, no.

Shortly thereafter began the Avignon period of the papacy. Clement V, the first of this group of French popes, was a native of Gascony and had been bishop of Comminges and archbishop of Bordeaux before his election. Crowned at Lyon in the presence of Philip, he strengthened his position and that of the French party by creating many new cardinals, among them the bishops of Toulouse and Béziers.[56] It was only natural that the university should avail itself of the opportunity to make known its wants, having a near neighbor in a position of such authority. Its requests were answered in three bulls of April 27, 1306, two of them directed to the students and one to the bishop of Toulouse. Besides granting a spiritual indulgence to the masters and students for attending the customary university Mass during Advent and Lent,[57] the pope conferred a judicial privilege as well. They were not to be cited in justice outside the city of Toulouse by authority of apostolic letters omitting express mention of exception to this indult.[58] The bishop was ordered at the same time to correct abuses in the licensing of physicians for the city. The pope had been informed that many had been practising with but slight knowledge of medicine. In the future no one was to do so who had not received license after an examination before the bishop and experts in the said art.[59] Clement V also occupied himself at this same epoch with

536, p. 461; and no. 537, p. 462. Pierre Flotte and Guillaume de Nogaret, two of the most prominent actors in the baiting of Boniface, are claimed by Gatien-Arnoult as products of the schools of Toulouse, because they were born in the region and noted lawyers, *Mémoires de l'académie des sciences, inscriptions, et belles-lettres de Toulouse* (1881), H., III, 1-20. See also Paul Fournier, "Guillaume de Montlauzon" in the *Histoire littéraire*, XXXV, 491.

[56] Bernard Guidonis, *Catalogue brevis*, Bibliothèque Nationale MS. lat. 4040.

[57] Fournier, *Statuts*, I, no. 525, p. 452, following Molinier, "Statuts et privilèges" in the *Histoire générale de Languedoc*, VII, preuves, no. viii, col. 439, has attributed this bull to Clement IV. In the latter, *Ysidulii* has been corrected to *Perusii*, in order to agree with the itinerary of that Pope. This error has been signalized by Denifle, *Les universités*, 27. Mas-Latrie, *Trésor de chronologie*, places Clement V at Ysduli on April 27, 1306. Baluze, in Bibliothèque Nationale MS. lat. 4222, attributed it correctly. The letter itself is also found at the Vatican in register 53 of Clement V, *epistola* cxxxii, f°45.

[58] Fournier, *Statuts*, I, no. 541, p. 464, has correctly attributed this to Clement V, citing "Arch. Vatic. Reg. Clem. V, an. 1, p. 1, ep. 145, f°45," which should be corrected to read Register 53, *epistola* cxxxxi, f°45. He has merely copied the edition of Molinier as "corrected" for Clement IV, however; for he dates the document *Perusii*, cf. "Statuts et privilèges" in the *Histoire générale de Languedoc*, VII, preuves, no. vii, cols. 438-439. This error is also cited by Denifle, *Les universités*, 27.

[59] Fournier, *Statuts*, I, no. 540, p. 464, quotes the document without address. This also has been "corrected" to read *Perusii*, but on his own authority as Molinier does not print the document. Denifle has corrected

a thorough reorganization of the *Studium* of Orléans. The latter school was directed to conform its organization, manner of lecturing, and statutes to those of the *Studium* of Toulouse and was confirmed by him in all immunities, privileges, and liberties which the other enjoyed. Three years later the *officialis* of Toulouse actually witnessed a transcription of the said privileges made by a local notary for transmitting to Orléans.[60]

With John XXII, a native of Cahors, upon the pontifical throne, the university again took the opportunity to gain further recognition. In bulls of November 13, 1316, he confirmed to "his dear sons, all the doctors and scholars studying at Toulouse," the liberties and immunities granted by his predecessors, all privileges conferred upon them by kings and princes and other secular powers, and at the same time wrote to the masters and doctors of Paris commanding them to send a copy of their privileges to Toulouse. This right, he explained, had been given to the latter *studium* by his predecessors, but the masters at Toulouse had complained to him that although they had requested a copy of such privileges on many occasions, none had ever been sent. Such being the case, he wondered greatly at their neglect to do so, as by it their liberties would in no way be impaired.[61] In December of this same year, the pope dispatched by special messenger a copy of the decretals of his predecessor, Clement V, to Toulouse where it was received at a ceremony in the Franciscan chapter house by an assemblage of six professors of law representing the university.[62]

Aside from the prestige and recognition received by the university during these years, there were also signs that it was growing. Guillaume de Cun in an *apparatus* on the first seven books of the *Codex*, written in 1316, recounts that the schools of Toulouse were crowded to overflowing and could not accommodate all of the students.[63] An encomium of Toulouse directed

this slip too, *Les universités*, 27. The rubric of register 53, *epistola* cxxxxv, f°45—save for the number of the volume, Fournier has given the correct reference in this instance—reads: "Venerabili fratri episcopo Tholosano."
[60] Fournier, *Statuts*, I, no. 19, p. 11; and no. 25, p. 25. The latter should read February 16, instead of the "16 janvier" that Fournier assigns to it. The document contained copies of five letters of Innocent IV—some of them mere confirmations of those of his predecessor—one of Urban IV, and two of Clement V—*ibid.*, nos. 519-525 and 541.
[61] Fournier, *Statuts*, I, no. 547, p. 496; and no. 546, p. 495. Another judicial privilege was extended by this Pope, *ibid.*, no. 548, p. 496; and the two bulls of Clement V in regard to the illegal practice of medicine, no. 559, p. 511; and in regard to indulgences, no. 560, p. 512, were renewed.
[62] Fournier, *Statuts*, III, no. 1901, pp. 521-522.
[63] "Dominus Guillelmus de Cumbo" is listed among the doctors of law who

to the *capitouls* of that city in 1319 by the infirmarian of Saint
Sernin, Pierre de Martiris, praises it in glowing terms, remarking
the "fountain of each law and of the divine" which irrigated
the city.[64] The flourishing state of the *studium* is also attested
to some extent by the fact that Guillaume de Montlauzon, who
had been professor of canon law at Toulouse before his nomination as abbot of the Montierneuf at Poitiers in 1319, gave
and endowed in that very year, for six poor students, his house
at Toulouse to be organized as a college after his death.[65] By
1329 the number of institutions in which poor students were
maintained from the rents of pious bequests of citizens of Toulouse had increased to six: namely, the hospice of Saint Raymond, the priory of the Daurade, the Hospital of Saint Jean, the
monastery of Saint Etienne, the priory of Saint Pierre de Cuisines, and the *Maynaderia* of Toulouse. Such endowments well
illustrate the importance of the university to the city.[66]

The removal of the Curia to Avignon also influenced the
growth of the *studium,* as the French popes, who were practically all natives of southern France, chose their relatives, friends,
and colleagues to fill the important administrative positions.
This made canon law all the more popular to those ambitious

witnessed the *Ad honorem Dei* statutes in 1314—Fournier, *Statuts,* I, no.
545, p. 495. The better reading *Cunho* is given in Bibliothèque Nationale MS. lat. 4221C, where the statutes run from f°18v°, col. 2 to
26v°. For his biography, consult Paul Fournier, "Guillaume de Cun,
légiste," in the *Histoire littéraire,* XXXV, 362 ff. He dates this *apparatus*
as one for the year 1316-1317. Edmond Cabié, "Guillaume de Cun de
Rabestens, professeur à Toulouse, 1314-1316" in the *Revue historique du
Tarn* (1876-1877), I, 227, devotes his principal effort to proving Rabestens as the birthplace of Guillaume. The *apparatus* itself was compiled
from the lecture notes of a student who had followed a course in the
Codex under Guillaume, and is found to-day at Basel, Universitäts-
Bibliothek, ms. C. I. 6, and also in an equally rare printed edition; see
article of Fournier cited above.

[64] Archives municipales de Toulouse, AA5 (1). "Inter urbes magnificas,
nostra et vestra civitas Tholosa affatim preconiis digna velut sidus nucans,
cultu decorata divino, fonte utriusque juris et divina irrigata, numerosa
populi caterva ac mercibus opulenta radios honoris ex hac fameque
fragranciam spargit et mittit per orbem." Quoted by Stephanus de Gano,
O.M., Master of Theology at Toulouse, in a treatise dedicated to Archbishop Bernard du Rosier of Toulouse, which bears the title *De funda-
tionibus tempore loco et nomine Tholose et Rome, Anglie, Britanie,
Narbonie et Parisius.*

[65] Fournier, *Statuts,* I, no. 699, pp. 654-656. He is mentioned as doctor in
decrees absent from the *Studium,* in the statutes of 1314—*ibid.,* no. 545,
p. 495. For his biography, see Paul Fournier, "Guillaume de Montlauzon,
canoniste" in the *Histoire littéraire,* XXXV, 467 ff.

[66] Fournier, *Statuts,* I, no. 558, p. 510, xii. The general chapter of St. Sernin
on June 8, 1328, included in its regulations the collegiates of St. Raymond,
Archives départementales d la Haute-Garonne, fonds Saint Sernin, 202,
f°8v°.

for rapid advancement. In his *apparatus* on the constitutions of Benedict XII, Guillaume de Montlauzon deplores this scramble for favor, for he refers disapprovingly to some students who had deserted Orléans for Toulouse and had abandoned civil law for decrees.[67] Special privileges were frequently given to favored ecclesiastics in order to allow them opportunity for advanced academic training. Guillaume Durant, nephew of the bishop of Mende, was granted by papal exemption in 1311 the emoluments of his canonicate and prebend in that diocese for a period of five years, during which time he was not obliged to attain the priesthood. This was evidently for the purpose of pursuing studies in canon law, for he was later master of that subject at Toulouse.[68] Even as early as 1304, Benedict XI had permitted Roger d'Armagnac, an archdeacon of Agen, to employ a substitute to visit his archdeaconry during the two years he should remain at a *studium* of civil law. Just two months later the same pope permitted the rector of a parish church in the diocese of Toulouse to study law for five years and receive the revenues of his church during that period.[69] In 1305, soon after his coronation at Lyon, Clement V granted to Gui de Montfort, son of the count de Comminges, the favor of studying in a school of law for a period of five years notwithstanding his duties as canon of Clermont. He had to be dispensed also in letters of the same date for holding various benefices and offices in spite of defect of years, "since you have only the tonsure and are about twelve years of age."[70] This maintaining of young clerks in the schools by conferring prebends on them and dispensing them from the duties of residence was greatly developed under the succeeding Avignon popes. Even when the long years of schooling were over, the holders of benefices did not return to their livings but continued to enjoy their revenues in prominent positions at the Curia. Hugues, son of Bertrand de l'Isle-Jourdain, was indulged in 1317 so that he could follow courses in civil law for five years and not be held to receive higher orders during that time, and by other letters was dispensed from residence and assured the

[67] Paul Fournier, "Guillaume de Montlauzon, canoniste," in the *Histoire littéraire*, XXXV, 487.

[68] Paul Violet, "Guillaume Durant le Jeune" in the *Histoire littéraire*, XXXV, 4.

[69] Charles Grandjean, *Le régistre de Benôit XI* (Paris, 1905), no. 357, col. 252, dated February 6, 1304; and *ibid.*, no. 635, col. 404, dated April 4, 1304.

[70] These two letters are found in a register of Clement V at the Bibliothèque Nationale, MS. lat. 4038B.

fruits of his benefices for the same period and purpose.[71] A canonicate, prebend, and cantorship in the church of Thérouanne had been conferred upon him in October of that year although he was but twenty-two and a canon of Narbonne.[72] Another student clerk was assured of his revenues for a *triennium* while following "scholastic disciplines," by papal letters of the same year. Two years later this privilege was renewed, and the letters were directed to the abbot of Saint Sernin at Toulouse, as well as to the student himself, which indicates his place of study.[73] That advancement came for law students at Toulouse as else-where, can be illustrated by Pierre Etienne, a Doctor of Decrees and cantor in the monastery of Saint Sernin, who was notified of his appointment as papal chaplain by letters of John XXII dated at Avignon, January 23, 1321.[74]

The great number of promotions which followed the change in the seat of the papacy must have been a great incentive to students at Toulouse. New sees were created in France to support the higher officials of the Curia so there were lucrative positions of all sorts, and advancement was rapid if one's knowl-edge of law was at all notable. John XXII in 1317 divided the enormous see of Toulouse into seven dioceses and in compensa-tion for this great curtailment of revenues and power raised Toulouse to metropolitan status. To this new province was added the bishopric of Pamiers which had already been sepa-rated from Toulouse under Boniface VIII. Among the early occupants of these new sees were Raymond d'Atho, formerly abbot of Saint Sernin, now raised to the bishopric of Mirepoix, and Pilfort de Rabestens, formerly canon of Saint Etienne, now raised to that of Pamiers.[75]

[71] Arnold Fayen, *Lettres de Jean XXII*, in the *Analecta Vaticano Belgica* (Rome, Brussels, and Paris, 1908), II, no. 448, p. 162; and no. 449, p. 163. The letters bear the date November 3, 1317.

[72] Fayen, *Lettres de Jean XXII* in the *Analecta Vaticano Belgica*, II, no. 430, p. 155. The letter is dated October 6, 1317. A prebend in the church of St. Gaudens in the Diocese of Comminges was conferred July 4, 1322, *ibid.*, no. 1064, p. 403; and a prebend in the church of Nar-bonne, where he was already canon in 1324. For this latter he had to lay aside all his other beneficies—*ibid.*, no. 1326, p. 490. The fruits of his benefices were assured him for another five year period, March 22, 1325 —*ibid.*, no. 1502, p. 554.

[73] Fayen, *Lettres de Jean XXII*, in *Analecta Vaticano Belgica*, II, no. 422, p. 152, dated September 29, 1317. He had been made a canon and re-ceived a prebend in the church of St. Jean at Liége, by letters of August 12, 1317—*ibid.*, no. 401, p. 139. The second letters are dated June 16, 1319—*ibid.*, no. 728, p. 301.

[74] Fournier, *Statuts*, I, no. 550, p. 496.

[75] *Chronicon S. Pauli Narbonensis, ad an.* 1317, in Catel, *Histoire des comtes*

About the same time, masters and students began to be called in for advice and they displaced the ordinary *jurisperitus* in a great many documents of record. A piece of legal business was enacted in the cloister of Saint Etienne in 1319 by the procurator of the chapter with the aid of a bachelor in law. In 1329 the cellarers of the same chapter named their "procurators, attorneys, defenders and special and general messengers" in the persons of Bernardus de Cava, *baccalarius in decretis,* and three *jurisperiti.*[76] Many of the episcopal offices also appear to have been reserved for the holders of legal degrees. In this same document there is a reference to the vicar general of the archbishop, Petrus Bergondionis, *legum professor.* During the third decade of the fourteenth century, degree holders begin to appear even in the lists of the *capitouls.*[77]

At about this same epoch, the first royal privileges for the *Studium* of Toulouse were given. Charles the Fair had visited Toulouse in February, 1324; and on his way to the north from Martel in the present Department of the Lot, had directed letters by which his seneschal at Toulouse was asked to take the doctors and scholars of the *studium* under a special royal protection and to guard their persons and goods against the violence and molestations of laymen. A year from the subsequent June he again directed orders to the same official and to the royal vicar, in answer to the request of the *capitouls* of the city, forbidding the former to impede or permit to be impeded the capitular jurisdiction over "lay students," their servants, or any other persons pleading the special safeguard conceded by royal letters to the university and students of Toulouse.[78]

de Tolose, p. 167. The bull of John XXII announcing this to the consuls and people of Toulouse is dated July 7, 1317, Bibliothèque Nationale MS. lat. 4223, f⁰102, "Datum Avinioni nonas Julii, pontif, nostri anno primo." For the new bishops, see Eubel, *Hierarchia,* I, 344; and 94 with footnote 3.

[76] Archives départementales de la Haute-Garonne, 46., XIX, liasse 6, titre 2. It is dated December 20, 1319, and the bachelor was Arnaldus Deubas. The second document is from the same repository—4G., XXI, liasse 1, titre 1.

[77] Germain de Lafaille, *Annales de Toulouse* (Toulouse, 1701), lists Guillaume du Pont, Knight and Doctor of laws, for 1318 and 1322; Pierre de Vaur for 1326; and Simon Bardin and Estienne Garric for 1329. Simon Bardin was bachelor in laws in 1311, Fournier, *Statuts,* I, no. 543, p. 467; and doctor in 1314, *ibid.,* no. 545, p. 495. He and Pierre de Vaur represented the city on official business in 1355, *ibid.,* no. 580, p. 533; and he was *capitoul* a second time in 1340.

[78] Fournier, *Statuts,* I, no. 552, p. 497; and the document cited in footnote 1. Gadave, no. 49 catalogues this latter after the *Livre blanc de la maison communale,* Archives municipales de Toulouse, AA3, no. 213, p. 292.

Although the first decades of the fourteenth century were prosperous for the university as a whole, it must have been affected to some extent by the series of calamities that befell Toulouse. In the spring and summer of 1310 floods in the region ruined crops and caused such a scarcity of wheat and wine, and a corresponding rise in the price of food, that no one could remember having seen a summer to equal it. The measure of flour sold at 13 pounds *tournois;* "and what was yet graver, wheat was not found for sale, nor bread at the ovens, and the poor—like beasts—were compelled to eat grass. A great many left Toulouse because of this famine." An epidemic came the following year, as might be expected. This affected the rich as well as the poor and was particularly virulent at Toulouse. According to the chronicler, there was scarcely a house which had not had one fatality. The scarcity of wheat and wine continued but not to the same extent as in the preceding year, for the measure of wheat sold at but 6 pounds *tournois*. By the following spring, however, grain began to appear more abundantly in the markets about Easter; and the price dropped to less than half, which saddened greatly the hoarders who had hopes of a famine market. The university was so well established by this time that its existence does not seem to have been gravely threatened by these events. In fact in the spring of 1311 the masters and students met in general congregation to frame a very important set of statutes. The actual attendance may have dropped off during the years of famine and pestilence, but the statutes of 1313 and 1314 give ample proof of the short duration of their effect upon the *studium*.[79]

Between 1309 and 1329 the activity of the masters and students at Toulouse was exceedingly great. No doubt the growth of the university in numbers and importance during the preceding decades had rendered its constitution, probably at best merely an agglomeration of ancient statutes and local customs, extremely inadequate. At any rate beginning with 1309 the first of a long series of attempts was made to organize and digest into a semblance of form, statutes whereby the *studium* should be governed. In this year regulations were enacted for the arts faculty. In 1311, 1313, and 1314, there were attempts at providing written constitutions for the university as a whole. In 1324 and 1328 there were special series of statutes concerning

[79] *Praeclara Francorum facinora,* in Catel, *Histoire des comtes de Tolose,* 153-154; and Fournier, *Statuts,* I, nos. 543-545, pp. 467-480.

the beadles, while in the last named year the ceremonial regarding examinations was again revised. In the following year, the faculty of arts required yet further attention, and the *studium* as a whole had by this time so hampered itself with statutes, all to be observed by strictest oath, that a thorough-going reorganization was necessary.[80] This was the work of a papal commission consisting of two cardinal-bishops, Gaucelin Deuze, titular of Albano, and Pierre Desprès, titular of Praeneste. The former had already regulated academic difficulties at Orléans in 1300 and 1321, while the latter had been professor of civil law at Toulouse in 1314.[81] Their regulations were transmitted for publication to the archbishop of Toulouse, Guillaume de Laudun, a former Dominican master of theology, who had but recently been translated to Toulouse.[82] A letter of John XXII authorized this prelate to publish, interpret, and modify them as he saw fit. Thus after nearly twenty years of disagreement and uncertainty, the university celebrated its first centennial by a complete papal reorganization.[83]

---

[80] Fournier, *Statuts*, I, nos. 542-545, pp. 465-480 ff.; nos. 553-555, pp. 497-500 ff.; and no. 556, p. 501.

[81] For the former at Orléans, see Fournier, *Statuts*, I, nos. 55-56, pp. 46-49; no. 59, p. 53; no. 63, p. 55; and nos. 65-70, pp. 57-61. The career of Petrus de Pratis well illustrates the points made above regarding advancement through academic activity. He is listed among the doctors of civil law in the *Ad honorem Dei* statutes of 1314—*ibid.*, no. 545, p. 495. On September 16, 1316, he was made canon in the church of Tournai, *non obstante* two rural churches with care of souls in the Dioceses of Toulouse and Narbonne—Fayen, *Lettres de Jean XXII* in the *Analecta Vaticano Belgica*, II, no. 93, p. 28. He was given a prebend in the church of Saintes, March 14 following, *non obstante* the three offices already held—*ibid.*, no. 272, p. 85. On August 13 of the same year he is addressed as papal chaplain and confirmed in the provostship of Clermont, *non obstante* his four other offices, but is advised to resign the church de Calviaco in the Diocese of Toulouse—*ibid.*, no. 403, p. 140. In October, he is addressed as papal chaplain resident in Saintes—*ibid.*, no. 429, p. 154. On May 31, 1318, his former canonicate and prebend at Clermont were "vacantes perpromotionem Petri, episcopi Regensis."—*ibid.*, no. 588, p. 228. Qualified as "Petrus (Desprès de Montpezat)" he appears in Eubel, *Hierarchia*, I, 417, under the bishops of Riez. He was translated to Aix-en-Provence, September 3, 1318, *ibid.*, 96; and raised to the cardinalate in the third promotion of John XXII in 1320, as cardinal priest of Santa Pudentiana, *ibid.*, 15. He was afterwards made cardinal bishop of Albano (1323), *ibid.*, 37; and then vice-chancellor (1325); dying September 30, 1361.

[82] Eubel, *Hierarchia*, I, 527, under the archbishops of Vienne; and 488 under those of Toulouse.

[83] Fournier, *Statuts*, I, no. 557, p. 503.

CHAPTER 4

THE MONASTIC ORDERS AND THE
UNIVERSITY DURING ITS FIRST CENTURY

MONASTIC establishments and their schools played an important part in the early history of the university, and none was of greater influence than the Order of Preachers or Dominicans. Of only slightly earlier foundation than the University of Toulouse itself, and with its mother-house in that very city, this order had grown with enormous strides until it comprised a vast religious organization with convents even in the more remote parts of Europe. Its founder, Saint Dominic, had devoted a great portion of his life and energies, it will be remembered, to preaching and teaching for the avowed purpose of counteracting heresy. From the very beginning, emphasis had thus been placed upon intellectual pursuits. Recruits for the ranks of these preaching friars were sought from the first among the masters and students in the best known schools of the time. The appeal must certainly have been a strong one, for the letters of the priors-general frequently recount the numbers who sought entry to the order after having heard a single sermon.[1] Paris and Bologna, because of their distinction in the intellectual world, soon became the most important convents of the order. The friars in these cities entered actively into university life and occupied prominent chairs of theology in both institutions. It was from the Dominican house in Paris that the earliest masters of theology were summoned when the *Studium* of Toulouse was founded. John of Saint Gilles, who succeeded Roland of Cremona there, was the master under whom the latter had been licensed at Paris.[2] He remained at Toulouse until 1235, and was followed by Laurentius Anglicus, but thereafter the series of master-theologians seems to break off; and the convent of Toulouse turned its attention primarily to inquisitorial matters. As this corresponded exactly with the decline of the *studium*

[1] Rashdall, *The Universities of Europe,* II:I, 13; and Denifle, *Chartularium,* I, no. 49, p. 106, and no. 52, p. 108.
[2] See *supra,* p. 53, footnote 63.

82

between 1235 and 1240, there was no reason why masters in theology should be continued, so the university faculty of theology disappeared not to be revived for over a century.

In order to understand the position of the school that persisted in the Dominican convent at Toulouse, it is necessary first to know something of the general educational system of the order. The general chapters which met each year in a different convent of this wide-spread organization early began to make provision for the instruction of novices and friars. To keep them as much as possible out of secular schools, an elaborate system of intramural education was soon provided. Beginning with the meeting at Bologna in 1233, the statutes of nearly every general chapter contain some regulations for their schools. At first they have to do mainly with providing books and masters. Later, courses of study and the location of the schools themselves are arranged. By 1246 the chapter general, meeting at Paris, made provision for the establishment of four special *studia* in the provinces of Provence, Lombardy, *Teutonia*, and England, to which each provincial prior could direct two students; while in 1255 the master of the order was counseled to provide competent lectors to any province lacking a suitable friar for a *studium*. Although the more important schools were later increased from time to time, the exact situation of a *studium generale* within its province is rarely mentioned. The convent of Toulouse was not the seat of one of these *studia generalia* until after 1304. Aside from this elaborate system of schools for the order as a whole, there was an even more complex system for the individual provinces. Here there were distinguished four different types of schools — novitiates, *studia* of arts, *studia* of natural sciences, and elementary theological *studia*.[3] These schools were carefully graded, and a stipulated time must be passed in each before entering a *studium generale*. Thereafter only the outstanding students were sent to Paris for the master's degree. Sometimes, however, they were obliged first to return to teach temporarily in their own provinces.

In this elaborate scheme, the convent of Toulouse played a very minor part. For the province of Provence there were assignments for arts' *studia* beginning in 1256, but Toulouse was not the seat of this school until 1270. In 1271 and 1274 lectors were assigned for such a school in that city. In 1275, however, the

---

[3] Consult Douais, *L'organisation des études*, 58-141.

school was transferred to Castres, never again to appear at Toulouse during the thirteenth or early fourteenth centuries. For the same period, Toulouse had its unique assignment in 1262 as a *studium naturalium.* Lectors and sub-lectors in theology were assigned more regularly from 1252 on, but as there were also such instructors assigned to many other convents in the vicinity with similar regularity, this *studium* must have had only local importance.[4]

The Franciscan friars also opened a convent at Toulouse in the thirteenth century. Members of this order were assigned as colleagues to the Dominican inquisitors to temper the extreme rigor of their zeal.[5] As early as 1247 certain meetings of the inquisition were in held "in schola fratrum Minorum Tholose," and the convent was soon listed among the four *studia generalia* of the order — the others being Paris, Bologna and Oxford. Fra Salimbene recounts how he met at Arles in Provence two former fellow-students from Pisa who were on their way to Toulouse to continue their studies before seeking the ultimate seal of Paris.[6] In 1285 at a chapter general held in Milan, the provinces which could send one student each to Toulouse were listed. Among them were Dacia, Austria, Cologne, France, Burgundy, Castile, Santiago, and the provinces of Saint Francis and of Rome. The province of Aquitaine — that of Toulouse itself — was further permitted to send a student to each of three other *studia,* Oxford, Assisi, and Bologna.[7] Despite its importance as a Franciscan *studium generale,* the convent of Toulouse in 1311 appears to have had no master in theology, for Arnaud Roiard is qualified as simple lector in the University statutes of that year, and his licensing was ordered at Paris only in 1314.[8] Constitutions concerning the Franciscans were transmitted to the doctors and scholars at Toulouse, Paris, Bologna, Rome, Naples,

[4] Douais, *L'organisation des études,* appendix IX, 179-180; appendix X, 207; and appendix XII, 235, where he gives a complete list of lectors for this convent.

[5] Guillaume de Puylaurens, chap. xliii (Bouquet, XX, 766).

[6] Felder, *Geschichte der wissenschaftlichen Studien im Franziskanorden,* p. 326; the reference to Fra Salimbene is cited in *ibid.,* p. 236.

[7] Cited by Felder, p. 361, from Franz Ehrle, "Die ältesten Redaktionen der Generalconstitutionen des Franziskanordens" in *Archiv für Literatur und Kirchengeschichte,* VI, 56.

[8] Fournier, *Statuts,* I, no. 543, p. 467. He was appointed to various commissions under John XXII, and was made archbishop of Salerno in 1321, and was translated to the See of Sarlat in 1330. His sermons—one addressed to the "universitati studentium Tholose"—are found in the Bibliothèque municipale de Toulouse, no. 329, f°33. See Charles Langlois, "Arnaud Roiard, Frère Mineur" in the *Histoire littéraire,* XXXV, 462.

Perugia, and Oxford by John XXII in 1324 in order that they might be read in the schools of those cities.[9]

The Carmelite friars, too, appear to have had a *studium* in their convent at Toulouse. They had been established outside the city somewhat later than their colleagues, the Dominicans and Franciscans, and were transferred inside the walls in 1264. In 1309 the Dominican, Franciscan, and Carmelite lectors were named as arbiters in the establishment of statutes for the faculty of arts, but Carmelite lectors or masters do not figure prominently until much later in the century.[10]

The Augustinian friars likewise established themselves near Toulouse during the thirteenth century. They moved within the walls in 1310. It is not until 1329, however, that there is mention of their lector in theology; but in a document of that year he was placed on a par with his Carmelite colleague, so perhaps this group of mendicants had founded a school at Toulouse even earlier.[11]

Although none of the orders actually permitted its students to take part in the secular schools at Toulouse, still the very presence of these private *studia* beside the university itself must have given it some added prestige. At any rate the lectors in theology in the local convents were accorded places of honor in the public exercises of the university. The names of the Dominican and Franciscan lectors head the lists of witnesses to the university statutes of 1311, appearing even before those of the actual masters themselves.[12] It is doubtful whether these lectors took much part in the purely academic exercises of the university, for the Dominican chapter general of 1280 had forbidden any lector to dispute with a master of theology without special permission of the provincial prior, except in places where a *studium generale* of the order existed. At Paris in 1306 this regulation was relaxed to include also a secular *studium generale*, but as there were no secular masters in theology at Toulouse, even this could not have directly affected the university.[13] Lectors in theology were not eligible for any of the administrative offices of the university, although by the statutes of 1313

[9] Denifle, *Chartularium*, II, no. 833, p. 276 and note.

[10] Emile Molinier in the *Histoire générale de Languedoc*, IV, note cxlv, col. 696; and Fournier, *Statuts*, I, no. 542, p. 465.

[11] Emile Molinier in the *Histoire générale de Languedoc*, IV, note cxlv, col. 693; and Fournier, *Statuts*, I, no. 537, p. 507, vi.

[12] Fournier, *Statuts*, I, no. 543, p. 467.

[13] Martène, *Thesaurus novus*, IV, col. 1801, no. 10; and col. 1903, no. 4.

they were obliged to be present at its special religious services on Sundays and feast days and at the funerals of academic personages. The university members themselves were likewise required to be present at the funeral of a lector. Lectors, like any other master or doctor, were also to be notified of a general congregation but "religious theologians of the pauper orders" were exempted from pecuniary fines for non-attendance at these congregations. The Dominican master or lector was further distinguished by being holder of one of the three keys to the *archa* or university strong box, which was to be conserved in their convent.[14]

To the existing schools of the friars was added between 1281 and 1286 a college for Cistercian students in the hospice of the monastery of Grandselve at Toulouse. The Cistercian general chapter of the former year had ordered the abbot of Grandselve to erect the necessary buildings and provide a suitable lector at Toulouse within a period of two years. The students who should be sent there were to enjoy all the privileges possessed by the College of Saint Bernard at Paris.[15] The great numbers who had collected in the city because of the *studium* in theology were given as the reason for this step. In the following January the abbot of Grandselve arranged with the abbot of Saint Sernin for the construction in the parish of the latter at Toulouse of a college where theology should be taught. By 1285 an agreement had been made whereby permission was gained to erect a church for this establishment.[16] Even by 1290 the Cistercians were not as yet able to furnish their own master for this house, for one of the *diffinitors* at the chapter general of the Dominican province of Provence in that year was qualified as teacher of the monks of Grandselve at Toulouse.[17] In 1302 the chapter general ordered that all abbots having more than twenty-five monks in

---

[14] Fournier, *Statuts*, I, no. 544, p. 474 ff. The paragraph numbers are 4, 13, 12 and 43 in this document.

[15] Statutes of the Cistercian chapters general in Martène, *Thesaurus novus*, IV, col. 1478, *ad an.* 1281. The house at Paris was in existence in 1227, see Denifle, *Chartularium*, I, no. 53, p. 109. There is another reference to Cistercian students at Paris just ten years later—*ibid.*, no. 118, p. 164.

[16] Catalogue de l'abbaye de Grandselve, no. dcccxciv, in the *Histoire générale de Languedoc*, VIII, cols. 1876–1877; and Fournier, *Statuts*, I, no. 529, p. 454 ff. This was confirmed April 8, 1287—Fournier incorrectly 1286.

[17] Percin, *Monumenta*, pars I, p. 64. "In hoc capitulo diffinitores fuere F. Guiamnus Avenionensis prior, F. Joannes Vigarosi prior Montespeliensis, F. Guillelmus de Sancto Genesio, qui tunc legebat Monachis Grandis Sylvae in Tolosa, fueratque Burdigalensis prior, et iterum lector Tolose, et F. Raymundus Hunaudi prior Tolosanus."

their houses should maintain one at the *studia* of Toulouse, Estella or Montpellier. This Cistercian house of studies was obviously private, for other regulations of the order forbade the admission of seculars or other clerks to their schools.[18] In the University statutes of 1313 there is also reference to the lector of Saint Bernard.[19] In 1322 the reformation of the Cistercian *studium* was committed to the abbots of Bonnefont, Boulbonne, and Bonneval, who were doctors in theology, and to the abbot of Grandselve. They were to forbid the students to go outside to hear courses in canon law, or even to incept under anyone who was not a Cistercian master.[20]

The monks of Cluny from the monastery at Moissac also maintained for their students at Toulouse a house in connection with the church of Saint Pierre des Cuisines. A "prior scolarium de coquinis" is listed in an early fourteenth century tithe assessment, and the monks of this establishment and of the Daurade, also a Cluniac appendage, are particularly mentioned in the university statutes of 1314.[21]

Even the regular canons of Saint Etienne appear to have been aroused to the needs of competing intellectually with the active and popular friars. Statutes of this chapter dating from November 12, 1279, provided that student-canons should be excused from Matins except in the case of feasts of nine readings. On these days they must rise and go to church but were permitted to withdraw at the "Te Deum laudamus." They were, moreover, excused from all canonical hours in which they should be in the schools or even when they should return from them.[22]

---

[18] Martène, *Thesaurus novus*, IV, col. 1500. Stellensi is Estella in the Diocese of Pamplona. This information is given in Benedict XII's reformation of Cistercian *studia*, *Bullarum Romanum*, III:II, 210. For the regulation against seculars in their schools, see Martène, *Thesaurus novus*, IV, col. 1384, a regulation of the chapter of 1245.

[19] Fournier, *Statuts*, I, no. 544, p. 475, par. 12.

[20] Martène, *Thesaurus novus*, IV, col. 1511. The monastery of Boulbonne is also said to have had a house in Toulouse where monks were sent for scholastic purposes—Fournier, *Statuts*, I, no. 530, p. 457. Its importance for the University was slight, and exact documents are lacking. Catel refers to this house at Toulouse on the street now bearing that name. He cites a testament of Raimond Mascaron of 1204, which I have been unable to locate—*Mémoires de l'histoire de Languedoc* (1643), p. 181. Auguste Molinier refers without citation to this college, in which a chapel was founded in 1270—*Histoire générale de Languedoc*, IV, note cxxiii, p. 611.

[21] Archives départementales de la Haute-Garonne, *Livre blanc de l'archevêché*, fº1ff. For the mention in the University statutes, see Fournier, *Statuts*, I, no. 545, p. 494.

[22] Archives départementales de la Haute-Garonne, 4G., II, liasse 7, titre 1.

The canons of Saint Sernin, not to be outdone by those of Saint Etienne, who were also followers of the rule of Saint Augustine, seem to have occupied themselves with intellectual pursuits also. Regulations passed in their general chapter of December 3, 1306, exempted certain canons and chaplains from a week's service at high Mass, as the student-canons who had to remain for "scholastic discipline" could conveniently fulfill their functions. Scholar-canons were also listed in another statute of the same year, for the religious of the monastery are grouped in three categories — "canon professed or novice or remaining in the schools."[23] The student-canons of both establishments were exempted by the university statutes of 1314 from regulations regarding the wearing of academic costume on certain occasions.[24] In 1324 there is extremely interesting evidence of the educational training expected of the canons of Saint Etienne, for a *rotulus* addressed to the Pope containing the statutes made at a recent chapter meeting listed all the newly-received with their ages and training. Of these, the mere boys were recorded as being able to read and chant, the youths in their teens were without exception either good grammarians or had studied that subject for a number of years, while those in their twenties were frequently students of law.[25] Hispan de Saishis, who was provost of this chapter from 1298 to 1302, had even attained the rank of doctor in decrees, and Geraldus de Lautrico, also a canon in this church, had a similar degree by 1314.[26]

In 1290 the chancellor, rector, and masters of the university had petitioned the Dominican provincial chapter for the appointment of a full master in theology at Toulouse. The response was that this could be done only by the master of the order, but that they would do what they could in the matter.[27] It was perhaps in answer to this appeal that "for the promotion of the *studium* of Toulouse, reverend father Raimundus Guilha, pro-

---

[23] Archives départementales de la Haute-Garonne, fonds St. Sernia, H., 202, f°3v° and f°5. This is from a copy of the statutes of St. Sernin compiled in 1422.

[24] Fournier, *Statuts*, I, no. 545, p. 494.

[25] Archives départementales de la Taute-Garonne, 4G, II, sac M., liasse 1.

[26] For Hispan, see *Gallia christiana*, XIII, col. 79. Geraldus in 1311 was one of the representatives of the chancellor for compiling the University Statutes—Fournier, *Statuts*, I, no. 543, p. 467. As doctor of decrees he heads the list of witnesses to the statutes of 1314—*ibid.*, no. 545, p. 495. There is a letter addressed to him as canon in 1317—Fayen, *Lettres de Jean XXII*, in the *Analecta Vaticano Belgica*, II, no. 267, p. 83.

[27] Fournier, *Statuts*, I, no. 532, p. 457.

fessor of the theological faculty" was assigned to that city in 1295.[28] The intention was evidently to establish a school of more importance than a mere particular *studium* of theology for the province, for both in that and the following year there was also a lector assigned to this convent for reading the *Sentences* "sub magistro."[29] Another indication that perhaps the house in Toulouse was being prepared for the establishment of a Dominican *studium generale* is the fact that in 1290, in compliance with the regulation of the general chapter at Ferrara requiring all *studia generalia* to maintain cursors for the reading of the Bible, cursors were established at both Montpellier and Toulouse by the provincial chapter of that year.[30] There is but one further reference to a master in theology thereafter until late in the fourteenth century, so the length of the sojourn of Raimundus Guilha cannot be definitely ascertained. Sublectors were appointed in 1299 and 1301 and both lector and sublector in 1303. In 1304 Toulouse was actually named a *studium generale* after the province of Provence had been divided and Toulouse had

---

[28] Douais, *L'organisation des études*, p. 236, quoting extracts from MS. 490 (I, 273) of the Bibliothèque municipale de Toulouse.
"1295.—Ad promotionem studii Tholosani Reverendum Patrem R. Guilha, professorem theologice facultatis, assignavimus pro doctore conventu Tholosano." f°376 B.
This brother had been lector in the *naturalia* at Toulouse in 1262, lector in theology at Narbonne in 1275, and had received his mastership at Paris—*ibid.*, appendices. He is listed by Bernard Gui, *Magistri*, in *ibid.*, appendix IV, 165. He died at Tarrascon, of which city he was a native.

[29] Douais, *L'organisation des études*, appendix XIV, 271. Arnaud de Près, the first of these two, had been full lector in the same convent from 1292 to 1294—*ibid.*, appendix XII, 236. The chapter general in session at Montpellier in the latter year had ordered his investigation and punishment for alleged irreverence to the cardinal of the order—Martène, *Thesaurus novus*, IV, col. 1859, no. 20. Perhaps it was as penance for this offense that he was thus reduced in 1295. He had been lector at Condom in 1265, at Bayonne in 1275, at Agen in 1280, at Cahors in 1282, at Bordeaux in 1283, before his appointment to Toulouse in 1292. Consult the appendices to Douais and see below for his later career. His successor in this office at Toulouse was Guillermus Petri de Godino of Bayonne in the province of Toulouse, who was lector in *naturalia* at Orthez in 1281, at Bordeaux in 1282, and at Condom in 1283—*ibid.* As bachelor he was named elector for his province to choose the master general in 1303—Martène, *Thesaurus novus*, IV, col. 1823, no. 24. He was licensed at Paris in 1324 and was afterwards lector at the Curia— Bernard Gui, *Magistri in theologia Parisius* in Douais, *L'organisation*, appendix IV, 166. In 1312 he was raised to the cardinalate as titular of Santa Caecilia and was later promoted to the See of Santa Sabina, dying June 4, 1336—Eubel, *Hierarchia*, I, 14.

[30] Douais, *L'organisation*, appendix XIV, 270. The codex containing these statutes has the remark on the margin: "Hoc anno primo incepit legi biblice in hiis duobus conventibus." The statute of the chapter general is given in Martène, *Thesaurus novus*, IV, col. 1836, no. 15.

been made the center of a new province bearing its name. In 1316 it was again listed as *studium* by the chapter of Montpellier and no doubt continued in that capacity. After 1312 the provincial chapters were no longer concerned with the appointment of lectors and sublectors, privileges reserved to the master of the order, but continued to name the cursors of the *Sentences* and Bible.[31] In 1311 the provincial chapter, "for the honor and promotion of the Toulouse *studium*," had ordained that when Guillaume de Leus, master in theology, should arrive in that city he might incept and could dispute with anyone as master. A lector for the convent was also assigned.[32] From the wording of the University statutes of 1313, it is obvious that the presence of a master in theology in the Dominican convent was not at all certain to be permanent, for the clause concerning him is modified with "or the lector, there being no master." The statutes of the next year when mentioning the Dominicans and Franciscans refer to lectors only, and thereafter no further references to a master of theology at Toulouse occur until much later in this century.[33] The convent itself was expanding at the turn of

[31] Douais, *L'organisation,* appendices XII and XIV, pp. 236 and 270; and Martène, *Thesaurus novus,* IV, col. 1961, no. 3.

[32] Douais, *L'organisation,* p. 129, footnote 6, citing Bibliothèque municipale de Toulouse, MS. 490, fº410 B. "Ad honorem et promotionem studii Tholosani, taliter ordinamus quod, cum frater Guillermus de Leus, magister in theologia, apud Tholosam pervenerit, ibidem incipiat et disputet de quolibet, et aliis, prout sibi visum fuerit, ut magister; et nichilominus, assignamus ibidem lectorem fratrem Dominicum Grimam." This brother Guillermus had been sublector at Toulouse in 1283 and had acted as lector at Castres and Narbonne, as sublector at the *studium generale* of Montpellier, and again at Narbonne, Carcasonne and Toulouse as lector, before receiving this appointment. Douais remarked that he knew nothing of Brother Guillaume de Leus, but the following references to W. de Levibus are to be found in the appendices of his *L'organisation.* Sublector at Toulouse in 1283, lector at Castres in 1285, lector at Narbonne in 1288, at Carcasonne in 1290, at Narbonne again in 1292, sublector at Montpellier in 1293, lector at Carcasonne in 1300, lector at Toulouse in 1303, and his assignment as master in 1311. See also Auguste Pelzer, "Guillaume de Leus (de Levibus), frère prêcheur de Toulouse" in *Studien und Texte Martin Grabmann zur Vollendung des 60. Lebensjahres von Freunden und Schülern gewidmet,* 2 Halbband, (which is Supplementband III. of *Beitrage zur Geschichte der Philosophie und Theologie des Mittelalters,* Münster i. W.), 1065-1079. His colleague Dominicus Grima had been sublector at Toulouse and lector at Perigueux and Bordeaux before his reappointment as lector for this year. The same appendices of Douais list him at Toulouse in 1301, at Perigueux in 1303, at Bordeaux in 1308, and again at Toulouse in 1311. He was later raised to the mastership at Avignon by John XXII, and made lector of the sacred palace, according to the additions of Bernard Gui to Etienne de Salanhac's *Magistri in theologia Parisius* in Douais, *L'organisation,* appendix IV, 167.

[33] Fournier, *Statuts,* I, no. 544, p. 478, "Vel lector, non existente magistro."

the century to accommodate this rise in importance, for in 1299 under Arnaud de Près as conventual prior, a new wing was constructed for a dormitory adjoining the school, and by 1307 under another prior, a portion of the cloister and another wing for a library with large quarters for schools on the floor above were completed. Under the predecessor of Arnaud a great bell for the use of the university had been made.[34]

The Dominican and Franciscan convents were also connected with the university in another way; their cloisters, chapter houses, and churches were frequently employed for congregations and other university functions, as the corporation of masters did not possess quarters large enough for such meetings until late in the fifteenth century. Congregations during the first decades of the fourteenth century were generally held in the Franciscan chapter house, but there is record of one which assembled in the Dominican cloister in 1328.[35] The daily requiem Mass for the university was assigned to the Dominican church by the statutes of 1311, and the Sunday Mass, at which the entire university was required to be present, was also to be celebrated in the same edifice by the regulations of 1313. The same statutes divided the solemnities for certain other feasts between the Dominican and Franciscan churches. From such evidence can be seen the importance of the convents in university life.[36]

Another clause also indicates this uncertainty: "per magistrum si fuerit, vel doctorum in defectum magistri vel lectoris in theologia proponatur," p. 480, par. 34. For reference to lectors in 1314, see *ibid.*, no. 545, p. 484, par. vii.

[34] Bernard Gui, *Historia fundationis conventuum ordinis Praedicatorum,* in Martène, *Amplissima collectio,* VI, 463. "Tempore sui prioratus (Arnaldi de Prato) facta fuit illa pars novi dormitorii, quae a meridie protenditur versus aquilonem, scilicet brachium unum crucis ex parte scholarum." Bernard Gui, *Priores in conventu Tholosano,* Bibliothèque municipale de Toulouse, MS. 490, f⁰121 B, cited in Douais, *L'organisation,* 39. "Hujus (Fr. Guillermi de Anhanis) tempore, facta fuit pars claustri de marmore, ex parte capituli, ante festum sancti Johannis Baptiste, et magna domus scolarum in solario; et desubtis facta et disposita libraria, ante nativitatem Christi, anno ejusdem Christi M⁰CCC⁰VII⁰." In regards the great bell, see *ibid.*, f⁰121A, cited by Douais, 130; and Martène, *Amplissima collectio,* VI. This is dated by the priorship of Bernard de Juzic (1294-1298). "Item, facta fuit illa magna campana pro universitate studii Tholosani." See also Fournier, *Statuts,* no. 543, p. 471, xiii.

[35] Congregations in 1311, Fournier, *Statuts,* I, no. 543, pp. 467-474; in 1314, *ibid.*, no. 545, pp. 480-495; in 1317, *ibid.*, III, no. 1901, p. 521; and in 1324, *ibid.*, I, no. 553, pp. 497-498 were held in the Franciscan chapter house. The congregation in the Dominican cloister is recorded in *ibid.*, no. 544, pp. 498-500.

[36] Fournier, I, no. 554, p. 474, par. 4. For further statutes on these matters see no. 545, p. 482, i, and p. 484, viii.

CHAPTER 5

PAPAL AND ROYAL INTERVENTION, A THEOLOGICAL FACULTY, AND COLLEGIATE FOUNDATIONS, 1329-1378

THE history of the university during the second century of its existence is varied and picturesque. It seems to have encountered about all the vicissitudes that a medieval university could suffer, but persevered in a generally even tenor. As the documents describing this period are extremely numerous, a much more microscopic picture of life within the university is possible. Just as at the beginning of its first century, the opening years of its second were clouded by grave forebodings, for the famous Berenger affair seriously threatened the university and its privileges. Indeed, had it not been for the protection afforded by the papacy, and the more self-seeking designs of royal justice which shattered municipal pretensions, the university might again have been dissolved as in its early years. As it was, the storm seems to have been weathered without much more than a ruffling of academic waters. It was not so with the city of Toulouse, however, as the most drastic punishment was meted out to the municipality.

As the details of this notable judicial process throw many interesting sidelights on the university, it seems well to trace briefly its various ramifications. There evidently had been a quarrel over the jurisdiction of lay students between the *capitouls* and the university. In 1324, a royal privilege, it will be remembered, had placed the doctors and students at Toulouse under the safeguard of the seneschal, while a year later another royal letter had explicitly exempted lay students from this provision. In 1331 Philip V confirmed the *capitouls* in this jurisdiction and specifically ordered his seneschal and vicar to desist from any interference.[1] Obviously the municipal officers were having difficulty in maintaining the peace, since various unruly elements when apprehended claimed exemption from their jurisdiction under pretext of the royal safeguard. It was this which

[1] See *supra,* p. 79; and Fournier, *Statuts,* I, no. 561, p. 512.

gave background to the famous case. It is difficult to arrive at
the precise sequence of events in this brutal affair and its still
more brutal aftermath, while to determine the exact truth from
the great mass of conflicting evidence is frankly impossible.

On the evening of Easter Sunday, which fell on April 19 in
1332, a group of young men and women were dancing in the
street before the hospice of the de Penne brothers, noble clerks
and students in residence at the university.[2] Among the merry-
makers were Amaury, viscount of Lautrec, with Auger Pouzols,
his squire, Aymery Berenger with Bernard de Mas, his squire,
and the squire of Raymond-Amiel de Penne, Peyrot, an illegiti-
mate connection of this noble house. François de Gaure, one
of the *capitouls*, accompanied by his squires and other retainers,
chanced to be passing through this part of the city and came
upon the group, all of whom were carrying prohibited arms.
An altercation arose over both the contraband arms and the
mockery shown toward the official by the revelers. One of the
capitoul's squires was wounded and left for dead, and François
himself was horribly mutilated at the hands of Amaury and Aymery Berenger. Perhaps fearful of the outcome of their escapade,
most of the group entered the hospice of their friends the de
Penne, where they soon learned that two squires of Olivier de
Penne had been arrested by the night watch. Bernard de Penne
had wished to go out immediately to their rescue, but seeing
that Aymery had his sword, he was forbidden to accompany
the rescue party. Later in the evening three *capitouls* came and
arrested Aymery Berenger and Peyrot de Penne, taking them
to the municipal prison.[3]

Although the next morning was still within the period of
Paschal immunity, the *capitouls,* considering the seriousness of
the offense and the great tumult that it had aroused among the
people, haled the accused before their court. Aymery there
appeared in a varigated lay habit and made his confession under
oath. The squires of François de Gaure were also summoned to
give evidence as well. The following day Aymery was again
before the court, this time augmented by a number of *jur-*

---

[2] They are named with their benefices and academic ranks in a bull of
John XXII, Fournier, *Statuts*, I, no. 565, p. 516.

[3] For these facts, consult the records of the trial as published in Fournier,
Statuts, I, no. 563, p. 513 ff., after the *Inventaire* of the Archives municipales de Toulouse as published by Monsieur Roschach. The proceedings
in this case are also found in a register of the same repository, dating
from 1563, (AA6, p. 49 ff.).

isperiti; and his confession of the previous day was read to him.
He was asked if there was anything to be changed or if he had
aught to offer in defense. He replied that he had not, and
placed himself at the mercy of the court. Peyrot de Penne was
also questioned at the same session. On Wednesday sworn
surgeons deposed before the court that François de Gaure,
though still alive, would probably never speak intelligibly
again for the wound he had received at the hands of Aymery
extended from his forehead to his beard about the nose and
lips, and eleven teeth had been broken by the violence of the
blow. Aymery was again given opportunity to enter a plea and
finally, after some deliberation, was sentenced to run through
the city of Toulouse from the gate of Arnaud Bernard as far as
the residence of François de Gaure, where his right fist would
be amputated; from there he should be dragged at the tail of
a horse to the scaffolds where he should be decapitated and
his head and body then hung. All of the goods of the accused
were to go to the royal treasury.[4] Aymery on hearing his fate
immediately appealed to the royal vicar and to the seneschal of
Toulouse but was denied the right of a rehearing. At this point
the allegations of the *capitouls* and the royal procurator are at
variance as to the good faith of the *capitouls* in notifying the
royal officials of the appeals. At any rate the appeals came to
naught, and the sentence was carried out explicitly.[5]

Meanwhile the university had apparently become implicated
in the matter owing to the arrest and incarceration of the de
Penne brothers, five of whom were its students. According to the
capitouls, these latter had not been arrested in the first place
but had been taken into custody the following day by the lieutenant of the royal vicar on suspicion of their implication in the
affair, because he had found arms sufficient to equip thirty men
in their hospice. As the brothers had preferred the municipal to
the royal prison, they had been housed in the former and treated
well. When the day of their hearing was postponed to the following Sunday so the archbishop could be present, they had
remained voluntarily in prison as they were afraid to leave be-

---

[4] *Ibid.*
[5] For the allegations of the royal procurator against the *capitouls* accused
of maladministration of justice, see the arrest of the *Parlement* of Paris
printed in Fournier, *Statuts,* I, no. 576, p. 528 ff. For the defense of the
capitouls, besides the above-cited arrest, see the two bulls of John XXII
issued at the request of the *capitouls—ibid.,* no. 568, p. 518; and no. 570,
p. 522.

cause of the popular tumult. Later they had been remitted under proper guard to the court of the archbishop. According to the petition of the de Penne, affairs occurred otherwise; and they were illegally captured and detained, the *capitouls* even refusing to remit them to the archbishop's *officialis* and thereby incurring excommunication.[6] The university had there taken a hand, seeing in the incarceration of five of its members a threat to its cherished privileges.[7] The subsequent quarrel grew so heated that the pope was requested to intervene. This he did by sending off three letters, dated July 18; one to the university urging moderation even if the *capitouls* did not render satisfaction, lest dissolution should follow; one to the *capitouls*, recounting the complaints against them and counseling satisfaction to the university that did them so much honor; and finally, one to Bertrand de Saint Genèse, one of his nuncios, ordering him to Toulouse as arbiter to settle matters peaceably.[8] The ecclesiastical court had demanded and ultimately received custody of all the de Penne, but many mutual recriminations were expressed on both sides. The papal nuncio was unable to arrange an amicable settlement and apparently withdrew, leaving the clerical court to act.[9]

The Berenger and de Penne affairs, although but slightly connected at first, soon became enmeshed owing to Peyrot de Penne. The university now vociferously claimed the clerical status of both Peyrot and the dead Aymery Berenger, even accusing the *capitouls* of having detonsured the latter, while the *capitouls* consistently maintained the lay character of both. Finally Peyrot was remitted to the *officialis* and the *capitouls* were absolved from excommunication, only to be re-excommunicated in letters from the pope reserving absolution to himself in their case. Despite their appeals to the Apostolic See and the several letters of John XXII to the archbishop of Narbonne ordering him to take cognizance and render decisions on the vexed questions, the *capitouls* failed to clear themselves. The university syndic was even able, on plea of clerkship, to have Aymery's body removed from the gibbet and given Christian

[6] Fournier, I, no. 568, p. 518; and no. 571, p. 523.
[7] Obviously the first letter of John XXII to the *capitouls* came as a result of the complaint of the University—Fournier, *Statuts*, I, no. 565, p. 516.
[8] Fournier, *Statuts*, I, nos. 564-566, pp. 516-517.
[9] Fournier, *Statuts*, I, no. 567, p. 518, records a meeting between the nuncio and the representatives of the *capitouls* on the twenty-second of August, where the latter objected to some of the statements in the apostolic letters they had received.

burial.[10] The *capitouls* by December had finally succeeded in having the sentence of excommunication by the bishop removed while their appeal to the Holy See was still pending,[11] but the principal questions were still undecided by the provincial curia of Narbonne in January, 1333. On that date the pope wrote to explain the absence of the de Penne brothers as not being contumacious but prevented through the power of the *capitouls*.[12] At the same time the bishop of Saint Papoul was assigned as assistant judge. The *capitouls* meanwhile were busy trying to clear up the cases against the other incriminated persons. Amaury de Lautrec had procured letters from the king remitting his case to the royal judge of appeals at Toulouse. On the complaint of the *capitouls* that their jurisdiction was being violated, the king ordered by royal letters of October 30, 1332, that his seneschal determine the truth in this matter.[13] Shortly after, the viscount complained to the pope that the *capitouls* had attempted to arrest him, disregarding his clerical status, and were preventing the trial of his squire, Auger, before the archiepiscopal court because the fever ran so high against him.[14]

The date of appeal to the *parlement* of Paris is unknown, but in August of 1334, Philip ordered the seizure of the means of eleven *capitouls* of Toulouse, who were imprisoned in Paris for the death of Aymery Berenger, clerk. In February of the next year one of the *capitouls* who had been imprisoned in Toulouse had not yet been transferred to Paris. His transfer was thereby ordered.[15] In July 1335, the *parlement* handed down a very severe judgment against the *capitouls* and the city of Toulouse for the part they had taken in the whole affair. It was decided that Aymery was a noble stranger and clerk in tonsure and therefore under royal safeguard and not justiciable before the *capitouls*. As the *capitouls* had denied all appeals, they were to render the body of Aymery for Christian burial, found

---

[10] Fournier, Statuts, I, no. 565, p. 516; nos. 568-570, pp. 520-522; and no. 596, p. 528.

[11] The pope had delegated several ecclesiastics of the diocese of Condom as judges, who ordered the clergy of Toulouse to read their letters of annulment dated December 17, Archives municipales de Toulouse, layette 74, (C 63/95).

[12] Fournier, *Statuts*, I, no. 571, p. 523.

[13] Found in the same sixteenth century manuscript which contained the proceedings of the trial of Aymery—Archives municipales de Toulouse, AA6, p. 63.

[14] Letter to the bishop of Saint Papoul ordering him to procede to trial, dated May 11, 1333—Fournier, *Statuts*, I, no. 572, p. 524.

[15] Fournier, *Statuts*, I, nos. 573-574, p. 526.

a chapel for the repose of his soul and distribute 4,000 *livres* among his relatives. The city was further punished by loss of its corporate privileges and the confiscation of all municipal property to the crown. The sentence was a severe one and rigorously carried out. Commissioners were appointed for this purpose by royal letters of August 7, and the city hall was in the hands of the king from October 7, 1335, until the following January. However, even as early as December, steps had been taken for the re-establishment of the *capitoulate*. Philip VI gave his commissioners permission to treat with the city in the same month, and the municipal franchise was repurchased at the cost of 50,000 *livres tournois*, which was later reduced to 46,000 *livres* with more liberal terms.[16] In January there were letters of remission signed by the royal commissioners, issued in the names of several of the former *capitouls*. In February, a delay having been encountered in the restoration of the *capitoulate* owing to the inability of the former *capitouls* to pay the heavy sums assessed against them on behalf of the relatives of Aymery Berenger, the city council agreed to engage the city for the remainder due.[17] But in all this there is no reference to the university. It had been the king's prerogative that had been violated, so it was the king's treasury that had profited. However, the university gained indirectly; for its royal safeguard was carefully respected by the *capitouls* a few years later in a case concerning the carrying of prohibited arms by a student and his consequent arrest. In fact, in this instance it was the student who was plaintiff against certain individuals who had formed part of the night watch. The case was tried before the seneschal's deputy, and the defendants were apparently acquitted. Also in the case of an assault upon a student by a burgher, the suit was heard by the seneschal; and when appealed to the *parlement* of Paris, the first decision was upheld.[18] Even in 1351, the royal safeguard for students was still functioning, for in the instance of the murder of a bachelor in law by a colleague of the same faculty in the church of the Taur, King Charles of Navarre, who was royal lieutenant for Languedoc,

---

[16] Fournier, *Statuts*, I, nos. 576-581, pp. 528-534; and no. 584, p. 534.

[17] Fournier, *Statuts*, I, nos. 586-587, pp. 536-537. Only one letter of remission is given in Fournier, but the original of his citation in the *Histoire générale de Languedoc*, X, p. 754 mentions three others.

[18] Document cited by Gadave, no. 83, found in the Archives municipales de Toulouse, FF 102. The trial dragged out through 1336 and 1337. The second case is given in Denifle, *Les universités*, no. viii, p. 59.

conferred the confiscations that ensued upon a certain knight and was confirmed in his action.[19]

Papal interest continued to be manifested in the university in the succeeding period, although naturally only when attention was called by some interested party. By this time it had become customary to petition Avignon for remedy in even the most trivial of matters. Among such matters for correction under Benedict XII in 1337 was an abuse practiced by certain doctors and masters and common in medieval universities in general, the employment of undue influence upon students coming to study in the schools. For the future, this was strictly forbidden under suitable penalties by papal letters of that year. In pursuance of these instructions the university shortly undertook to regulate the related question of the ownership of hospices and schools by its members.[20] In 1341, horrified by the extortionate financial demands at doctoral examinations which hindered worthy candidates from presenting themselves, Benedict forbade that such practices continue on pain of excommunication, and ordered the archbishop of Toulouse to publish his letter and return certificate of its solemn publication.[21]

The king also intervened in university affairs in 1338, when as an economy expedient on behalf of students who found the financial strain burdensome, the masters had arbitrarily reduced the rental rates on hospices in the city. In this instance, the *capitouls* complained to the king that the rent for lodgings, ordinarily fixed by a committee of four representing equally the city and the *studium,* had recently been changed by the *taxatores* of the latter acting alone, in spite of the protest of their colleagues from the town. This measure the masters had caused to be observed, though without right, through the backing of the archbishop's curia. This was to the prejudice of the *capitouls.* The king therefore ordered his seneschal to confer with the royal procurator to decide if the matter pertained to royal jurisdiction. In case it did, the seneschal was not to permit any arrangement concerning lodgings to be made except concordantly by all the *taxatores.* In case they were unable to

---

[19] Royal *vidimus* confirmed to the value of 300 golden florins and dated July, 1352, of an original of Charles of Navarre for October, 1351, in the Archives Nationales, JJ 81, no. 459, f°228.

[20] Denifle, *Les universités,* no. ix, p. 59; and J. M. Vidal, *Benôit XII—Lettres communes* (Paris, 1903-1911) I, no. 5166, p. 487. The university regulation is found in Fournier, *Statuts,* I, no. 596, p. 561.

[21] Denifle, *Les universités,* no. xi, p. 61.

come to an agreement, he was to submit the case for arbitration to the royal master of works. The scale of lodgings which had formerly existed was to be restored and the court of the archbishop was to be forbidden further interference.[22]

Under Clement VI papal interest in the university was more perfunctory. Aside from two confirmations having to do with the establishment of new colleges, he seems to have acted only in regard to the customary dispensations for students to claim the fruits of a benefice *in absentia* and with individual advancements in various faculties. In 1344 he conferred on all legitimate students and masters of the *studium* such a dispensation from residence for a period of three years. In 1346 this same privilege was renewed for a period of five years after the completion of the triennium already granted.[23] Such dispensations must have been renewed from time to time even before this pontificate, for John XXII had addressed a similar letter to the *Studium* of Toulouse in 1331, wherein he extended this privilege for another triennium. In the letters of Clement, only the highest cathedral and collegial officers were excepted.[24] In the individual advancements, Clement VI might seem to be interfering somewhat unwarrantedly in the academic machinery of the *studium*, but as it possessed as yet no theological faculty, most of these, which were fairly frequent over the next few years, should be ranked merely as favors to the convents of the mendicant friars located in the city.[25] Another case of similar import, though on behalf of an individual rather than his convent, was a special permission to read canon law at Toulouse or elsewhere given to a Cistercian monk, despite the statutes of his order to the contrary.[26] However, in one instance the pope did carry a matter entirely over the heads of the university authorities in a dispensation to a law

---

[22] Archives municipales de Toulouse, AA(28). An original on parchment, signaled by Gadave, no. 87.

[23] Fournier, *Statuts*, I, no. 601, p. 564, gives *five* instead of *three* as the number of years for the indult to run. It is incorrectly dated as well, for the document is of Clement's third year. *Ibid.*, no. 603, p. 565, is misplaced for it concerns the University of Montpellier, not Toulouse. *Ibid.*, no. 607, p. 566, is also incorrectly dated, being of the fifth year.

[24] Fournier, *Statuts*, I, no. 562, p. 512.

[25] Denifle, *Chartularium*, II, no. 1083, p. 546, and Fournier, *Statuts*, III, no. 1904, p. 523; Denifle, *Chartularium*, II, no. 1084, p. 546, and Fournier, *Statuts*, III, no. 1905, p. 523; *ibid.*, no. 1906, p. 523; *ibid.*, I, no. 606, p. 566; Vatican Archives, *Supplicationes* (Clemens VI) V, f°234; and *ibid.*, VIII, f°17v°. A Carmelite lector of Toulouse was permitted magisterial honors in Montpellier in 1344—*ibid.*, V, f°167.

[26] Vatican Archives, *Supplicationes* (Clemens VI), V, f°234.

student who had been licensed at Toulouse. This clerk from the
diocese of Tarragona had taken the customary oath to make his
solemn inception only at Toulouse. Later, however, some of his
friends promised to pay the expenses of this very burdensome
ceremony in the *Studium* of Lerida in Catalonia. The pope was
petitioned and granted a dispensation from this oath to the
chancellor. This, of course, fell within the ordinary dispensing
rights of the papacy at that time, so could not be questioned.[27]

In 1353 a long supplication roll of the university to the recently elected Innocent VI throws much light on affairs in the
studium. In the first place there is a request for certain favors
in guise of benefices or ecclesiastical offices for specified members. In addition to these individual advancements, the *studium*
also desired certain corporate privileges. It was requested that
the archbishop of Toulouse be authorized to correct, annul, or
change statutes, dispositions, and ordinances in need of reform.
This was to be granted in regard to those which could not conveniently be observed. A conservator of all apostolic privileges
was also sought, for which authorization was given for a period
of five years; the archbishop or his *officialis* was, at university
request, to be made judge for all secular and religious students
in things touching the statutes or status of the *studium*.[28]
Furthermore, Innocent granted the usual dispensations for fruits
of benefices of masters and students for five years on condition
that they had obtained the permission of their own prelates to
study at Toulouse and a judicial privilege of not being cited outside Toulouse in cases arising from contracts made within the city
or from delicts committed within its walls.[29] Like his predecessor
Clement, Innocent also interfered at least once in the granting
of degrees, for in 1355 he ordered the chancellor to concede the
license and doctoral honors in civil law to a priest of the diocese
of Albi who had undergone "secret examination." On the face

[27] Fournier, *Statuts,* I, no. 590, p. 538. Fournier has misattributed this document to Benedict XII.

[28] Denifle, *Les universités,* no. xii, p. 62. From the official response to the last
request, Fournier, *Statuts,* I, no. 609, p. 567, it is made clear that in the
past certain students had contemned the authority of the archbishop to try
them. Permission for the archbishop to modify the statutes is to be found
in *ibid.,* no. 610, p. 567.

[29] These additions to the *rotulus* as printed in Denifle are to be found with
the document itself in the Vatican Archives, *Supplicationes* (Innocens VI)
XXV, f°s49v°-51v°. The *capitouls* had sought and received somewhat
similar privileges to the last mentioned above, one month earlier. By this
no citizen of Toulouse could be cited outside the city in any case by
apostolic letters—*ibid.,* f°5v°. This indult was to last for fifteen years.

Papal Intervention 101

of it, this would seem an even more highhanded proceeding than the others, for no explanation is offered.[30]

Under Urban V, the university again received the now customary dispensations in order to permit its members the perception of fruits of benefices while resident in the *studium.* On the first occasion it was even asked that the ordinary exceptions for dignitaries and high elective offices be waived and also for benefices having "care of souls." Indeed, a *non obstante* for the lack of permission from one's proper prelate was also sought, and — what is more surprising — was presumably granted. In March of 1365, some eight months before the privilege would expire, it was renewed for another triennium with express exception of pontificals in cathedrals and the principal dignitaries in collegiate churches.[31] Again in February of 1367 the same privilege was conceded, although the reason for its being given one year in advance of the expiration of the earlier grant is not explained. In August 1369 this was again extended owing to the fact that the previous privilege was about exhausted.[32] University matters needing correction were also drawn to the attention of Urban, for in 1365 he directed a reproving letter to the university because it had come to his ears that many students had spent enough on sumptuous garments to have kept them a whole year. Consequently they had been unable to complete their work in the *studium.* Since, through the negligence of the rector and university, statutes prescribing garments to be worn in the *studium* had not been made in the past, it was ordered that new statutes be enacted and transmitted to the pope who wished to see them.[33]

Gregory XI, the last of the legitimate line of Avignon popes, granted, for a period of five years, the now customary extension of the rights to perception of the fruits of benefices for ecclesiastics resident in the university. Indeed, as far as Toulouse was concerned, he played a very minor rôle with only an occasional intervention in the newly established faculty of theology and authorization for the foundation of new colleges.[34]

[30] Cited without reference by Denifle, *Les universités,* p. 36. I was unable to locate the document at the Vatican.

[31] Fournier, *Statuts,* I, no. 656, p. 599. The document has "Fiat ad triennium." The renewal is given in *ibid.,* no. 665, p. 609.

[32] Fournier, *Statuts,* I, no. 671, p. 617, where the document is misdated February 12. The twelfth kalend of March is, of course, February eighteenth. See *ibid.,* no. 680, p. 622 for the second renewal. The reason for this is explained in no. 683, p. 623.

[33] Denifle, *Les universités,* no. xiii, p. 64, dated November 26, 1365.

[34] Fournier, *Statuts,* I, no. 688, p. 625. The register of Gregory XI here cited

The chancery records of the Avignon popes, however, contain another type of document which throws considerable light on university personnel during this period. From time to time, usually just after the accession of the new pope, the French universities submitted supplication rolls asking for ecclesiastical preferment for their members. Three such rolls of the University of Toulouse have been conserved for this epoch. There is indication of another sent to Benedict XII.[35] The roll sent to Benedict XII, presumably in 1334, contained the names of at least seven masters, for that many faculty members of Toulouse were provided with canonicates or benefices between January 9 and February 10, 1335. This list included two regent doctors of law, a non-regent doctor of law, and a doctor of canon law, all teaching in the civil faculty; a doctor of both laws teaching in the canonical faculty, and two masters of grammar who had taught long years at Toulouse. There is, of course, no proof that these seven comprised the total on the university *rotulus* of that year; but at any rate all of the existing faculties save arts and medicine were at least represented. The roll sent to Innocent VI in the first year of his pontificate had twenty-five names, from which it can be inferred that there were at least three doctors of canon law, two of civil law, two masters in medicine, one in arts and medicine, one in arts, and two in grammar actually teaching in Toulouse at the time. Two other doctors of law, one of them the archbishop's *officialis* and two other masters in medicine are also listed. Besides the faculty members previously mentioned, the list also included a master of arts who had "read ordinarily in the *studium* for a long time" and was now bachelor in decrees, and a master of grammar, also bachelor in decrees, who had likewise "read ordinarily for a long time" and was now treasurer of the university. Two licentiates in decrees, perhaps recent graduates, a bachelor in decrees who was also university syndic, two bachelors in law,

has been recatalogued as no. 185 of the Avignon Series. See *infra*, p. 110, p. 114 and p. 116 for Gregory's intervention in other matters.
[35] The series of *Supplicationes* as conserved at the Vatican begins only with Clement VI, Berlière, "Suppliques de Clement VI" in *Analecta Vaticano Belgica*, I, xxix. There is indication from the registers of common letters of Benedict XII that at least one *rotulus* had been directed to an Avignon pope before that time, for the names of seven masters regent in the *Studium* are included in letters dated early in 1335, conferring canonicates with expectancies of prebends, Vidal, *Benoit XII-Lettres communes*, I, no. 558, p. 63; no. 315, p. 41; no. 570, p. 63; no. 1041, p. 100; no. 1201, p. 114; no. 1203, p. 114; and no. 1214, p. 115.

and a monk and two clerks, who are not even described as students, completed the list. As all faculty members may not have been seeking preferment at this time, it cannot be categorically assumed that the whole teaching force of the *studium* is here comprised. However, it is to be noted that all faculties are fairly well represented.[36] The first supplication roll to Urban V in 1362 was about the same length, having twenty-eight names; in 1366 an additional list of seventeen names was sent to the same pontiff with but few duplications.[37] Of these three *rotuli* submitted to Innocent and Urban, the earliest gives the best idea of the teaching personnel, for a fair number of masters from each faculty is listed. Ten years later there is but one repetition of a name from the first list, but the distribution of faculty petitioners is such that it would seem that most of the decretists and legists were suitably provided with benefices, for masters from the lower faculties are most numerous.[38] The only repetitions on the third *rotulus,* aside from Guillelmus Galterius who had achieved his doctorate in decrees in the interim and was then rector, were masters of arts and grammar.[39] In this century which gloried lawyers, advancement was apparently slow in coming in the less practical branches of learning. Licentiates and bachelors in the legal faculties form the major part of the list of names in each roll, indicating that expectations were still good for those versed in law.

The Avignon popes continued to single out for honors ecclesiastics who had been connected with the *Studium* of Toulouse. In 1351 there is record of a permutation of offices in the cathedral chapter whereby the chancellorship passed from Raymond de Canillac, who had recently been created cardinal-priest of Santa Croce in Gerrusaleme, to Geraud de Lambis.[40] Not to be outdone by his predecessor, Benedict XII, Innocent VI also honored the university in 1362 by elevating to the cardinalate two of its masters, one of whom was actually regent there at the time. Guillaume Bragose was among the foremost canonists of his century, while the other, Hugues de Saint Martial, was a

[36] Denifle, *Les universités,* no. xii, p. 62.

[37] Fournier, *Statuts,* I, no. 656, p. 599; and Denifle, *Les universités,* no. xiv, p. 65.

[38] Astorgius de Galhaco, Doctor of Law, is number thirteen in 1353 and number three in 1362.

[39] Galterius was number ten in 1362, a Bachelor of Decrees approved by examination. As rector he is listed first in 1366.

[40] Archives départementales de la Haute-Garonne, 4G., carton 5, no. xi, liasse 1, titre 1bis.

doctor of civil law.[41] Pierre de Montrevel, a Doctor of Law who had formerly taught at Toulouse, was named bishop of Lectoure about the same time. As far back as 1342 he was *juge-mage* of Toulouse, and ten years later he was still holding this office and acting as lieutenant of the royal seneschal. As dean of Paris he was resident in Toulouse in 1362, but he resigned this office in the next year when he accepted his bishopric.[42] Gregory XI also honored two more masters of Toulouse in 1371 by elevating them to the cardinalate. One of these was Bertrand de Cosnac, a Doctor of Decrees, and the other was Guillaume Noellet, a Doctor of Law.[43]

Meanwhile, during the mid-part of the century, active steps were being taken to acquire a full-fledged faculty of theology for the University of Toulouse. Even before 1300, it will be remembered, the Franciscans had had a private *studium generale* in theology in the city, and the Dominicans and Cistercians both possessed conventual theological schools there. By the early fourteenth century, the Carmelites and Augustinians had followed the example of their mendicant brethren, but despite this accumulation of theological *studia,* resident masters were far from numerous. Apparently as a first step in the acquisition of a real faculty of theology, the chancellor, rector, and masters of the university in 1290 had petitioned the Dominicans to appoint a full master in theology for their convent in Toulouse. It was perhaps hoped to increase thereby the prestige of the local theological schools. This effort, although temporarily successful, did not achieve the desired end.[44] Even after Benedict XII had reformed the statutes of the Cistercians, whereby their convent at Toulouse was included among the *studia generalia* of the order, the university was not allowed to grant decrees in theology.[45] Just about a month after confirming this document in 1335, the pope reproved the chancellor of Toulouse for having raised a Franciscan friar to the rank of master in theology. He

[41] *Histoire générale de Languedoc,* IX, 744. The former figured as rector in the *rotulus* of 1353—Denifle, *Les universités,* no. xii, 63.

[42] Vatican Archives, *Supplicationes* (Clemens VI) I, f°103, dated August 1, 1342, is the request of the *juge-mage* for ecclesiastical office. Archives municipales de Toulouse, layette 11, gives his appointment as lieutenant of the seneschal in 1352. As dean of Paris still resident in Toulouse, see Fournier, *Statuts,* I, no. 657, p. 600. See also Douais, "Un nouveau collège universitaire à Toulouse, xive s.," in *Bul. Soc. arch. Midi France,* II, nos. 15 à 24, pp. 185-196.

[43] *Histoire générale de Languedoc,* IX, 837.

[44] See *supra,* chapter iv.

[45] *Bullarum romanum,* III:II, 210.

reminded him that such degrees were not customarily given at Toulouse since there were not a sufficient number of masters in theology to warrant it. In the future the chancellor was warned not to promote anyone in that faculty without the special permission of the Apostolic See.[46] The chancellor apparently objected to this order, for a month later another letter was dispatched from the Curia asking him to submit proofs for his claim of the university's ancient privilege in this matter.[47] Evidently these proofs were not satisfactory, for a theological faculty had to be organized at Toulouse some thirty years later. It would be interesting to know just who had brought this irregularity to the attention of the pope in the first place. Possibly the University of Paris was watching scrupulously over her privileges, although the pope does not divulge his informant.

The university continued its policy of building up the theological schools thereafter. In 1337 Benedict wrote to the archbishop of Toulouse recalling a certain statute of the third Lateran Council that had subsequently been confirmed by Honorius III but which was obviously not being followed at Toulouse. This required that a master in theology should be maintained by all metropolitan churches for the instruction of priests. The archbishop was warned by this letter to provide one and to endow him with the rents of one prebend.[48] A few months later the pope wrote again on the same matter and named the amount of the prebend to be given to the new master lest between the archbishop and his chapter a controversy arise which should hinder the work of the theologian.[49] Although all this had to do more directly with the provincial seminary for the training of secular clergy than with the university, still the appearance of a new master in theology and a new school in the city cannot have failed to concern it. It was perhaps at the instigation of the university that the first of these letters was

[46] Denifle, *Chartularium*, II, no. 993, p. 451; and Fournier, *Statuts*, III, no. 1902, p. 522.
[47] Denifle, *Chartularium*, II, no. 994, p. 452; and Fournier, *Statuts*, III, no. 1903, p. 522. Denifle remarks (footnote 1, p. 994) that the general chapter of the Franciscans, meeting in Bologna in 1313, had ordered the master to raise bachelors at Toulouse to magisterial honors at his discretion.
[48] Fournier, *Statuts*, I, no. 592, p. 539. *Ibid.*, no. 600, p. 564, and attributed by Fournier to Clement VI, is the identical document. Its *datum* phrase as well as subject matter is the same. This duplication is due to a binding error made in the archives centuries ago. The document is actually Benedict's.
[49] Fournier, *Statuts*, I, no. 583, p. 534. This is only approximately dated by the editor as 1335-1337. The identical document, again attributed to Clement VI, is found in *ibid.*, no. 604, p. 565.

sent, for on the very same day other letters were dispatched for the correction of matters within the *studium* itself after solicitation "by the doctors and students of Toulouse."[50] In 1346 again the doctors and masters, and even the *capitouls,* petitioned the pope that a mendicant licentiate resident in a convent of the city be permitted to teach as master within and without the *studium* of his order.[51]

Under Clement VI, the conventual schools of theology which did not as yet form an official part of the *Studium* of Toulouse were the recipients of many favors which increased their prestige. There is record for the Dominican convent of the transfer of a lector from Toulouse to Paris and the appointment of his substitute by the master of the order in 1340. The former, Girardus de Domario, became master-general himself in 1342 and was then raised to the cardinalate of Santa Sabina; while the latter, Bertrandus de Sancto Michaele, was in 1345 ordered raised to magisterial rank by the pope, if the Dominican inquisitor, who was himself a master in theology, should after examination find him capable.[52] Even earlier in this same year Clement had given permission for Raymundus de Parisius, O.P., to assume magisterial honors at Toulouse under someone of his own order.[53] The Franciscan provincial minister for Aquitaine was also authorized to be raised to the same dignity under a professor of theology of his order in 1344. As the papal letter was directed in this instance to the archbishop of Toulouse, and as the Franciscan convent there was a *studium generale,* it is obvious that the ceremony was to take place in Toulouse.[54] The Carmelite convent, too, was similarly honored a few years later, for Guillelmus Durandus, lector in theology at Toulouse, at the request of a cardinal-patron, was ordered raised to the magisterial rank after examination. Although the supplication had requested the degree from Montpellier, the papal letter named Toulouse in its place.[55] Another Carmelite friar and professor

---

[50] Fournier, *Statuts,* I, no. 599, p. 563. This again is a document of Benedict misinserted in a register of Clement VI.

[51] Fournier, *Statuts,* I, no. 605, p. 566.

[52] Denifle, *Chartularium,* II, no. 1036, p. 500 and footnote 3, citing Douais, *Les frères prêcheurs en Gascogne,* p. 405. See also Fournier, *Statuts,* III, no. 1906, p. 523; and the *Supplicationes* (Clemens VI) X, f°44v° of the Vatican Archives.

[53] Vatican Archives, *Supplicationes* (Clemens VI) IX, f°17v°.

[54] Denifle, *Chartularium,* II, no. 1083, p. 546; and Fournier, *Statuts,* III, 1904, p. 523, who misquotes the document.

[55] Denifle, *Chartularium,* II, no. 1084, p. 546; and Fournier, *Statuts,* III, no. 1905, p. 523.

in the house of his order at Toulouse was permitted by apostolic letters to present himself for examination for the mastership in theology in 1346.[56] In 1345 a petition to Clement VI by the king and queen of distant Hungary requested the mastership in theology for a friar of the Brother Hermits of Saint Augustine. From this it is learned that the friar had passed twenty years studying at Paris and teaching in diverse *studia* of the Kingdom of Hungary and at Toulouse, where he would have been the first licentiate of his order had the university had the right of conferring degrees in that faculty.[57] Another Augustinian friar, a licentiate who had also studied at Paris and had taught theology for twelve years at Toulouse, was given permission by the pope in 1346 to assume the mastership in Toulouse with all the apostolic privileges attached to the Parisian degree.[58]

In 1360 the University of Toulouse made formal petition to Innocent VI for a real faculty of theology. As an alumnus of the *studium* he had recently established a new college at Toulouse, so perhaps the moment was thought propitious for requesting another favor. The petition recounted how the university had for a long time been recognized as a center for all Languedoc, yet in spite of the many proficient theologians resident in its convents, it still lacked the privilege of granting degrees in this science, even though such a faculty had been provided of old by Count Raymond and confirmed by the papacy. In these times, the document continues, many were unable to go to Paris; and even if they did go they were unable to obtain the mastership because of the prerogatives of that university. As many were thus drawn from Toulouse, the pope was requested to concede a *studium generale* in theology and to authorize the chancellor to grant the license and magisterial dignity with the counsel of the masters. As a final argument against the elusiveness of Paris, the two universities granting such degrees "in the island of England" were cited.[59] In response to this appeal, a bull was issued granting the favor sought. In it were marshaled with true legalistic exactitude all the authorities for such an act, from the original establishment of Romano, through the

---

[56] His petition was made by the *capitouls* of Toulouse, Vatican Archives, *Supplicationes* (Clemens VI) XI, f°106. The papal letter of notification is in Fournier, *Statuts*, I, no. 606, p. 566.

[57] Denifle, *Chartularium*, II, no. 114, p. 571. He was later raised to episcopal rank.

[58] Fournier, *Statuts*, I, no. 605, p. 566.

[59] Fournier, *Statuts*, I, no. 640, p. 592.

extension of all Parisian privileges by Pope Gregory IX and Pope Innocent IV. Out of sentiment for his alma mater and in response to the request of the rector and *capitouls,* the pope granted among other things the privileges of assuming masters from elsewhere, or of creating new ones from suitable candidates for the new faculty.[60]

Urban V played an active part in organizing the new faculty of theology at Toulouse, for he directed numerous letters to the chancellor, recommending candidates for licensing as masters in theology. In December, 1364, he so designated Thomas de Reati of the Hermits of Saint Augustine and Petrus Sabaterius of the Friars Minor. Both were to be permitted to lecture on the *Sentences,* and if deemed suitable were to be admitted to the mastership after diligent examination.[61] Four other papal candidates were presented in that same year for the license in theology, three Franciscans and one Dominican. In the year following, another Friar Hermit of Saint Augustine was similarly advanced with a special mandate for his presentation since the regulations of his order forbade this advancement at Toulouse.[62] Having his attention thus called to the prohibitions of certain orders that militated against their members' receiving the magisterial honor at Toulouse, Urban directed letters to the general chapters of both Augustinian and Franciscan friars, ordering them to include Toulouse among the *studia* where their members could attain the mastership. In 1366 two more Augustinians were recommended to the chancellor for similar honors.[63]

It was perhaps to give impetus to the study of theology in Toulouse that Urban V in the summer of 1368 sanctioned the translation of the body of Saint Thomas Aquinas to the Dominican church at Toulouse. This was arranged at the solicitation of Elias, the Dominican provincial for the province, and the relics were received with great solemnity January 28 of the

---

[60] Fournier, *Statuts,* I, no. 641, p. 592. This favor to Toulouse seems to have been resented at Paris—Du Boulay, *Historia universitatis Parisiensis,* IV, 364. See also the comment of Denifle in the *Chartularium,* III, no. 1257, p. 75, footnote 1.

[61] Fournier, *Statuts, I,* nos. 663-664, p. 608. It is remarked in a footnote that this document (no. 663) was not found in the Vatican. The folio reference was misread as 154 whereas actually it is 184. The register containing this document has been renumbered since as 159. The document is also misdated as of October 14, whereas it is really of December 12.

[62] Denifle, *Les universités,* p. 36; and the Index to the Avignon Series of the registers of Urban V (Register 159, f°241).

[63] Denifle, *Chartularium,* III, no. 1302, p. 125; and Denifle, *Les universités,* pp. 36-37.

following year.[64] The pope had recommended at the same time that the doctrines of the great theologian be propounded and studied. Probably the minor recurrences of heresy in the region had aroused attention, for in 1353 Guillaume Bernard de Puy, a Franciscan friar, had had to be examined by the vicars of the archbishop and inquisitor of Toulouse for heresy in the matter of the poverty of Christ and the sacrament of the altar. In 1372, some four years after the translation, erroneous doctrines of some sort were still taught there, for Gregory XI ordered the archbishop and the inquisitor of that city to punish certain seculars and regulars who were acting against apostolic doctrine "in their preaching, disputations, responsions, determinations and lectures."[65] What these errors were is not stated, but in May of 1389, Friar Richard Marie, O.P., was examined by a certain doctor of decrees in Rouen, because he preached badly of the Blessed Virgin. In the course of this examination, the accused alleged that the University of Toulouse had approved these conclusions which were those of his master, one John of Montesono.[66]

At any rate, the faculty of theology had grown large enough to require statutes for its governance by the end of 1366, for in December a special congregation was held in the Franciscan convent to publish them. At that time the theologians present were ten in number, although obviously the minister of the Franciscan province of Aquitaine and the provincial of the Augustinian friars were degree-holders only and not occupied with teaching in the schools.[67]

---

[64] Fournier, *Statuts*, I, no. 677, p. 620; and Martène, *Amplissima collectio*, VI, 417, "In conventu Tholosano collocatum MCCCLXVIII in festo Agnetis secundo."

[65] Reference to these matters is found in the Vatican Archives, *Supplicationes* (Innocens VI) XXV, f°15v° and f°125v°, dated March 15 and April 15. See also Rainaldus, *Annales ecclesiastici*, XXVI, no. xxxv, p. 229, cited by Chatelain, *Les statuts et privilèges*, p. 12.

[66] Denifle, *Chartularium*, III, no. 1673, p. 520, citing D'Argentré, *Coll. jud.*, I², p. 135-138.

[67] Fournier, *Statuts*, I, no. 670, p. 611. To the eight names listed as "conventuum Tholose magistri in sacra theologia," the Bibliothèque Nationale MS. lat. 4221C, f°35, adds those of Bernardus Barrani and Franciscus de Fabrica, both Franciscans. The former is one of the Franciscans licensed in 1364—Denifle, *Les universités*, p. 36. In the edited document of Fournier there is some hesitation shown about the last name on the list. It reads, "Bernardus provincialis (Pinali)." Obviously the editor was hazarding a correction from *Pinali* to *provincialis*, failing to observe that he had already listed one provincial of the Order of Brother Hermits of Saint Augustine. Baluze in transcribing this document (Bibliothèque Nationale MS. Lat. 4222, f°84) has copied *Bernardus Pinali* but then barred it, evidently suggesting this false correction of the later editor. Bernardus Pinali is con-

The interest of Gregory XI in the new faculty of theology at Toulouse appears to have been more to use it as a convenience than to give it substantial aid, for on two occasions in 1371 he wrote to the chancellor on behalf of students who had completed their work elsewhere but for whom it was inconvenient to return for magisterial honors.[68] He also interfered on several occasions, in all probability at the request of the persons concerned, ordering in one instance the recognition of a Franciscan theologian after examination by the university, and even stipulating the schools in which he should teach, and in others making special demands for bachelors to enable them to complete their work toward the license more expeditiously. Nor was the faculty of theology the only one so treated, for in 1373 the same pope ordered the recognition of a doctor of laws by the chancellor and rector.[69]

Another feature of the growth of the university during the mid-years of the fourteenth century was the multiplication of collegiate institutions for the housing of students. In the course of the first century of its existence, provisions had been made on several occasions for the charitable maintenance of pauper students in the hospitals and monastic houses of the city. To these had been added in 1242 and 1319 respectively the colleges of Vidal Gautier and Montlauzon.[70] Between 1337 and 1382 there were eight new collegiate foundations, several of them large and of ample endowment, which certainly augmented the prestige of the *studium*.

The earliest of these was the College of Verdale, founded by Arnaud de Verdale, a professor of both laws and clerk and councillor of the king. In December of 1337, Arnaud drew up his last will and testament. As that document very figuratively states it, he "having awaited like another Jacob for a deformed Lia (Civil Law), and having consecrated matrimony in the church of Toulouse on the twenty-fourth day of January in the year of our Lord 1331 by receiving the doctorate in both laws, and finally having had from the said two sisters twelve perpetual sons, had decided to make provisions from their dots for those twelve perpetual sons." Therefore for the repose of the soul of

firmed as the correct reading by the papal letter of 1365 raising him to mastership at Toulouse, Vatican Archives, Urban V, Register 159, f°241.
[68] Fournier, *Statuts*, I, no. 685, p. 623; and Denifle, *Les universités*, p. 37.
[69] Fournier, *Statuts*, I, nos. 687 and 689, p. 625; Denifle, *Les universités*, p. 37, who cites two cases; and Fournier, *Statuts*, I, no. 691, p. 626.
[70] See *supra*, pp. 58, 64-65 and 76.

his cousin, Pierre de Verdale, Doctor of Decrees and abbot of the monastery of Nicolo of the Order of Saint Augustine, and also for those of his relatives and benefactors, he liberally endowed a college for twelve students in his house at Toulouse. That the house was already established at the time of the drawing of the will is further proved by a letter of the archbishop of Toulouse, dated almost four months earlier, whereby he granted to Arnaud, "who is known to have and to have had a house for students called Verdala, situated in the *carreria de Botatis,* in which are twelve students," permission to construct a chapel for morning and evening services. In 1343, after Arnaud had been raised to the see of Maguelonne, he prevailed upon Clement VI to confirm his foundation.[71]

Two other colleges were founded at Toulouse during the next decade. In 1341 Benedict XII at the request of "his dear sons of the *Studium* of Toulouse," ordered the archbishop of that city to give permission for the construction of a chapel for a college of poor students founded by Pierre Berenger of Toulouse by his testament. As the dot for the chapel had been provided by the donor, instructions were given for its erection in the parish of Saint Sernin. The doctors and students had to petition again to Clement VI, and were answered by letters of 1344 in the same tenor; for it would appear the monastery had been hindering its construction.[72] This foundation was probably the reparation for an attack upon a student made by members of the night watch under the direction of the *capitoul,* Pierre Berenger. Litigation in this matter was in course in 1336, so the college must have been founded within a few years of the conclusion of the lawsuit.[73] Meanwhile in 1341 another prelate, Gaubert, archbishop of Arles, who had formerly been a student at Toulouse, made arrangements in his testament for the foundation of a college there. The date of the opening of this college cannot be ascertained; but the archbishop of Toulouse in 1345, at the request of Gaubert, now translated to Narbonne, gave permission for the chaplains of this College of Narbonne to hear confessions and administer the sacraments.[74]

[71] Fournier, *Statuts,* I, no. 593, p. 539; no. 591, p. 538; and the request for papal confirmation, in the Vatican Archives, *Supplicationes* (Clemens VI) IV, f°179. The actual confirmation itself is given in Fournier, *Statuts,* I, no. 597, p. 561.

[72] Fournier, *Statuts,* I, no. 594, p. 556; and no. 598, p. 563.

[73] See *supra,* p. 97.

[74] Fournier, *Statuts, I, no.* 595, p. 556; and no. 602, p. 564.

Far more important, however, than any of these was the great papal foundation of Innocent VI, who had received his degree in civil law at Toulouse. The earliest document to intimate that the pope was contemplating such a foundation dates from the sixth of November, 1358, for on that day Cardinal Audouin, delegated by Innocent for the purpose, constituted a procurator for acquiring certain lands and rents. In the same month, letters of the dauphin as regent exempted from exactions of the royal treasury the house selected at Toulouse for the new college when it should be acquired.[75] Shortly after that, Charles granted the same privilege for other lands up to 500 pounds annual rent for the endowment of the college.[76] Although the act of purchase for a mansion of a knight of Toulouse, made by the cardinal in the pope's name, is dated from the cloister of the Augustinian friars at Toulouse on December 3 of that year, the official foundation was delayed until September of the year following.[77] Meanwhile and throughout the succeeding years, Innocent not only authorized the expending of money for the purchase of lands to support his college but also endowed it with numerous ecclesiastical livings in the neighborhood as they fell vacant.[78] On October 27, 1359, Audouin was given full powers to appoint and correct the scholars and priests of the new institution and also to make statutes for them, and on the eleventh of November the scholars took possession of their house, and two of them were designated as priors.[79] Naturally the new foundation was showered with privileges and attentions. Audouin was given even more ample powers of direction by the pope before the year was out, and the cardinal of Santa Anasta-

[75] Bibliothèque Nationale MS. lat. 4223, f°64v°; and Fournier, Statuts, I, no. 612, p. 568.

[76] Fournier, Statuts, I, no. 613, p. 568. The house was amortized by the dauphin in September, 1359, ibid., no. 616, p. 570, and the amortisation confirmed by King John himself in 1362, ibid., no. 655, p. 599.

[77] Fournier, Statuts, I, no. 614, p. 569, has incorrectly dated this as of June 8, 1359, doubling the date of the following document, also one of the cardinal's, but made in Avignon. Bibliothèque Nationale MS. lat. 4223, f°101 gives the correct date for this and also for its ratification by the knight's lady on the same day. Record of the foundation is found in Fournier, Statuts, I, no. 617, p. 571.

[78] Fournier, Statuts, I, no. 615, p. 569; no. 620, p. 579; no. 621, p. 579; no. 629, p. 584; no. 630, p. 584; and nos. 643-644, pp. 594-595. For the ecclesiastical livings united to the college, see ibid., nos. 618-619, pp. 577-578; no. 622, p. 580; no. 632, p. 588; no. 637, p. 590; and no. 647, p. 596.

[79] Vatican Archives, Innocent VI, Avignon Register 141, f°33v°. "Datum Avinion. vi kal. Novembris anno septimo." The statutes of Audouin were communicated to the college, May 8, 1360—Fournier, Statuts, I, no. 631, p. 585. For the opening of the college, see ibid., no. 624, p. 580.

sia, the archbishop of Auch, the bishop of Albi and Etienne Aubert, a papal notary, were named to succeed in order at his death. The archbishop of Toulouse and bishop of Albi were also named protectors of the college and conservators of its privileges early in 1360, and the bishops of Carcasonne and Pamiers were added to the list in December.[80] The members of this college, other than the priors, were not to be cited in suits concerning the institution, and even the latter were not to go outside the city in such a suit. In personal cases the collegiates could not be subpoenaed outside the city without the express permission of the Holy See. The archbishop and his *officialis* were also authorized to absolve collegiates from excommunication or interdict incurred for irregularities. The college chapel itself was not to be interdicted by the ordinary nor even by apostolic letters not making express mention of this concession.[81] The college was furthermore to be exempted from the payment of all first fruits of ecclesiastical benefices and from the application of the reservations of the Apostolic Camera. Permission for the reception of the fruits of personal benefices up to 39 pounds *turonensium* annually was extended to the members themselves for a period of ten years.[82] Even the collectors of tithes and of the thirtieths for the ransom of the king were warned by the archbishop of Toulouse in 1360 that the benefices of Saint Martial were exempt for one year, and one of the college's priories was excused from the episcopal visitation of the same prelate.[83] The bishops of Albi and Carcasonne and the archbishop of Toulouse subdelegated their powers as conservators and judges of causes to long lists of ecclesiastics in dioceses neighboring on Toulouse in 1362, 1369, and 1370. This was probably intended to give protection for the widely distributed properties of the college. Even the regent Charles also showed his interest by placing the collegiates and their property under special safeguard.[84]

[80] Fournier, *Statuts*, I, nos. 625-627, pp. 580-582; no. 650, p. 597.

[81] Fournier, *Statuts*, I, nos. 634-636, pp. 588-590.

[82] Fournier, *Statuts*, no. 638, p. 590. The document is not given and the editor's summary is a trifle vague, so I quote the index of the registers of Innocent VI of the Avignon Series on this point. "Ad perpetuum rei memoriam remissio omnium fructuum primi anni beneficiorum ecclesiasticorum quorumcumque apud sedem apostolicam seu alibi vacantium, et reservatorum Camerae Apostolicae applicandorum, facta collegio et domui Sancti Martialis Tholosane. Datum Aven. iv nonas Septembris." See also, Fournier, *Statuts*, I, nos. 648-649, pp. 596-597.

[83] Fournier, *Statuts*, I, no. 633, p. 588; and no. 639, p. 590.

[84] Fournier, *Statuts*, I, no. 657, p. 600; no. 679, p. 621; no. 682, p. 622; and *Ordonances des rois de France de la IIIe race jusqu'en 1514* (Paris, 1723-1849) III, 395.

Drawing inspiration from Innocent VI who had been so energetic in the support of his collegiate foundation in Toulouse, the pope's two nephews, who had been appointed cardinal-provisors to that institution, founded in turn colleges of their own in the same city. Audouin Aubert, cardinal-bishop of Ostia, was the first to follow this example, when in 1363 he drew up his last will and testament, arranging that after his bequests had been made whatever remained should be used to found a college for grammarians and logicians at Toulouse in such numbers as his means would permit. Four years later, the cardinal of Nîmes, one of his executors, requested Charles V to amortize certain property for a college he was about to establish in Toulouse for ten students in canon and civil law "as the executor of several deceased."[85] That it was Audouin's college here intended is clear from a letter written in the same year by two of his cardinal executors giving authority for certain procurators to act in their name in matters concerning this foundation. The fact that its founder was dead made the work of organizing very slow, for in 1371 Gregory XI wrote to the cardinal of Nîmes giving him full powers to act alone in this matter as the other executors were either dead or difficult to assemble.[86] The College of Maguelonne — it was named after the French see occupied by Audouin — was presumably opened in the autumn term of 1374, as Gregory XI in that year appointed the abbot of Saint Sernin and the provost and chancellor of the church of Toulouse as conservators of the goods of the college and of its members.[87]

Meanwhile Pierre, cardinal-priest of Santa Anastasia, had assumed on the death of Audouin the powers of provisor of the College of Saint Martial as his uncle Innocent VI had directed. The cardinal was apparently very active in this capacity, for he issued new statutes for the collegiates in 1364, and in 1373 he was taking measures to recover from the priors of the college

---

[85] Fournier, Statuts, I, no. 659, p. 601; and no. 672, p. 617.
[86] Fournier, Statuts, I, no. 673, p. 618; and no. 686, p. 624.
[87] The document is incorrectly inventoried in Fournier, Statuts, I, no. 693, p. 627. In the Vatican Archives the register noted in his citation has been recatalogued as 193. The index of the Avignon Series describes this same document as follows: "Conservatoria ad triennium pro collegio, domus scolarium clericorum Tholosanorum per bone memorie Audoynum episcopum cardinalem Ostiensem canonice fundate, quo ad bona ad collegium, domum ac scholares predictos spectantia, directa abbati monasterii Sancti Saturnini Tholosani ac preposito et cancellario ecclesie Tholosane. Datum apud Villam Novam Avenionensis diocesis iv kal. Octobris anno quarto."

money which had been left by Innocent for the construction of a chapel but which had been diverted to other uses.[88] Two years later it is learned from royal letters of amortizement issued by Charles V that Cardinal Pierre himself had purchased a house in Toulouse and had collected lands to endow a college of his own. In 1379 the Avignon anti-Pope Clement VII granted official permission for the creation of this college for two priests and twelve students in civil or canon law at the cardinal's request, and in the following year he confirmed the purchase of a dwelling in Toulouse to house the college.[89] It was two years, however, before the official foundation occurred. Pierre, like Audouin, then named his college for his see, that of Pamplona. The cardinal of Santa Anastasia continued to have interest in the colleges of Toulouse, for he acted in official capacity as provisor of Saint Martial in directing letters of expulsion in 1384; and in drawing up his testament in the next year, he especially safeguarded the possessions of the College of Saint Martial and bequeathed two-thirds of his estate to his own foundation.[90]

Another ecclesiastic to follow in the footsteps of Innocent VI in providing for worthy students of Toulouse was Talleyrand, cardinal-bishop of Albano, who commenced work for his foundation in 1362. Strangely enough it is only by accident that the purpose of his numerous purchases of land and houses in that city is learned, for although the cardinal drew up his will in 1360 there is not the slightest mention of a collegiate foundation there.[91] In 1363, however, a royal amortizement for this property by King John refers to it as being for the use of a congregation of poor students.[92] By December of that year Talleyrand had

---

[88] Pierre de Selve, born at Monteruc in Limousin and nephew of Innocent VI, was named bishop of Pamplona and then of Saragossa under John XXII. He was made archbishop of Bourges under Gregory XI. Innocent named him cardinal-priest of Santa Anastasia in 1355. Lehondes, "Collège de Pampelune" in *Bul. Soc. arch. Midi* (1909) Ser. 2, xxiii, 488, gives the details of his biography. For his work at St. Martial, see Fournier, *Statuts*, I, no. 662, p. 606; and no. 690, p. 625.

[89] Fournier, *Statuts*, I, no. 695, p. 629; no. 698, p. 653; and no. 702, p. 662.

[90] Fournier, *Statuts*, I, nos. 706-707, p. 667. The former is merely an inventory reference to the latter. See also *ibid.*, nos. 710-711, p. 674.

[91] From the *Inventaire de collège de Perigord*, made in 1372 and conserved in the Archives départementales de la Haute-Garonne, it is learned that the cardinal made purchases of houses in Toulouse in 1362 and 1363. The cardinal's will is referred to in Fournier, *Statuts*, I, no. 642, p. 594, but the will itself in Bibliothèque Nationale MS. Lat. 4223, f°110, gives no information on this score.

[92] Fournier, *Statuts*, I, no. 660, p. 604. In January, 1365, a codicil was added to the original testament, having a clause which is described in the *Inventaire* of the college (f°2), "Sommes après ses dettes sont payée d'etre

appointed procurators, giving them full powers of governing his college at Toulouse and of administering the business connected with it. The cardinal's executors worked diligently after his death in 1365 to amass further properties and rents for the support of the college.[93] The actual opening of the institution occurred only in 1375, when Gregory XI stipulated that twenty students should be housed in the college, to be called of Perigord, and that its chapel, dedicated to Saint Front, should be served by four chaplains. The statutes which follow are the almost literal reproduction of those of Saint Martial. Cardinal Pierre, nephew of Innocent VI and provisor of Saint Martial, who was even then contemplating a similar foundation of his own, was given the right of reforming the new establishment. The first prior was named shortly after, as a document made in his name is dated December 3, 1375.[94]

Pierre de Montrevel, bishop of Lectoure and a doctor of law who had formerly taught at Toulouse, in drawing up his last will and testament at Avignon in 1370, created a small college for four students and two priests in his house in Toulouse. One of the latter was to teach the students until they were ready to study law and thereafter to act as tutor for them, while the other was to manage the affairs of the house. The original students in the college were to be relatives of the testator, but if they were lacking, the quota could be completed from specified monasteries and thereafter from the *seneschausée* of Toulouse. After private legacies had been met, the college was to be his universal heir.[95]

employées à l'augmentation du nombre des chanoines reguliers de Nostre Dame de Chancelade ou au profit du collège de Perigord, si ses executeurs testamentaires le trouvent plus a propos." The document itself is missing in the Archives, but it is evidently the same codicil that has been transcribed by Baluze in the Bibliothèque Nationale MS. lat. 4223 at f°115. The clause there reads; "Et si executoribus nostris videatur expedientius ipsam ordinationam nostram fieri in ecclesia Sancti Frontis Petragoricensis quam in ipso monasterio de Cancellata."

93 Fournier, *Statuts*, I, no. 661, p. 605; and nos. 674-678, pp. 618-620. Pierre de Furno, chaplain of the late cardinal and named as procurator by him in 1363, continued to function from 1365 to 1371 in the name of the cardinal's executors—*Inventaire de collège de Perigord*, f°9v°, 10, 11, 14v°, 33, 47, 61, 71v°, 90, 94 and 95. In 1373, one of the executors himself acted as purchasing agent, *ibid.*, f°9v°. Pierre had presumably died, for two years later there is record of an arbitral award between his heirs and the college— *ibid.*, f°9v°.

94 Fournier, *Statuts*, I, no. 694, p. 627; and *Inventaire de collège de Perigord*, f°102.

95 Douais, "Un nouveau collège universitaire à Toulouse, xivᵉ s.," in *Bul. Soc. arch. Midi France*, II, nos. 15 à 24, pp. 185-196. He was named conservator of the college of St. Martial in 1362, Fournier, *Statuts*, I, no. 657,

The conventual establishments of Saint Sernin and Saint Pierre des Cuisines were still maintaining their student members throughout this period. The regulations for students emanating from the chapter meetings of the monastery of Saint Sernin in 1337 and the years immediately succeeding would indicate that the schools in this house were carefully administered. In the first named year, the chapter authorized the creation of a library either in the quarters then used as a classroom by one of the canons, to whom another classroom should be assigned, or in an entirely new structure to be erected in a suitable place. To the books already left them, Hugues II, the existing abbot, added five other volumes.[96] In the following years regulations for scholar and bachelor canons, observed early in the fourteenth century under Raymond Atho, were repromulgated. The chapter meeting of 1339 was closed because no business remained for consideration at the moment, and its prorogation would inconvenience certain priors who intended returning to their priories and the students who would be impeded in their studies.[97] That the Cluniacs still maintained their house for students at Toulouse is confirmed by several references to the students "in domo Coquinis."[98]

Some religious establishments of this period were not so meticulous in fulfilling their obligations to students. As early as 1329 the university reform statutes had admonished the rector to inspect the houses for poor students at least once in his rectorate, and to report any delinquencies to the bishop or to his *officialis*. The houses for poor students that had received gifts and legacies from laymen are listed as six in number, and are enumerated as the houses of Saint Raymond, the Daurade, the Hospital of Saint John, the Cathedral of Saint Etienne, Saint

---

p. 600. The testament is printed in full in the article cited above. *See* supra, p. 104 for further details of the biography of the founder.

[96] This entry is from a copy of the capitular statutes of St. Sernin made in 1422, and now conserved in the Archives départementales de la Haute-Garonne, fonds Saint Sernin, H., 202, f°30.

[97] Archives départementales de la Haute-Garonne, fonds Saint Sernin, H., 202, f°94v°-95 give two almost identical copies of these regulations. Only the latter is dated. The 1339 entry is found in *ibid.*, f°33.

[98] A letter of Benedict XII in 1341 refers to the "administrationem monachorum dicti monasterii (Moissac) in domo de Coquinis Tolosan studentium," Vidal, *Benôit XII*, II, no. 8496, p. 326. A supplication to Clement VI, dated July 11, 1343, mentions the "prioratus . . . existens in civitate Tholosano in domo de Coquinis pro monachis predictis studentibus in civitate predicta," Vatican Archives, *Supplicationes* (Clemens VI) IV, f°69v°. There is another reference to the "prioratus studencium S.Petri de

Pierre des Cuisines, and the Maynaderia.[99] Saint Raymond as such a foundation dated from at least 1233, but the foundations of the others cannot be precisely dated. The Daurade was a Benedictine establishment, the hospital was a center for the military-monastic Knights of Saint John, and a chapter of Augustinian canons regular presided over Saint Etienne. Perhaps these three had added students to already existing hospices at the exhortation of Pope Innocent IV in 1245. The house of Saint Pierre des Cuisines is obviously the house for Cluniac student monks from Moissac, which is first mentioned in the statutes of 1314. Although the College of Vidal Gautier was to be set up in the vicinity of Saint Pierre des Cuisines, according to the testament of its founder, and was to use that church for its weekly requiem Masses for the repose of his soul, there is no further reference of any kind to this college. The Maynaderia is doubtless the popular designation for the College of Montlauzon, as that institution was to be set up in the *bastide* of that name outside the gates of Toulouse at the direction of its founders.[100]

In 1337 Benedict XII appointed a commission of prominent ecclesiastics of Toulouse to investigate the alleged misuse of certain rents left by benefactors to support poor students, with instructions that they report their findings to the Curia. The prior of the Daurade and Bernard Hugo, a canon of Saint Etienne, are specifically named among the three commissioners. It could well be that the pope was giving a gentle hint to two of the institutions listed as remiss in 1329 to amend their practices.[101] The Daurade, Saint Raymond, and the Hospital of Saint John were again remiss in this matter of supporting poor students in 1360, for a supplication to Pope Innocent VI listed them along with other unnamed houses. The pope designated

Coquinis" in a supplication to Innocent VI in 1353, Vatican Archives, *Supplicationes* (Innocens VI) XXV, f°134.

[99] Fournier, *Statuts,* I, no. 558, p. 510.

[100] For the earliest reference to St. Raymond, see Auvray, I, no. 1673, p. 932. The letter of Innocent IV is in Fournier, *Statuts,* I, no. 520, p. 450. For references to the student monks of the Daurade and the Cuisines, see *ibid.,* no. 545, p. 494. For Vidal Gautier and Montlauzon, see *ibid.,* no. 517, p. 447; and no. 699, p. 654.

[101] Fournier, *Statuts,* I, no. 599, p. 563. Fournier attributes this document to Clement VI; but this is in error, for it is actually a letter of Benedict XII, and is so listed by Denifle, *Les Universités,* no. x, p. 60, and by Vidal, *Benôit XII-Lettres Communes,* I, no. 5123, p. 482. It is dated by both as of November 28, 1337. Fournier in his no. 582, p. 534 lists the same document but only from an entry in the Vatican Index for the registers of Benedict XII. He remarks that the letter itself was missing. On consulting

the abbot of Saint Sernin and the chancellor of Toulouse to correct these matters. In 1366 it was again Saint Etienne, the Daurade, and Saint John of Jerusalem that were not supporting poor students, according to a supplication of the university to Urban V. He entrusted the matter this time to the *officialis* of Toulouse. Even the collegiate foundations were having similar difficulties about the same time, for letters of Urban V appointed a committee to investigate the disorders in certain colleges which were reported by the rector and university as being in a bad state and unable to support their members. They are named as Saint Raymond, Narbonne, Verdale, Montlauzon, and Pierre Berenger; and the provost and chancellor of the church of Toulouse, and its *officialis* were empowered to investigate and settle these matters.[102] On the same date a second commission was named to act as conservators in reclaiming the distrained property of the same houses. This commission consisted of the bishop of Rieux, and the provost and chancellor of Toulouse.[103]

The most frequent offenders judging from this series of documents were Saint Raymond, the Daurade, and the Hospital of Saint John. All three were mentioned in the statutes of 1329, and in the supplication to Innocent VI in 1360; while Saint Raymond was also included among the colleges in the two letters of Urban V in 1364, and the Daurade and the Hospital of Saint John were again listed as remiss in the supplications to Urban V in 1366. The cathedral church of Saint Etienne was listed in 1329 and 1366 and perhaps again by implication in the appointment of inspectors in 1337. In this instance, by similar im-

---

the register of Clement VI which Fournier cited for his no. 599, I discovered that the page which contained it had obviously been rebound in this volume by error. There was no continuity with either the preceding or following pages, and both caligraphy and the ink employed were different. The same page also contained a letter to the bishop of Basel listed as missing in the Index of Benedict XII's registers.

102 Fournier, *Statuts*, I, no. 640, p. 591; and Denifle, *Les Universités*, no. xiv, p. 65. For the colleges, see Fournier, *Statuts*, I, no. 667, p. 609. The Maynaderia is here mentioned just before Montlauzon. Perhaps the scribe was confused by the double designation for the same institution?

103 Fournier, *Statuts*, I, no. 666, p. 609 is erroneously summarized. Fournier refers to the Avignon Series of Urban V, X, f°399, but consulted only the Index, which reads, "Conservatoria ad quinquenium pro universitate studii Tholosani, directa episcopo Rivensi et proposito ac cancellario Tholosano. Datum Avenione ii nonas Martii, anno tertio." The register itself— now renumbered 159—throws a very different light on the functions of the conservators. Both no. 666 and no. 667 bear identical dating phrases. Denifle, *Les Universités*, p. 28, indicates no. 667 as a bull of the second year although placed in a register of the third. Presumably both should be dated as March 6, 1364.

plication, the Daurade would be included a fourth time. The College of Montlauzon was remiss in 1329 and 1364, but Saint Pierre des Cuisines was mentioned only once. Apparently the Cluniacs needed but one warning. The record for the rectoral visitations of colleges in 1373 shows that the College of Saint Raymond was still badly provided with bread and wine and was three students above the number permitted by their statutes. The College of Montlauzon, also disorderly in 1364, was likewise maintaining two students above the permitted number.[104]

[104] Fournier, *Statuts*, III, no. 1907, p. 523.

CHAPTER 6

THE DISORDERS OF SCHISM AND
WAR, 1350-1427

ALTHOUGH the long struggle of the Hundred Years' War had broken out between the French and English in 1338, the first ten years of the conflict did not concern Toulouse directly. In 1349 or 1350, however, Henry of Lancaster did lead a raid which ravaged the countryside and even burned the *faubourgs* of the city. In 1352 once again Toulouse was fearful of siege, so the citizens destroyed all houses outside the walls. Three years later the Black Prince came within a league of the city in one of his expeditions but passed eastward instead.[1] These raids were especially destructive of property in the country; the walled towns offered ample protection for the burghers. Those, however, whose income was derived mainly from rural estates must have been fairly hard hit financially. The cathedral chapter of Toulouse was among this number, for it petitioned for dispensation from a ruling of John XXII requiring a personnel of fifty canons and asked that their maximum be set at thirty for the future. It was presumably this financial stringency that caused the cathedral chapter to be numbered among monastic institutions not maintaining the required quota of poor students in 1366.[2] Even at that the Toulousain offered more protection than the dioceses farther west. A student of Cahors besought dispensation for having accepted the fruits of his benefices after leaving that *studium* in 1346 for fear of the enemy. In that same year a clerk of the diocese of Agen apparently remained to resist instead of taking flight, for another was requesting the benefices he had forfeited by fighting in the wars against the English. In 1353 a Benedictine monk from the monastery of Clariac in the same diocese asked papal permission

---

[1] Denifle, *La guerre de cents ans et la désolation des églises monastères et hôpitaux en France*, II, 64, 66 and 88.
[2] Denifle, *La guerre de cents ans*, II, 64; and Denifle, *Les universités*, no. xiv, p. 65.

for his transfer to a house of the same order in the diocese of Toulouse, alleging as his reason the wars that raged.[3]

Notwithstanding her comparative protection from the actual sufferings of the campaigning, Toulouse, like all other parts of France, must have felt the pressure of the very necessary financial exactions. In 1346 the provinces of Narbonne and Toulouse and five dioceses of the province of Auch had sought papal permission to pay a royal subsidy. The quota for Toulouse was set at 8,000 *livres tournois* and was to be paid in two installments. It was most specifically signified that the money so raised was not to be used for war, obviously to satisfy canonical scruples.[4]

The Black Death reached Toulouse in 1348. Its havoc is eloquently testified in a petition of the *capitouls* to the *parlement* of Paris some half century later, in an attempt to compel certain colleges to contribute to the city taxes. Before the plague, it is stated, more people lived outside than within the walls. Such a mortality cannot have failed to have affected the university but precise documents are lacking.[5]

As the years passed and the war with the English dragged on, the outlook at Toulouse was far from cheerful. The diocese was ravaged by Spanish companies of freebooters in 1365.[6] In that very year Urban V not only appointed conservators to reclaim the properties of several colleges, as already has been explained, but a few weeks later named the same group of ecclesiastics as conservators of university privileges because the masters and students had complained that these were not being observed.[7] That the precious prerogatives of the university were seriously jeopardized is given more conclusive proof in the official summary of such privileges published at about this date by the subexecutors and judges designated by the archbishops of Narbonne and Toulouse and the bishop of Carcasonne, delegates of the Holy See. This copy of privileges was addressed to all rectors and chaplains and also especially to the beadles of the venerable *Studia* of Toulouse, Montpellier and Cahors. It seems that the addressees had received earlier monition on the same subject, but in spite of this warning the university was still complaining of maltreatment. The specific charges

---

[3] Vatican Archives, *Supplicationes* (Clemens VI) XII, f°148v° and f°159; and *Supplicationes* (Innocens VI) XXV, f°161.
[4] Vatican Archives, *Supplicationes* (Clemens VI) XII, f°95.
[5] Fournier, *Statuts*, III, no. 1913, p. 562.
[6] Denifle, *La guerre de cents ans*, II, 400.
[7] See *supra,* chapter v, p. 119; and Fournier, *Statuts,* I, no. 668, p. 610.

in this instance were that students had been arrested and imprisoned, wounded, and even killed, and their property seized, when they bought and sold necessaries under exemption from tax impositions, and that food had been withdrawn from the city in time of scarcity to the detriment of the students. Those who continued to ignore these privileges and to harm the university members were to be publicly excommunicated. Obviously lay tax collectors were using extreme measures to compel all to contribute to the war chest.[8]

In 1372 affairs had reached such a state that the citizens of Toulouse and its neighborhood appealed to the *officialis* of that city for protection from the depredations of both clerks and laymen. It would seem that neither houses nor farms were safe from trespass and that at times entry was made with force and violence. Furniture and other goods were frequently appropriated from houses, and the fruits of orchard, vineyard, and field carried off, to omit all reference to the damage to trees and gates. In order to remedy these matters, the *officialis* addressed his admonition to the chaplains of the parish churches of Toulouse and to the beadles of the *studium,* warning them to publish in their churches and in the schools that for all such depredations satisfaction should be rendered within four days on pain of excommunication. In case the amount of the damages could not be amicably settled, the aggrieved parties were to appear in the archiepiscopal court on the second juridical day following the publication of the warning. Meanwhile further depredations were strictly forbidden. No intimation is given in this document as to the cause for this lawlessness, but it may be presumed that the disorders consequent to war had caused hardship and because of scarcity many who did not have wherewithal to purchase food simply rifled fields and barns.[9] Just two years later actual famine conditions reached Toulouse and the *capitouls* were forced to take desperate action to relieve matters. A special committee was appointed to procure grain wherever possible for resale at the common stone for public utility. In order not to overtax municipal finances, it was ordered that strangers who were able to buy food for their own use be expelled from the city.[10] Affairs must have been very bad in

[8] Archives municipales de Toulouse, layette 47 (C 20/133).
[9] Archives municipales de Toulouse, layette 48 (C 49/21).
[10] François Galabert, *Album de paléographie et de diplomatique relatifs à l'histoire du Midi de la France,* fasc. premiere, XIV⁰ s., planche v, no. 5. The original is found in the Archives municipales, BB., f°16.

the Midi, for two masters, sent by the university as messengers
to the Avignon anti-Pope Clement VII in 1379, requested the
grace of certain benefices for their friends and servants who had
sustained such perils and labors in coming and going from the
Curia.[11] The evils of the day made so great an impression on a
Dominican theologian of Toulouse that he composed in the same
year, a work on the Apocalypse to show how its prophecies were
being fulfilled and referred with feeling to the schism which
was rending Christendom and the tribulations that were affect-
ing the whole world.[12] The enmity between the duke of Berry,
royal lieutenant in Languedoc, and the count of Foix was a
further cause for discord in the south in 1380 and 1381. The duke
was closely allied to the Armagnac faction which made him most
unpopular with the count. The latter persuaded the Estates of
Languedoc meeting in Toulouse to grant him money for men at
arms to put down the *routiers*. This was done; and what is
even more surprising, the royal officers at Toulouse seem to have
sanctioned this treaty, which practically amounted to a war
against the duke of Berry. The king was furious when he
learned of this, and the duke soon appeared on the scene and
compelled the people of Toulouse to obey him.[13] A few years
later both masters and students found themselves so financially
embarrassed as to incur excommunication for not contributing
their share to a papal subsidy. This had been imposed in order
to effect the evacuation of men at arms who had been occupying
certain cities and fortresses in the provinces of Bourges, Narbonne, Toulouse and Bordeaux. In 1387 the vicar-general of
the see of Toulouse addressed his letters patent to the clergy
of the diocese authorizing the absolution of such persons from
the excommunication so incurred, on condition that the sums
owed be paid by the ensuing Easter.[14]

The university members were not only averse to paying papal
subsidies but also soon after were contesting the right of the
city to tax them. Litigation on this point stretched over a great
many years. In order to repair the ravages of war, the *capitouls*
of Toulouse had adopted the expedient of diminishing the measure of wine. This the students refused to obey. When the city
appealed to the pope, orders were sent to the archbishop of

[11] Vatican Archives, *Supplicationes* (Clemens VII) XLIX, f°203.
[12] Bibliothèque municipale de Toulouse, MS. 57, f°2, col. I.
[13] A. Baudouin, "Querelle du comte de Foix et du duc de Berry" in *Mem.
Acad. de Toulouse* (1871) Ser. G, III, 360-378.
[14] Vatican Archives, *Instrumenta miscellenea,* 3300.

Toulouse in March of 1392, informing him that students were to be compelled to follow local customs. Letters of the same date notified the *officialis* of Toulouse that he was no longer to recognize as students, citizens of Toulouse who were married and had heard law or theology for a few hours in order to claim exemption from taxation.[15] As the *capitouls* had appealed to the pope, the university now appealed to the king. Royal letters dating from September 24, 1392, took the rectors, masters, doctors, licentiates, bachelors, and students of the university with their servants and familiars and even their property under royal safeguard; and the seneschal and vicar of Toulouse were charged with special attention to their protection.[16] This was but the opening of the controversy, however. A few weeks later Charles VI at the request of the chancellor, rector, and university issued further instructions in this matter. The *studium* had complained that the immunities, privileges, and liberties which it had enjoyed from time immemorial had been impeded by the farmers and collectors of royal subsidies. Even the special grants of Charles and his father, and of the latter's lieutenants in Languedoc, Louis, the former king of Sicily and John, the duke of Bourges, had been violated. The university, anxious to have its prerogatives respected, had then caused certain of these tax farmers and collectors to be excommunicated. They in turn had complained to the royal officers, and the chancellor and rector had been requested to have these excommunications withdrawn. The tax farmers had been so vexed that they secured this mandate and had it published in the squares of the city, with threats of suspension of privileges and removal from royal safeguard, and of injunction against holding congregations, and any other scholastic acts. The university, thus threatened with deprivation of all her legal weapons, had immediately appealed to the king. As a result Charles issued special letters covering the points concerned. In the future the chancellor or rector and university and its students, two syndics, two notaries, two stationers, two parchmenters, and the greater *banquerius* or treasurer were to be quit of all subsidies and impositions, even for war or defense, upon wines, grains, vegetables, and any other things coming from benefices, or anything which they should expose for sale without fraud. In addition all privileges

15 Archives municipales de Toulouse, layette 48 (C 49/13) and layette 47 (103 D).
16 Fournier, *Statuts*, I, no. 721, p. 681.

were reconfirmed, all actions taken against the university repudiated; and the royal officers were given special orders to protect
it. Letters of the same date informed the vicar of his appointment as conservator of university privileges.[17] That university
members had been employing the privilege of royal protection
for their property even before this time is illustrated by a unique
document conserved among the records of the College of Maguelonne. Guillelmus Dominicus, a student, applied in 1381 to the
seneschal of Toulouse for letters of safeguard for his property,
which consisted of three houses in Toulouse. Armed with this
letter and accompanied by a royal officer, the student had had
attached to the doors of his houses in high and conspicuous
places the royal symbol of the *fleur-de-lys* as warning.[18]

That all did not move smoothly even after these confirmations in 1392 is apparent from the lawsuits arising the next year
over identical questions. On the thirteenth of March the syndic
of the university accompanied by certain masters appeared in
the court of the seneschal and demanded execution of the royal
letters mentioned above. They were assigned a day for hearing
on this matter, at which time the syndic for the city and several
capitouls also appeared and entered a vigorous protest, asking
for a delay in order that the city might have time to present its
case. The syndic also requested that legal counsel be accorded
to him and that the counsellors so named be required by oath
to aid him in every way, for all the practicing attorneys were
university graduates and bound by oath not to act against it.
The royal procurator of Toulouse also entered his objections
to the execution of the king's letters, alleging that they had
been dishonestly obtained, and particularly insisting that the
soquetum, the tax on wine, did not properly belong to the king,
so that he did not have the right to grant exemptions thereto.
It was further stated that if the university were so exempted.
all the taverns of the town would be forced to close. The
collector of war taxes also interposed his objections and asked
time to present his case. When the municipal syndic again
besought the court to grant him legal counsel, the judge named
a doctor of law and six licentiates as advocates, who excused
themselves as university graduates. In order to block the syndic
even further in this matter, the party of the university produced

[17] Fournier, *Statuts*, I, nos. 722-723, p. 684.
[18] Fournier, *Statuts*, I, no. 704, p. 663. Dominicus in 1376 was prior of this
college, *ibid.*, no. 696, p. 630.

the procurator of the chancellor who formally objected to the employment of university graduates for such a purpose. Three days later, March 22, the university syndic was again before the court demanding execution, while the municipal syndic reiterated his earlier objections and appealed to the king and the *parlement* of Paris. The court finally named advocates for the city, ordering the university graduates to fulfill these functions on pain of being deprived of advocacy in court, and gave copies of the royal letters to all seeking them. At the following meeting of the court on March 27, the municipal syndic was still complaining that those appointed to give him legal aid had refused to act, although one of the licentiates appointed at the previous session did present a few arguments in his behalf. These were mainly the two precedents that the *soquet* had been levied against the patriarch of Alexandria during the period of his administration in the see of Toulouse and against other ecclesiastics publicly and without comment. It was further diplomatically urged that as the lord king never violated the rights of others, and as the *soquet* was not his, the university had obtained its letters under false pretense. The right of the *capitouls* to levy war taxes on all persons was further claimed by authority of earlier royal letters.[19]

On April 17 a brief of the municipal claims was presented to the court. Here the whole history of this tax was discussed in detail. The *soquet*, it argued, was imposed upon the retail sellers of wine in order to maintain the fortifications of the city; and for this tax the royal consent had been obtained. It was collected through diminishing the measure of wine; thus the buyer and not the seller was affected. The university as a seller could in no way consider this a burden. Furthermore, the *capitouls* had had the right of collecting such a tax on the wine of clerk and layman for sixty years, and the archbishop and other members of the clergy had paid it. When the College of Saint Martial had contested this right before the duke of Anjou and before Pope Urban, the city, not the college, had been sustained. The cathedral chapter also had been forced to pay this tax even with appeal pending. The *soquet* had been confirmed by the royal seneschal and had been openly published by him. The university had not objected at that time. Meanwhile, the students had been violating this law to the great detriment of

---

[19] Fournier, *Statuts*, III, no. 1911, pp. 529-540.

merchants by underselling them, and had even sold the wine of their friends under the same pretended exemption. This was also to the detriment of the royal treasury for it received one-fourth of the receipts which amounted to 2,000 *livres* in a year. The sum lost by the city in three months was estimated at 4,000 *livres*. In their efforts to stop this leakage in municipal revenues, the *capitouls* had obtained letters from the king forbidding ecclesiastics and colleges from this practice, and had had the letters duly published. The university knew of this and had not objected. Thus, the recently obtained royal privilege giving such exemption to university notaries, parchmenters, and syndics as well as to actual members of the *studium* was contested as being fraudulently obtained through misrepresenting matters to the king. This was the more unjust, the brief continued, as the university as a whole was not at all injured, for most of its students came from long distances so had no wine to sell in the city anyway. At the conclusion of the reading of this long list of grievances, the municipal syndic was given one day to correct his brief and present a copy of it to the university. The case dragged on until May, several extensions having been granted. On the seventh of that month the municipal syndic appeared with royal letters granted at Abbeville six days earlier, ordering the seneschal to render judgment in this matter, for the king had heard that the university held a great part of the city and often maintained taverns there to the detriment of other wine merchants. The judicial record closes with the remission of the case to the court of the seneschal for the following Friday.[20]

In the meanwhile another suit had arisen between the university and the *capitouls* over other tax exemptions claimed by the university. There were several points in dispute. First, there was the question of the *collects,* which the *capitouls* claimed they had the right of imposing on the patrimonial property of all married or unmarried clerks who were students at Toulouse, particularly if they were not regent doctors. They also claimed the right of collecting the *cosset* or milling tax on grain, and the *soquet* from these same persons. It would seem that the university had lost its suit on the latter before the seneschal, for his decision is quoted. This information comes from a document contained in a parchment roll, which was apparently the brief presented by the syndic of the city to a

[20] Materials derived from the document mentioned above.

group of legal experts chosen concordantly by the university and the city to settle these matters.[21] The pleadings on these points were very similar to those on the *soquet* already quoted. The *capitouls* claimed that they had been confirmed in their right of exacting *collects* from unmarried clerks as far back as 1280 and that on several occasions the archbishop had been forbidden to impede the collection of such a tax, namely in 1337 by the seneschal, and in June of 1387 by the *parlement*. In 1390 the king had ordered all clerks to pay the tax according to the orders of the *parlement*, and in 1392 the *officialis* had been forbidden any impediment in the collection of such rights. In 1368 a special royal letter had commanded clerks and colleges to pay *tailles* and *collects* on patrimonial wealth, and in 1372 a similar letter in regard to the *taille* had been sent to other members of the clergy. In 1377 this demand had been renewed, and in 1379 the *capitouls* were given royal authority for the collection of the *taille* from ecclesiastics. Thus the university was alleged to have no right to pretend immunity on the pretext of clerical privileges. Furthermore, to come even closer to the case in point, three former professors of law in the university were cited as having contributed to the municipal *collects* and imposts even while they were teaching in the *studium*. Additional arguments were also adduced on the question of the *soquet*. A decision of Pope Urban compelling the College of Saint Martial to employ the prescribed measure for wine, and a case between the chapter of Saint Etienne and the *capitouls* having similar outcome are mentioned. It is also learned that as a result of the attempt of the *capitouls* at enforcing the collection of the *taille* from three individuals, the university had held that its rights were endangered and had threatened cessation for the Tuesday of Holy Week unless the pledges exacted were returned within the week. When this proved unavailing the cessation of all scholastic exercises actually resulted, although, if the brief may be followed, illegally.[22]

Early in the fifteenth century, the university was still embroiled with the royal officials of Toulouse in the matter of its privileges and exemptions in respect to war taxation. It seems

[21] *Archives municipales de Toulouse*, layette 79. The document itself has no date but contains references to dates, the latest of which is 1392. The decision of the seneschal in the case of the *soquet* would probably date from 1393.

[22] Materials derived from the document cited above.

that the seneschal and the judges of appeals, civil causes, and criminal causes of Toulouse had intervened in cases concerning the university to the detriment of its special royal safeguard of 1392, whereby the vicar of Toulouse and his lieutenant had been named conservators of its privileges.[23] By royal letters of 1407 this violation is forbidden for the future. No appeals are to be heard thereafter by any of the designated judges in matters concerning the university, nor may they take part in such questions save in the case of an appeal to *parlement*. The vicar was furthermore warned that he was not to act as ordinary judge for such suits but simply as conservator and guardian of university rights.[24] A letter of special safeguard dating from 1408 is extant, which was issued by the vicar of Toulouse functioning as university conservator in behalf of a bachelor of decrees. From this is learned just how far the royal protection extended, for it is specified to apply to his family, rights, things, and goods; and judges and royal officers are ordered to protect them. The royal insignia of the *fleur-de-lys* is to be placed on all his goods, houses, gardens, granges, fields, woods, meadows, vines, and other possessions, and his messengers are to be similarly safeguarded. Judges are forbidden to take cognizance in cases brought against this student, but are to remit them to the court of the vicar. The royal injunctions of the previous year were thus faithfully followed.[25]

This long legal quarrel between the municipality of Toulouse and the university was paralleled by a similar dispute between the municipality and the colleges, in which the university also intervened. Here again the subject was one of taxation. It seems that certain colleges had refused to pay the *tailles* or *collects* that the *capitouls* had imposed to defray the expenses of the city government. When the city had requested and received authority from the king to enforce payment through the seneschal, the procurator of the university had impeded

[23] Fournier, *Statuts*, I, no. 723, p. 684.
[24] Archives municipales de Toulouse, GG., 76, f°3. This document is also to be found in the *Ordonances*, IX, p. 200. Fournier, *Statuts*, I, no. 763, p. 726 notes a reference to this document in Brillon, *Dictionnaire des arrêts*, VI, 935, but considers it a mistake because kings did not yet make declarations on the subject of universities. There is a slight discrepancy in dating between the manuscript at Toulouse and the documents quoted in the *Ordonances* and Brillon. It results from a confusion of the copyist between the day of the month and the year of the reign. The last two give both as "xxvii," while the manuscript gives both as "xvii". The twenty-seventh year of Charles' reign was 1407, of course.
[25] Fournier, *Statuts*, III, no. 1919, p. 638.

execution of the royal letters and had obtained others directed
to the vicar, by which the colleges were to be held quit. When
the *capitouls* complained that these last had been obtained by
misrepresentation, Charles VI then ordered his seneschal to
proceed, disregarding the letters of the university procurator
and vicar of Toulouse.[26] Objection was taken in several instances
when the seneschal tried to enforce these letters, and the cases
were appealed to the *parlement* of Paris. These cases were
ultimately quashed when the principal cause itself was finally
brought up in appeal.[27] From the elaborate brief that the
capitouls of Toulouse presented to this court many further details of the dispute are obtained. For instance, here for the first
time the names of the colleges party to the suit are given. The
list included that of Maguelonne, Pampelune, Saint Martial,
and Perigord, four of the largest and most recently founded
colleges. It is also learned that the university itself joined the
colleges by sending its syndic. The pleadings of the municipality
for its rights to taxation are very carefully developed in this
document, and incidentally the counter-pleas of the colleges are
outlined in the rebuttal arguments.

The city first reiterated its demands that the colleges be
forced to contribute with the burghers and citizens of Toulouse
to pay their reasonable share of charges and *tailles* for charitable
purposes and public works, such as the repair of bridges, gates,
walls and ditches, and public ways; and also to meet the special
sums enjoined upon the city by the king. It was furthermore
urged that the colleges be forced to meet all arrears and pay
their assessments pending the decision. Cited as special reasons
for such action on the part of the *parlement* were the loyalty
of the city to the king, its seigneur, and the extremely small
revenues which did not suffice to pay the salaries of its officers.
Nor were these emoluments of a very munificent sort, for the
capitouls received an ordinary robe and a furred robe each year,
a torch of wax to the value of three *livres* each month, and
two *livres* of spice at Lent. The diminution of municipal revenues was laid to the great ruin suffered by the city over a period
of fifty years. There had formerly been many nobles and knights
with holdings around Toulouse and houses in the city, but these

---

[26] Archives municipales de Toulouse, AA 37:19. The original on parchment
is dated February 13, 1409.
[27] Data gleaned from the pleadings of the *capitouls*, Fournier, *Statuts*, III,
no. 1913, p. 583.

had decreased to six knights and ten squires, for the colleges
now held all their land. Formerly the city had been full of
people and had had large *faubourgs;* but now a third part of
both were uninhabited, owing to the great mortality of 1348.
Outside the walls in the *faubourgs* toward the chateau Narbonnais, only about thirty houses were now occupied. As result
of the war and its ravages which had turned the neighborhood
into a wilderness, the need for defense was greater than ever.
That part of the *seneschausée* situated between Toulouse and
Montauban had suffered not only from the enemies of the king
but also from the expenses of quartering the royal armies and
from wartime taxation. Fortresses held by the enemy, such as
those of de Penne in the Albigeois, of Lourdes, of Montauban,
and others, had been centers for ravaging bands which greatly impeded the merchants as there was no market for grain and wine
at Bordeaux and Bayonne. Furthermore, the war had caused a
great lack of silver, oil, salt, cattle, spice, and other merchandise.
The silver had been drawn to Flanders to buy cloth and to Paris
to the king and *parlement.* Toulouse had done her best to regain
these fortresses for the king and had been ravaged to her very
gates, and her citizens had been exposed to imprisonment and
murder by the English. Indeed, all her levies for fortifications
and reparations had been necessary, for without the resistance
of Toulouse, the English would have overrun Carcasonne and
Beaucaire to the river Rhone. At that very moment, because
of her poverty, the bridges and walls of the city were in ruin
in spite of the expending of 4,000 francs on the former and
100,000 *livres tournois* on the latter in the last thirty years.
Of the five bridges, only two were passable, and one of these
lacked an arch and was so badly in need of repair that its reconstruction was estimated by masons of Toulouse, Avignon,
and Lyons at 760,000 *livres tournois.* Two hundred thousand
livres tournois were required at the moment for repair of the
walls. During the same period of thirty years the city had paid
200,000 *livres* for the defense of the realm. Consequently the
citizens had been impoverished and had turned over their possessions to monasteries. As a result, the monasteries and colleges
held nearly all the land that was formerly taxable. During the
course of the war, lands and rents without number were purchased for the support of colleges despite the prohibition of the
king of Sicily, the duke of Anjou. These institutions were now
very rich and possessed fine mansions but refused to pay their

share of municipal taxes. As they held property formerly taxable, they should be compelled to do so, for the *capitouls* have had the right for a hundred years to impose taxes on laymen, clerks, and students. As citations of precedents in this matter, many instances of the compulsion of ecclesiastics to pay are noted, among them the case lost by the bishop of Toulouse in 1280 to prevent the taxing of married clerks. The colleges themselves had paid taxes several times, so the right to tax them had been clearly established. In 1379 and again in 1386 the city had received permission to force the colleges and monasteries to pay imposts for its defense and fortification. Students also had been forced on occasions to pay taxes on the milling of wheat and on the retail selling of wine. The College of Saint Martial itself had lost its case in the matter of the tax on wine.

The following section of this lengthy brief is devoted to the enumeration of sums assessed by king, municipality, and pope over a period of thirty years. Toward these assessments the colleges had in most cases refused to pay their share. For instance the College of Perigord had paid 5,768 *livres*, 6 *sous tournois,* and still owed 3,903 *livres,* 3 *sous,* 9 *deniers tournois;* the College of Pampelune had paid 3,720 *livres,* 3 *sous,* 6 *deniers,* and owed 1,834 *livres,* 15 *sous,* 6 *deniers;* and the College of Maguelonne had paid 3,801 *livres,* 4 *sous* and owed 2,324 *livres.* It was estimated that collegiate holdings were so extensive in the city that the burghers held but a paltry tenth of the revenues. To substantiate these claims, long lists of the properties of these institutions were inserted as evidence of their ability to pay. In summary of the municipal allegations, it is argued that these colleges were really inhabitants of Toulouse because they had been founded over ten or twenty years, that properly speaking they were not churches, but colleges of clerks and laymen who contracted marriage when they wished, and that priests were present in these institutions only for the purpose of saying Masses for the scholars. As to the university, it was a useless party in this dispute because nothing had been demanded of it.

The arguments of the university and colleges submitted in defense can be traced, though somewhat less clearly, from the rebuttals that form the last portion of this document. These seemed to rest largely on the fact that the immunities of Toulouse were identical with those of Paris, which was considered questionable by the *capitouls* since the university had made so little use of them. To the allegation that the University of

Toulouse, like the University of Paris, was exempted from payments, the response was that it had never used this privilege;
and furthermore the city was trying to collect from colleges
only, not from the university or its students. To the plea that
these colleges were founded for poor students, the city claimed
that it was asking nothing of the students in the colleges but
from the rents of the colleges which were temporal revenues,
not benefices. Beside the collegiate claims of inability to pay
such taxes was set their great wealth. To their protests that the
count of Toulouse and the pope had given immunity to all
students, the *capitouls* insisted that such rights belonged only to
the king. To their allegation of royal confirmation of such
immunities, it was argued that the confirmation of what was nul
could not hold, and that the king would not do anything preju-
dicial to the citizens without consulting them. To their claims
that their lands had been amortized by the king came flat denial.
If he had amortized them it would apply only to personal and extraordinary charges and not to patrimonial and real, and, if actually done, should be revoked. All rights of freedom from contribution on analogy with colleges in Paris and Montpellier were
denied, because Parisian colleges did not possess castles, cities,
and lands of the ancient contribution. Furthermore, the College of
Cluny had been compelled to contribute for the repair of public
ways. It was likewise denied that the city had other revenues sufficient to repair its walls and that it had spent money uselessly on
pleadings and journeys. These revenues would not even pay its
officials, they had been so greatly diminished by wars, mortalities, and the great fire which had burned the *rue des Changeurs*
five years back. It was specifically denied that the *capitouls*
received an annual emolument of 40, and the syndics of 50 *livres*.
As final argument the brief asks what means would be available
to the colleges housed in the city in case it were destroyed, and
calls upon the royal procurator for his fullest support of the
city's demands in this taxation problem.[28]

This litigation before the *parlement* of Paris dragged on for
several years. Evidently careful investigations were made before

[28] The four preceding paragraphs are derived from the brief as printed in
Fournier, *Statuts,* III, no. 1913, p. 560 ff. The document is dated "1406(?)"
by the editor, but contains a reference to the royal letters to the seneschal
in 1408, obviously those of February, 1409 cited above. Letters to the
seneschal dated January 7, 1410, (Archives municipales de Toulouse,
AA37:25), asking that he seek information upon the matter of the suit
between the *capitouls* and the colleges which had refused to pay taxes, for
transmission to his court, would definitely date this brief as of 1409.

the decision was actually rendered, for there are extant letters of the king to his seneschal of Toulouse, which require that officer to investigate the truth of the allegations of the *capitouls* and to transmit his findings to the court, and also letters of the same seneschal delegating this business to the royal judge of Verdun, since his own business was so pressing.[29] These both date from early in 1410, but in May, 1413, the suit must have still been in progress, for royal letters directed to the four colleges inform them that the *capitouls* were forbidden to impose the *taille* upon their properties pending litigation in the *parlement* of Paris. As so frequently occurs in the records of medieval lawsuits, the final decision in this interesting case is unknown.[30]

In 1426 the university was again embroiled in a very serious quarrel with the citizens of Toulouse in a matter arising at least in part out of the violent prejudices of wartime psychology. This dispute was more along the lines of the celebrated Berenger affair of the previous century than of the comparatively mild civil suits on taxation questions that had been brought up as a result of the protracted warfare with the English. The principal point at stake in the Saint Cricq affair was the academic privilege of royal safeguard for students, which the university claimed had been wantonly disregarded. At the same time the *studium* was also defending its use of the right of cessation to enforce justice against the *capitouls* and citizens of Toulouse for the second time in less than forty years.

The whole affair, it would seem, had very trivial origins. Two tailors of Toulouse had been annoyed at the attention paid their wives by a pair of students who were retainers in the household of the prior of Saint Cricq, himself also a student in the university. The outraged husbands had complained of this unseemly conduct to the prior but on failing to gain satisfaction had taken revenge into their own hands by waylaying one of their tormentors in the streets on two occasions within a fortnight. On the second attempt the student had taken refuge in the church of Saint Sernin while his assailants secured the intervention of Petrus Ramundus de Aurivalle, nephew of the *juge-mage* of Toulouse, who apparently bore a grudge against

---

[29] Archives municipales de Toulouse, AA 37:25. Original on parchment.
[30] Fournier, *Statuts,* I, no. 777, p. 739. This is a mere summary with reference to the *Grand Inventaire de Sainte Catherine* of the Archives départementales de la Haute-Garonne. Folio 2v° of the latter gives the additional information, "pendant la litispendance au parlement de Paris."

the prior of Saint Cricq. At any rate he entered the church and violated its right of sanctuary by injuring the student in the scuffle which followed. Evidently there was a feud in progress directed by Aurivalle and his friend Rosset, both of whom were in the king's service, against Saint Cricq. The two young officers through their important connections in the region, had been able to secure immunity from arrest at the hands of the municipal police even though each maintained a considerable group of liveried retainers within the confines of the city. At any rate during the trial which followed, they were accused of plotting against Saint Cricq and of setting ambushes in the streets to waylay his followers. The prior and his friends were in turn denounced by the officers as "native-born Englishmen" and the former particularly charged with evil life and the abduction of several women.

In the rioting which followed the attempt of Saint Cricq to escort his injured friend from Saint Sernin to his hospice, another of his retainers was wounded at the hands of Rosset and his liveried followers. Thereafter the two officers sought the backing of their friends and relatives in public office, including two of the *capitouls* and two sons of the *juge-mage*, for a further attack upon the prior. The following morning the university became implicated in the matter. It seems that Bernard de Rosergue, a canon of Saint Etienne and regent doctor in the university, was on his way to the Dominican chapel for the university Mass after celebrating his own at the cathedral, when he heard that a student had been wounded in a brawl and that Aurivalle and Rosset were attempting an illegal congregation against the prior of Saint Cricq. He immediately hastened to the *juge-mage* to lodge a complaint, and was told by that officer that Aurivalle and Rosset had already complained of the students but that he would do what he could. Rosergue continued to the chapel for the university service and deliberated thereafter with his colleagues as to what action should be taken. It was decided to demand justice next morning, but after dinner the canon was disquieted by the news that Aurivalle and Rosset had assembled a great multitude, so he hastened to the house of Saint Cricq and told him to seek refuge with the Franciscans. Then Rosergue continued to the city hall to protest. Here he found some of the *capitouls* already congregated, but they showed no interest in his demands for protection. The legality of this meeting at the city hall was hotly disputed later by the two parties to the case.

The prosecution claimed that it was a fraudulent affair which the plotters were attempting to mask by having a fencing master stage an exhibition there, so that they would have an excuse for the gathering. The three or four *capitouls* present, the prosecution argued, did not constitute a quorum sufficient for legality, for that required the presence of at least eight. The defense was equally insistent that it was only after the university's complaint to the *juge-mage* that the *capitouls* had congregated to see if they could prevent violence and that a canon of Pamiers and two students had likewise requested action of the *juge-mage*. As to the fencing exhibition, it had been announced for a week so was no cloak to a conspiracy. Strangely enough, the defense also tried to make it appear that Rosergue was complaining of the congregating of armed men by Saint Cricq, when the former reported the affair to the *juge-mage*. It was argued that as a result of this protest the *juge-mage* had sent the sub-vicar of Toulouse and another to warn the prior and his followers, and that he himself had only followed after the sub-vicar at the suggestion of the canon of Pamiers. The sub-vicar went first toward the city hall, commandeering the services of several citizens along the way. Before the church of the Taur this party met two of the *capitouls*, accompanied by Aurivalle and Rosset, coming from the city hall with a large following. The *capitouls* subsequently claimed in defense that the crowd had followed out of curiosity and had not been required by them, and that their own group had consisted of not more than twenty persons. They were on their way, they explained, to the house of Saint Cricq to attempt to avoid scandal. The sub-vicar on his part forbade Aurivalle and Rosset to proceed further with the *capitouls*, so they turned aside; and the *capitouls* and sub-vicar continued to the prior's, accompanied by about forty people.

When the *capitouls*, the *juge-mage*, and the sub-vicar reached their destination they heard a great tumult in the neighboring College of Narbonne and hastened there immediately. It would seem that the party with Aurivalle and Rosset, when deflected, had encountered one of the prior's retainers as he was going to the Franciscan church for sermon and vespers. One of this party, presumably the son of the *juge-mage*, recognized him as a friend of Saint Cricq and would probably have killed him but for the intervention of a passing priest. Thereafter all bore down upon the College of Narbonne and attacked it. It was the noise of this tumult that had summoned the sub-vicar and his group from the neighboring street. Presumably the prior and his friends had sought refuge within the college, and this had come to the ears of Aurivalle and Rosset. At any rate, while one group attacked the gate of the college, the other broke into the garden of the Franciscan convent nearby in an attempt to force an entry. The prior and his followers had fled from the threatened college by a back way and sought refuge with the Friars Minor.

The College of Narbonne was evidently the scene of a grave disorder. The intruders overcame a servant who tried to stop their entry and then broke the locks and entered the chambers of the students. In one room, that of Navarrus Rossus, procurator of the count of Foix, they found arms, and beat the unfortunate student about the head. Meanwhile the *capitouls, juge-mage,* and the sub-vicar arrived on the scene. The prosecution insisted on including the *capitouls* in the attack on the college, alleging that the *juge-mage* had thrown stones on the roof of the college to break the tiles and that both the *capitouls* and the party of Aurivalle and Rosset had carried off books from the library and chapel utensils as well as arms belonging to the collegiates. The defense, on the other hand, held that the *capitouls* had entered the college only in form of justice and had used no undue force. They admitted it was possible that the door of the college had been pierced with a lance, because resistance had been offered, but denied that the captain of the night guard had entered the college and also that anything had been carried away. The *capitouls*, it was explained, had searched all who had entered the college in the presence of the collegiates to prevent that very thing. It was furthermore denied that the *juge-mage* had thrown stones on the roof of the college, but that this had been done by a fifteen year old servant of the prior of Saint Cricq, and the former had only thrown a stone to make him desist.

The prosecution, moreover, asserted that one of the *capitouls* had broken weapons belonging to the count of Foix and had urged that all the students be killed and their bodies thrown into the river. When a student had protested at the cries, "to the Garonne! to the Garonne!" he would have been killed but for the intervention of the sub-vicar. The latter also had to protect the college servant from injury at the hands of the night watch. In the mêlée a companion of the sub-vicar had been wounded. The *capitouls* disclaimed vigorously in their defense that they had broken any arms belonging to the count and asserted that

Navarrus had destroyed these himself and had hidden a harness belonging to the prior of Saint Cricq in his chamber, telling them he had some silver vessels belonging to the cardinal of Foix.

From the College of Narbonne the *capitouls* proceeded to the convent of the Franciscans, still in search of the prior. They entered the church of the friars although a sermon was in progress and then violated the cloisters by breaking in a door of the refectory. Stephanus de Gano, the friar guardian of the convent, finally produced the prior of Saint Cricq after they had promised to do him no harm, and the prior himself had agreed to go to prison if they could prove any blame against him. After warning the prior, the *capitouls* returned to the city hall, where they made a rather tardy threat to Aurivalle and Rosset against further disturbance of the peace. In the meantime, however, Aurivalle had entered the shop of a furrier and had dragged his son, a bachelor in law, out into the street beating him severely. Only the intervention of neighbors prevented homicide. On the following day, one of Aurivalle's retainers pursued the same student with leaden knuckles and would have injured him, had not he sought refuge in his father's home. It seems that his offense had been in declaring that Aurivalle wanted to run the whole city.

Evidently a petty reign of terror followed. The university claimed that its students did not dare to appear in the streets, for Aurivalle and his friends rode through the city showing their power. When the university attempted to lodge a complaint with the seneschal on the following Tuesday, it found the doors of the court locked, so had to seek out instead two judges of the *seneschausée* who had no jurisdiction in Toulouse. No justice was obtained by these efforts because Aurivalle and Rosset prevented anything being done. It was alleged that the *capitouls* refused to act when complaint was made to them, because Aurivalle was the nephew of the *juge-mage* and two of the latter's sons had been his accomplices. The masters were merely derided for their efforts. In desperation the university threatened cessation in two weeks' time unless justice were done. As no action was taken, the cessation was put rigorously into effect, even sermons being forbidden on the pain of excommunication. Rosset meanwhile had continued to threaten the prior of Saint Cricq, and Aurivalle had been reported to have said he would ring the bell of the night watch in the church of the Taur so that the university would know with whom it had to deal. He would arouse the whole populace to destroy the university. Fearing further violence, the university appealed to *parlement,* and after five months' cessation the case finally came up in that court. During this period Stephanus de Gano and Ramundus Gauterius, two Franciscan friars, were excommunicated by the university for disobedience to its commands to cease preaching. This was carried out notwithstanding their papal authorization as preachers and their exemption from all ecclesiastical judges save the general of the order. It would seem that the university, although in cessation, had used the solemnities of a bachelor for promulgating its decree.

Thus far the matter is seen to be an extremely complicated affair, embracing an enormous number of plaintiffs and defendants. The pleadings, counter-pleadings, and rebuttals make up a most complex lawsuit record. It is difficult to say which party or parties were at fault and which innocent. As in all such quarrels there was obviously error on both sides. During the protracted trial much seems to have been extravagantly charged and much reasonably explained both for plaintiffs and defendants. It is interesting to compare the justifications of the accused for their actions with the interpretations of these actions by the prosecution. On the whole the accused seem to have succeeded fairly well.

When the case first came to trial before the *parlement* meeting at Béziers in December, 1426, the university refused to accept the submission of one of the accused and, refusing all offers of compromise, insisted that it preferred a little justice through litigation to double or triple the damages through settlement out of court. Thereafter, when the representative of the *capitouls* demanded the distribution of counsel and the court responded, the university protested the assignment of its graduates on the ground that their oaths to the chancellor forbade their undertaking suits against the university. The court overruled this objection, and three days later the case was resumed with the appearance of the chief parties to the litigation. The syndics of the university, of the canons of Saint Sernin, of the College of Narbonne, and of the two wounded students, assisted by the royal procurator, appeared as plaintiffs against a group of thirty individually named defendants. The advocate for the plaintiffs, after describing the grievances of the university, accused the *capitouls* of blocking justice and stipulated the damages he wished assessed against the defendants on behalf of

each of the injured plaintiffs. It was likewise demanded that
until satisfaction had been made, the accused be held in prison,
that the university be free of the jurisdiction of the *capitouls*
during the remainder of the suit, and that the *juge-mage* and
capitouls be forbidden to embarrass the university further. It is
interesting to note that the Franciscan convent does not appear
among the plaintiffs, although it had been subjected to violence
as well as Saint Sernin and the College of Narbonne. The
reason for this absence was, of course, the quarrel between the
university and the Franciscans over the right to preach during
the time of cessation. The prosecution even claimed that the
two friars frequented Rosset and Aurivalle.

Two days later when the case was resumed the university
brought up more grievances. The *capitouls*, it seems, had considered reprisals against the *studium*. They threatened with-
drawal of the use of mills for grain, of ovens for bread, and a
ban on outside supplies for university members. The royal
procurator for this reason demanded that the *capitouls* recall
the dispersed students and assure them of protection. Having
finished with the defendants, the procurator then requested that
the university not be permitted to extend its cessation to sermons, and that the excommunications against the Franciscan
friars be recalled.

*On Friday, December 20, the defense was allowed to plead.
This was done in masterly fashion by Brolhet, in spite of his
connection with the university. No wonder the syndic of the
university had protested the latter's assignment to the party
opposed. Brolhet admitted that the accusations against the defendants were great and well known but insisted that they should
not be considered necessarily true. The defendants, he urged,
had always honored the university, and they wished to come to
an understanding with it now. The chief points brought out by
the defense advocate tended to show that the *juge-mage*, the
capitouls, and the others had been acting only to prevent rioting
on that fateful Sunday, and this at the request of the university
itself. In order to exculpate the *capitouls*, it was alleged that
the prior of Saint Cricq and his friends were English and trouble-
makers. Two student friends of the prior were even then with
the English at Curvorivo. The university's claim that it could
not gain justice at the court of the seneschal on the following
Tuesday because the doors were locked against them was untrue,
since the offices of the court were never ordinarily open on that

day. Moreover, the judge of Verdun and the lieutenant of the seneschal had committed two men immediately to hear their complaints. It was the university which had required instant amends without hearing a word of defense, and when this was refused a cessation had been declared. It was asked that the court excuse the defendants of blame and collect the costs from the plaintiffs. The defendants were quite willing to make their own amends to the university and college. Meanwhile the cessation should be raised, at least in so far as to permit the doctors to preach. Furthermore, it was denied that the university privileges included that of cessation, or that any but good, honest students were included in the royal safeguard. These the prior and his companions were certainly not. As the *capitouls* were neither present at, nor responsible for, the wounding of the prior's friends, this should not be held against them. Najac, the *capitoul*, had neither broken the weapons of the count of Foix nor wounded Navarrus. Indeed, the latter had not been killed as the plaintiffs intimated, but had died several months later after an epidemic. The university had no reason to inculpate the *juge-mage*, for he had done his duty well and had advised his sons and brother to submit.

The party of the university declared in response that it had no authority to cancel the cessation, but that from grants of Innocent IV, Boniface VIII, and Benedict XIII, the university legally possessed the right of cessation. The congregation which had voted cessation had been attended by sixty masters and doctors, and the university had ample power to excommunicate those disobedient to its commands. Sermons were included in cessations at Paris, so could be included as well at Toulouse. At Paris, it was added, even the king could scarcely have a Paschal sermon in time of cessation. At Toulouse the university had given special permission for Christmas sermons, except to the excommunicated Franciscans.

At this point the royal procurator interposed a word in defense of the two friars. He argued that the university should require justice before cessation, and even before appeal to higher courts. That such a cessation should occur within fifteen days of the act itself made the university judge of the matter in dispute. The cessation, furthermore, should include scholastic acts only, and should not be extended to sermons. It should be enforced gradually and not entirely on a given date. The excommunication of the Franciscan preachers over their appeals was inexcusable; and they should be immediately absolved, and the cessation raised.

At the next session of the court, the university procurator continued his pleas. He was on the defensive and presumably answering objections of the opposing counsel in the matter of the riots. In the first place, he questioned the jurisdiction of the *capitouls* and denied that the royal safeguard was limited to good students. Though the university had no intention of sustaining evil students, even though the prior were evil, the *capitouls* had no right to hold an illicit congregation. The university was merely acting as father or mother in protection of its children. Even the English were to be included in the university safeguard. The precedent for this was set in the time of the duke of Anjou, when an imprisoned student from Bordeaux was released. A student from Bayonne had similarly been released at another time. Moreover it was explicitly denied that the prior and his friends were English, but instead were relatives and subjects of the count of Foix. The prior's two brothers were not at Curvorivo, but in the service of the king. Furthermore he was a noble and good student, the possessor of many books. It is admitted that he may have had a harness and sword in his house, but not many. The university knew nothing about the charges of abduction and of pro-English sympathizing brought against the prior by the defendants. The servant who alleged the latter should have denounced him to the proper authorities at the time, but he did not do so. The acts of procuration for syndics by the university, in spite of the cessation, and by the College of Narbonne, although but three students remained in residence, were clearly justified. Furthermore all knowledge of the relations between the friends of Saint Cricq and the wives of the two tailors was disclaimed on the part of the university, and it was intimated that these students had acted only in self-defense. This in no way exculpated Aurivalle and Rosset from plotting against them, nor the *capitouls* from joining in the plot. The university as a whole had always been faithful to the king and had never sustained the English. Malice had certainly been borne against the prior by both Aurivalle and Rosset, and the university only took his part because her privileges had been violated. The *capitouls*, indeed, had not cleared themselves from abetting the former, for they had not placed the tailors in prison until after several days had elapsed, and they had been released later by Aurivalle and his friends. As further proof of malice, statements of other partisans of Aurivalle and Rosset were cited. One of these was reported as saying that could they find the prior and his friends they would kill them even though the *bereti,* meaning the doctors and masters, were there. Another had advocated sounding the tocsin if students showed any resistance. If one of the defendants was touched by a student, they said they would kill him. The university procurator concluded by objecting to the triviality of the excuses for non-appearance of Aurivalle, Rosset, and some of the others. It was urged that they be declared in contempt of court and adjudged guilty of breaking the royal safeguard and *lèse-majesté.*

The royal procurator then took up the case, affirming the infraction of royal safeguard by the accused and defending the prior and his friends from the charges of treason, which he averred were due to malevolence on the part of enemies. The *capitouls* were merely trying to excuse themselves by maligning the prior. Again it is reiterated that even if the prior were English and were he not included in the royal safeguard, the defendants could not excuse themselves for their delicts. Judgment was demanded for the grave abuse of justice.

The rebuttal for the defense in this instance seems rather weak and frivolous. It denied that the prosecution had enough evidence to continue the case and affirmed that the *capitouls* had jurisdiction by day and by night. The character of the prior was further attacked. It was denied that he was a relative of the count of Foix, for the count had told the *juge-mage* that for the first offense the prior should have been drowned. The region of Saint Cricq itself was declared to be in the land of the English because an expedition to that region had netted the capture of twelve Englishmen. After this the prior was quoted as reporting to Lord Tortanerius de Lesmith, the English seneschal, that he believed his brother to have been captured, thus proving the prior to be English. Furthermore, the two tailors were justified in their actions by the attacks of the students on their wives; and the students were guilty as rebels, so not worthy of the royal safeguard. Quite decidedly Aurivalle had not plotted all night with Rosset; and as to the alleged threat of ringing the bell of the Taur, the reference was probably to a bell named for his father and used as curfew. The said bell was never employed as tocsin. Both Aurivalle and Rosset were of notable families, and the latter had not wounded the prior's friend but acted only in self-defense. Nor were the *capitouls* guilty of sedition; they had merely gone at the request of Rosergue to prohibit scandal, and had not been forbidden to proceed when they met the sub-vicar. In fine, the prior and his two retainers were at the bottom of the whole affair, and the *capitouls* had just cause in proceeding against them. All, on a previous occasion, had been banned at the sound of the horn from Toulouse with another Englishman named Prat. Furthermore, Rosset and Aurivalle as men of the king had a right to go through the city armed, and had not answered the university's citations to appear at Monterapido because it was a league distant from Toulouse and they were afraid of the English. The tailors had not been freed from prison at the behest of Aurivalle and his friends but by the other *capitouls*.

At the end of the pleading, the court asked for all documents and forbade either party to go against the other on pain of 100 marks. Through February, March, April, and May the case was continued for the defendants who had not appeared at the previous hearings. Then unfortunately the record ceases, leaving the outcome unknown. From the course of the pleadings summarized above, however, a few suggestions may be hazarded. Whether the prior and his friends were disloyal or not cannot be decided. Certainly the charges of the defense on this score were of the feeblest sort and based on vaguest hearsay. How Saint Cricq's not being related to the count of Foix, as claimed, could prove loyalty or disloyalty to France is not at all clear. The term "native-born English," as applied to the prior and his friends by the defense, surely could mean nothing more than native to the English held regions of southern France. The only English name to appear in the whole court record is that of Lesmith, the seneschal. The extent of the prior's alleged relations with this official is not very incriminating at that, for it is reported that he told the seneschal that he believed his brother had been captured in a raiding expedition. It is also seriously to be questioned how the knowledge of such a conversation could have come to the ears of the defense in the first place. It has all the earmarks of hearsay. Surely the defense must have been hard put to prove disloyalty on the part of the prior. What is more likely is that they were trying to justify mere suspicions of this on the part of the *capitouls*. However, the university itself, although claiming the prior innocent and a good student, rather qualifies his complete exoneration by claiming that even if the charges were true, the actions of the *capitouls* were to be con-

demned. On the whole, no very damaging evidence was produced against him. On the other hand, the charges of plot and
conspiracy on the part of Aurivalle, Rosset and the *capitouls*
seem to have had some basis of fact. There was certainly some
bond of relationship among them. It was not denied that Rosset
had come from supper with one of the *capitouls* on the night
when the prior's friends had been waylaid in the streets. Another
of the accused likewise admitted the gathering in his home, and
his wife's unwillingness to lend a harness during his absence.
Rosergue had certainly found a small group of *capitouls* at the
city hall when he went there to protest on the following day,
although the defense insisted that the fencing exhibition was no
ruse, but had been announced a week in advance. The *capitouls*
also seem to have shown great zeal in warning the prior and to
have been most remiss in restraining his enemies, even after the
protest of Rosergue. In fact, Aurivalle and Rosset and their
friends seem to have accompanied the *capitouls* until forbidden
to go further by the sub-vicar. They were only warned by the
capitouls after the disturbance was entirely over. On the other
hand, the defense of the *capitouls* seems to clear them of any
part in the disorders at the College of Narbonne and at the
Franciscan convent. They seem to justify their actions there on
the score of policing the city, and admit that violence may have
been done before they arrived on the scene. On behalf of the
capitouls, it might also be suggested that they acted hastily and
with the best intentions, having listened to the complaints and
suspicions cast on the prior and his friends by Aurivalle and
Rosset. Wartime psychology and patriotic indignation, but not
malice, had led to their mistake. Thereafter, disinclination to
listen to the charges against their noble friends, Aurivalle and
Rosset, and the feeling that they had been scrupulously correct
would naturally have led the *capitouls* to deny the university's
demands for redress of grievances, and thus would have brought
about the cessation. Feelings then rose higher and higher until
a complete impasse was reached. That the error of the *capitouls*
was one of judgment and not of deliberate conspiracy is thus
fairly clear. However, it seems to have been rather a grievous
error, for the prior and his friends seem to have been the really
injured parties as far as physical violence was concerned. Rosset's injury in the street brawl was obviously not serious, but
two of the prior's retainers had certainly suffered at the hands
of their enemies. There is very little evidence that the prior was

collecting an armed band in his house, as was charged by the defense. His flight to the College of Narbonne and then to the Franciscan convent do not bespeak pugnaciousness. The other injured parties, the two tailors, are never connected with Aurivalle and Rosset in any coherent way. On the whole, the affair probably had no deeper motivation than a soldier-student brawl.

That the university should feel itself injured by these events is not surprising. It had called upon the *capitouls* and *juge-mage* for protection of its students, and instead, one of its colleges had been violated. Then all its demands for justice were impeded, giving still more color of conspiracy to the whole affair. The excommunication against the Franciscan preachers was perhaps hastily taken, but such questions had frequently arisen between secular and regular at Paris in times of cessation, so it is not surprising in this instance.

The line taken by the defense in the course of the trial at Béziers may allow for the drawing of some further inferences. One of the accused who was not a *capitoul*, so could not plead policing duties, seemed to consider submission the better way out. The *capitouls* themselves were a little slow in coming forward, but finally did appear for the most part. The weakest point in their defense was the insistence that their action had been taken solely at the request of the university, whereas their inhibitions seem to have been directed primarily to the students and not to their opponents. Neither Aurivalle nor Rosset appeared in their own defense, but sent their excuses, which seem weak. The prior himself did not appear for the prosecution, as he personally had received no injury, but one of his wounded companions was in court as plaintiff.[31] It would be gratifying if documents were extant to permit the tracing of the resumption of university life after this rather lengthy interruption, but such is not the case.

In addition to these difficulties arising from the war, the University of Toulouse was also implicated in the great papal schism which occurred during a part of this same period. At the election of the anti-Pope Clement VII, the mad rush for ecclesiastical preferment on the part of students in French universities grew to even larger proportions, and the supplications

[31] These materials have been drawn from the record of the suit before the *parlement* at Béziers in 1426 and 1427—Fournier, *Statuts*, III, no. 1915, pp. 597-633. The original document is conserved in the Archives départementales de la Haute-Garonne, bearing the dates 1426-1427.

of these *studia* must have required rolls of giant size to include the names and qualifications of all the benefice seekers. In 1378, the first year of the schism, the University of Toulouse submitted an enormous *rotulus* containing some 1,285 names to the Avignon chancery.[32] The anti-pope, who would naturally want the support of the great universities of France in the struggle with his Italian rival, apparently lent willing ear to the requests for preferment from their members. In fact, the register of supplications into which this *rotulus* was transcribed at the Curia bears the preliminary notation of acceptance dated from November 22 of that year for graduates, great nobles, and students who had "heard" a sufficient time for acquiring a degree; and from the twenty-sixth for the others. These annotations were revised in 1380, in all probability for sake of equity among the rival universities of Toulouse, Angers, Montpellier, Cahors, and Avignon, to have the date for doctors and licentiates as of the eighteenth of December, 1378; for bachelors, great nobles, and masters in arts as of the twentieth; and for ordinary students as of the twenty-fourth.[33]

Rotuli bearing such requests had been sent on several occasions by the University of Toulouse to Avignon popes, but never with such wholesale petitions. From this *rotulus* of 1378 a fair idea is gained of the teaching personnel of the *studium,* for aside from spiritual indulgences for five members of the comparatively recently organized faculty of theology, there were listed six regent doctors in canon law, and two each in civil law, arts and grammar. Four other holders of doctoral or magisterial degrees are also noted, but in all probability they were nonregent. The first comprehensive view of the student element in the university is also given in the same petition. Canon law, as might be expected from the great number of regents in that faculty, was the most popular branch with nineteen licentiates. Civil law lagged far behind with a paltry seven, and arts had only three. With baccalaureate rank were 154 decretists, 62

[32] Fournier, *Statuts,* I, no. 697, p. 631 ff.
[33] Vatican Archives, *Supplicationes* (Clemens VII) L, f°99. "Datum Fundis pro graduatis et magnis nobilibus ac scolaribus qui audierunt tempore sufficienti ad gradum habendum, decimo, et pro ceteris sexto kal. Decembris anno primo. E.B. . . . Dominus noster ordinavit iii kal. Aprilis pontificatus sui anno secundo quod Rotuli studiorum Regni Francie, videlicet Tholosani, Andegavensis, Montispessulani, Caturcensis, Avinionensis, datum habeant, videlicet pro doctoribus et licenciatis, xiiii, pro bacallaris et magnis nobilibus ac magistris in artibus xii°; et pro scolaribus quibuscumque viii° kal. Decembris anno primo."

legists, and 47 artists. The undergraduates were in somewhat different proportion with 401, 130 and 246, respectively, and an additional 295 students in the faculty of grammar. In 1387 another *rotulus* was submitted to the same pope, bearing some three hundred names in all. The teaching staff in this case is almost the same size as nine years earlier, but only six names of masters are repetitions of the earlier list.[34] The student enrollment in the nine years had fallen off greatly, owing doubtless to the resumption of hostilities between the French and English and the consequent disorders, for a list of only three hundred names follows, including all branches.

Clement VII also intervened in the local affairs of the *studium* when the scandal that had arisen at Paris between the Dominicans and that university spread to Toulouse. The pope gave mandate to the chancellors of the two universities to act in repressing either seculars or regulars who should "sustain errors" in that dispute. Presumably the strong Dominican group in Toulouse had meant the carrying of the Parisian quarrel into the southern *studium*. In 1391 the pope requested the same chancellors to concede to a Dominican the right to read the *Sentences* extraordinarily and take the magisterial grade in either university, but later in the same year this candidate was given the privilege of reading and the mastership at either Avignon or Montpellier, so perhaps conditions at Toulouse and Paris were not too propitious.[35]

The later Avignon popes seem also to have put their dispensing powers to rather political uses on several occasions, availing themselves of the support given them in the south to reward their northern partisans. A case before the *parlement* of Paris in 1392 between the University of Orléans and one of its former students clearly illustrates these methods. Jean de la Coste, who had been licensed in Orléans, had been dispensed by Clement VII from his oath to complete in that *studium* the work for the doctorate, and thereafter attained his degree at Toulouse. The defendant alleged that he had gone to Toulouse

---

[34] This *rotulus* is cited by Denifle, *Les universités*, p. 36, and found in the Vatican Archives, *Supplicationes* (Clemens VII) LXXII, f°ˢ344-364v°. Johannes Pagesii, M.A., is rector in both cases and first on the list. The other duplications are Petrus Aldeberti, O.P., Master in Theology (number three on both lists), Chatardus Aycardi, Doctor of Decrees (numbers 15 and 21), Guillelmus Vayssere, Master of Grammar (number 16 in both cases), Petrus Arpajonis, Master of Grammar (numbers 17 and 22).

[35] Denifle, *Chartularium*, III, no. 1582, p. 532; and no. 1591, p. 542.

only in obedience to the order of the pope and had dared to take the doctorate under Astorg de Gaillac, for otherwise he should not have been received there as regent. As the pope had dispensed him from his oath and had notified Orléans of this fact, and as he had been commanded to go there for the doctorate on pain of disobedience, he felt himself excused. Furthermore, the same case had been appealed to the court of Rome, and he should not be held in two courts for the same matter. With his statements the *parlement* apparently agreed.[36] Jean de la Coste rose rapidly at Toulouse, for he was one of the rectors for the year in 1392. His advancement was doubtless due to the fact that he was nephew of the titular cardinal of Santi Giovanni e Paulo.[37] A royal letter of 1396 also gives evidence of interference in university affairs on the part of Benedict XIII. Jean de Moravie, a former and somewhat rebellious student of the University of Paris, had sought from the pope a chair in the University of Toulouse. His plea was granted by discharging Fors Senc de Pardiac, Master in Theology, who had occupied one of the chairs there for a long time. The royal letter demanded that the former incumbent be maintained in his rights and was evidently obeyed, for the professor was later confirmed by Benedict himself in 1404.[38]

The supplications sent to Clement VII and Benedict XIII by the university indicate that it too was perfectly cognizant of the fact that the Avignon papacy was anxious for support at any cost. The demands made of Clement VII in 1392 seem rather broad. He was asked to dispense the doctors so that they might hold two or more incompatible benefices for the space of three years, and to excuse masters and licentiates that they might not be forced to continue teaching to the detriment of their search for preferment. Furthermore, the teaching faculty requested that the pope not prefer bachelors and scholars who had obtained *anteferri* clauses to the doctors, masters, and licentiates not having such preference.[39] The supplication to Benedict XIII in the first year of his pontificate contains no such extraordinary requests but is enormously long and includes even simple students in arts and grammar. It is interesting to note

---

[36] Du Boulay, *Historia universitatis Parisiensis*, IV, 679. This Jean de la Coste later defended Benedict XIII in the Council of Paris in 1398.

[37] Fournier, *Statuts*, III, no. 1909, p. 525; and no. 1912, p. 541.

[38] Antoine Thomas, "Lettres closes de Charles VI et de Charles VII addressées à l'université de Toulouse" in *Ann. Midi* (1915-1916), xxvi, 181.

[39] Fournier, *Statuts*, III, no. 1909, p. 525; and no. 1910, p. 528.

that another supplication to this same pontiff in 1403 requests only privileges of spiritual indulgences in connection with its equally lengthy list of benefice seekers.[40]

In regard to the attempts to heal the schism, the University of Toulouse, not to be outdone by Paris, had entered actively into the discussions even as early as 1397. The southern *studium* seems from the very beginning to have been an ardent backer of the Avignon candidate, Benedict XIII, and to have supported him in his refusal to accept the suggestion that he abdicate. Vital de Castelmoron, a doctor of decrees and former professor in the university who, as canon of Saint Etienne, rose first to be vicar general of the diocese and later to the provostship of the cathedral, was sent by his archbishop as representative to an assembly at Paris in the following year, where this question was discussed. It is notable at this time that the universities of Toulouse and Montpellier both definitely refused to sanction any subtraction of obedience from Benedict.[41] Quite obviously they had no desire to lose the advantage of having as a near neighbor a pope who was only too willing to grant them favors. Again in 1402 the university took sides on this same question, sending a letter to the king in favor of Benedict by one of its masters, Guigo Flandrin, a doctor in decrees, who had apparently carried a letter on behalf of the university in 1398 much to the ire of the masters at Paris who responded on behalf of the subtraction.[42] It was probably as a result of this constantly proffered advice that obedience was finally restored to Benedict in the following year. The royal letters make express mention

---

[40] Fournier, *Statuts,* III, no. 1912, p. 525 ff. Denifle, *Les universités,* 36, footnote 2, cites a *rotulus* of the *capitouls* for certain doctors and nobles which I lacked time to locate at the Vatican. For the 1403 *rotulus,* see *ibid.,* no. xv, 67.

[41] *Histoire générale de Languedoc,* IX, 974. Vital was a native of Toulouse (Lafaille, *Annales,* I, 161), who had received his academic training in the city. He was listed as bachelor in decrees in a University document as early as 1378 (Fournier, *Statuts,* I, no. 697, p. 632), and nine years later he is found among the regent doctors in the same faculty (Vatican Archives, *Supplicationes* (Clemens VII) LXXII, f°344). The following year he was vicar general (Vatican Archives, *Instrumenta miscellanea,* 3300), an office which he was still holding in 1395 (Fournier, *Statuts,* I, no. 731, p. 690; and no. 735, p. 692). Shortly after he became provost (so designated in a document in the Archives départementales de la Haute-Garonne, 4G., XXIX, liasse 10, pièce sans numero, dated March 12, 1398; "Acta fuerunt hec Tholose die duodecima mensis martii anno ab Incarnatione domini millesimo millesimo trecentesimo nonagesimo septimo.")

[42] *Histoire générale de Languedoc,* IX, 990. Fournier, *Statuts,* I, no. 750, p. 702, citing Duboulay, *Historia universitatis Parisiensis,* V, 25 and 30, refers to the same response.

of the acquiescence of certain universities of the realm, namely Toulouse, Orléans, Montpellier, and Angers.[43] About this same epoch also, Guigo Flandrin seems to have been rewarded by the pope for his partisan endeavors, for he appears on a *rotulus* of the university qualified as auditor of the Sacred Palace.[44] Both the university and its messenger were shortly to have ample proof of the grudge borne them in this matter by the Paris *studium*. In 1406 before the *parlement* of Paris, the irate masters brought suit claiming that the letter of the University of Toulouse at the time of the subtraction of obedience to Benedict XIII in 1398 had been defamatory. It also alleged in defense of their own position that the pope had been approached most honorably and requested to withdraw so as not to cause a schism, and that when this had been refused, then only had a congregation been held and obedience withdrawn. The language of the letter from Toulouse in response to this subtraction had been most violent and opprobrious, and the procurator quoted a long, fiery passage in proof of his statement. The decision in this suit was unfavorable to the defendant, for copies of the said letter were ordered burned publicly at Paris, upon the bridge at Avignon, at Toulouse, Montpellier, and Carcasonne. The parlementary arrest even included the name of the bearer of the original document, Guigo Flandrin. Two years later Guigo was again denounced as abettor of Benedict and accused of being in part author as well as bearer of the offending letter of the university.[45]

Meanwhile there was trouble at Toulouse over the succession to the see of that city in 1406. Vital de Castelmoron, provost of Saint Etienne, had been elected by the chapter, but Benedict XIII insisted on translating Pierre Ravot, the bishop of Saint Pons, who was also an alumnus of the university, having been a doctor of decrees and later chancellor there. Ravot had gained rapid advancement under Benedict XIII, acquiring the see of Mâcon in 1395 and later the bishopric of Saint Pons. The university espoused the cause of Ravot, and a papal notary, with the assistance of Jean Corneille, a canon of Saint Sernin

---

[43] *Ordonances*, VIII, 593, letters dated May 28, 1403. The *Histoire générale de Languedoc*, IX, 993, notes this under the year 1404, but includes Paris and omits Orléans and Angers.

[44] Denifle, *Les universités*, no. xv, p. 67. He was a nephew of John, titular of Santi Giovanni e Paulo, Fournier, *Statuts*, III, 1912, p. 541, so rose rapidly like his cousin Jean de la Coste.

[45] *Histoire générale de Languedoc*, IX, 999-1000, 1002; and Fournier, *Statuts*, I, no. 760, p. 718.

and regent Doctor in Decrees, who was acting as lieutenant for the rector, Abbot Aimery Nadal, managed to assemble a congregation of professors and students to install Ravot. Philippe Bonne, the *juge-mage* of Toulouse, who attempted to stop this, was murdered, and order was only restored by the royal forces.[46] Vital was translated to Saint Pons, but returned to the see to which he had been elected when Ravot was forced from the province in 1408. Ravot was not deserted by his patron but shortly raised to the cardinalate, where he was commonly known as the cardinal of Toulouse.[47] It was possibly in connection with the rioting in Toulouse that occurred during this disputed possession of the see that the *capitouls* and inhabitants were forbidden to attend the academic ceremonies in the *studium*. At any rate, the ban was raised by letters of the duke of Berry, dated from Paris the nineteenth of April, 1407.[48]

At the Council of Pisa in 1409, the university continued to play its part, for among the delegates from the province of Toulouse, along with six prelates and two doctors, were two other doctors from the university. One of the latter was Johannes Gassis, O.F.M., a professor of theology in the *studium,* although, according to Lafaille, it was the archbishop, Vital de Castelmoron, who was requested by the professors to present their instructions to the council.[49] An unnamed delegate of the university took part in the proceedings at the thirteenth session of this council on May 29, but his discourse is not recorded. Also present at the council, but as legate of Benedict XIII, was Jean de la Coste, the former professor at Toulouse whose magisterial honors in that *studium* had so antagonized the University of Orléans.[50]

[46] *Histoire générale de Languedoc,* IX, 1000. Pierre Ravot as professor is mentioned in University documents dating from 1378 and 1394—Fournier, *Statuts,* I, no. 697, p. 630; and no. 731, p. 690. For his acquisition of the see of Macon see Denifle, *Chartularium,* III, no. 1582, p. 533. Jean Corneille was bachelor in decrees and in arts in 1387, Vatican Archives, *Supplicationes* (Clemens VII) LXXII, f°346v°; and regent doctor in decrees in 1403, Denifle, *Les universités,* no. xv, p. 68.

[47] *Eubel, Hierarchia,* I, 426 and 515; and Baluze, Bibliothèque Nationale, MS. lat. 4222, f°A.

[48] Archives municipales de Toulouse, AA46(52). Original on parchment.

[49] Martène, *Amplissima collectio,* VII, 886; d'Achery, *Spicilegium,* I, 958; and Lafaille, *Annales,* I, 161.

[50] Martène, *Amplissima collectio,* VII, 1094; and *Histoire générale de Languedoc,* IX, 1157. The career of Jean which had commenced under the patronage of Clement VII, was continued under the latter's Avignon successor, Benedict XIII. Jean was cantor of Bayeux in 1401 and later bishop of Châlons and Mende—Baluze in Bibliothèque Nationale, M.S. lat. 4222, f°A.

Toulouse was also represented at the Council of Constance which was convoked for 1414. There are references to these delegates in the proceedings of that body for March 19, 1415, and for May, 1417.[51] Records of the deliberations of the ecclesiastical committee of the province of Toulouse for July 18, 1416, list the provincial representatives in residence at the council, among them one Gerard Faydit as ambassador of the university. The question before the committee had to do with the legitimacy of the election of these delegates. It was debated whether it would be better to reëlect the existing representatives, or to recall them and choose anew. The possibility of retaining the bishop, since he held an important position in the council, but of appointing another abbot and clerk was also discussed. Evidently Faydit was not maintained in his position, for in 1418 he was acting as ambassador of the University of Paris to Martin V.[52] Jean Corneille, the doctor in decrees who had supported so whole-heartedly the candidacy of Pierre Ravot for the see of Toulouse in 1406, apparently replaced Faydit as the representative of the University of Toulouse.[53] After the election of Martin V in 1417, the ambassadors of the university submitted a *rotulus* to the new pope requesting many special privileges, so evidently it had abandoned the cause of Benedict, who still stubbornly held to his dignity. The chief partisans of the Spaniard at Toulouse, Jean de la Coste and Guigo Flandrin, the nephews of the cardinal, had left the *studium* long before this, so presumably the university had been won to the conciliar cause.[54] The latest letters of Benedict to the university or its colleges date from February of the year 1407, when special privileges were conferred on the *studium* and the College of Maguelonne at their own request.[55]

---

[51] Denifle, *Les délégués des universités francaises au concile de Constance,* 31, citing Finke, *Forschungen und Quellen zur Geschichte des Konstanzer Koncils* (1889), pp. 169 and 200.

[52] Marténe, *Thesaurus novus anecdotarum,* IV, 349; and Denifle *Les universités,* 38, footnote 1. Faydit, a canon of Bayeux had read less than five years in 1404, when he was petitioning Benedict XIII to dispense him from the statutes of Toulouse which required seven before admission to examination and the license. He is listed simply as councillor of the University of Toulouse in 1407 with no indication of his academic rank—Fournier, *Statuts,* I, no. 766, p. 728.

[53] Baluze, Bibliothèque Nationale MS. lat. 4222, f°A, citing *To* XII *Conciliar. pag.* 1630.

[54] Denifle, *Les universités,* no. xx, p. 75. Flandrin still had his substitute at Toulouse as late as 1407—Fournier, *Statuts,* I, no. 766, p. 728.

[55] Denifle, *Les universités,* no. xix, p. 73; and Fournier, *Statuts,* I, no. 770, p. 732.

Benedict XIII at all times seems to have been most complacent in granting university requests. In 1404 he had conferred upon the university the right of having four notaries for its business. The original holders were named in the papal letters and given exclusive privilege in university business. Later, in 1407, two other notaries were added to this list at university request, and their previous acts for the university ratified.[56] In 1404 also, the pope conferred upon the university, again at its request, the parochial church of Saint Anian in the diocese of Toulouse, whose fruits and rents were stated as not worth more than 100 *livres*. Possession of this church was to be had only at the death of the incumbent rector, with provision for the reservation of a certain sum for a perpetual vicar.[57] This is apparently the first property to be owned by the University of Toulouse. In turn the pope himself occasionally requested a favor of the university in the guise of special privileges for students in theology. Between 1403 and 1406, four Dominicans were given permission to read the *Sentences* in preparation for the license, and in 1405 a Benedictine monk from Limoges was ordered admitted to examination before three masters, preparatory to reading the *Sentences* and magisterial honors.[58] On another occasion in 1404, Benedict confirmed a regency in the theological school of Saint Etienne to a Franciscan master.[59]

The kings of France also honored the university on several occasions during this period. Charles VI visited Toulouse in December, 1389, and was greeted in the new royal hall by Gaucelin de Bosquet, professor of law and rector of the university. As a result of this visit, Louis, duke of Turenne, was named special protector of the university, and many new petty privileges were also conceded.[60] When Charles VI in 1411 resumed personal direction of affairs in Languedoc from the unpopular duke of Berry, he recommended his new commissioners to the university and asked that it give them all aid,

---

[56] Denifle, *Les universités*, no. xix, p. 73.
[57] Denifle, *Les universités*, no. xvii, p. 71.
[58] Denifle, *Les universités*, p. 37; and Archives departementales de la Haute-Garonne, Saint Sernin, liasse 5, titre 11 (reproduced by Galabert in *Album de paléographie et de diplomatique*, XVe siècle, planche v, no. 1).
[59] Denifle, *Les universités*, 38.
[60] Fournier, *Statuts*, no. 716, p. 768. The manuscript copy in the Archives départementales de la Haute-Garonne, which is one of the references given by Fournier for his edition of this document, reads "Anno Domini millesimo trecentesimo octuagesimo nono." See the notice on this discourse by Thomas in *Bul. soc. archéol. Midi France* (1884-1885 June), XIX 37.

counsel, and comfort.[61] In 1419 with the Dauphin Charles as regent, the university was ordered to send its delegates to confer upon the question of the liberties of the French church with the papal representative, the bishop of Leon.[62]

[61] A. Thomas, "Lettres closes de Charles VI et de Charles VII addressées à l'université de Toulouse" in *Ann. Midi* (1915-1916), 183. Gadave, no. 115 has misdated these letters by suggesting 1389, although M. Thomas avers that the events calling them forth were well known.
[62] *Ibid.*, 186.

CHAPTER 7

ADMINISTRATIVE DIFFICULTIES IN *STUDIUM* AND COLLEGES, 1380-1450

D URING the period of seventy years be-
tween 1380 and 1450, the University of Toulouse and its colleges
were troubled with many internal disorders that did not arise
directly either from schism or war. Local administrative difficulties in the *studium* itself, in the faculties of theology, arts
and grammar, and in many of its colleges required constant
efforts of reform.

The university in 1391 found itself in difficulties over the
observance of ancient statutes and petitioned the pope for
assistance in the matter. Many of the apostolic privileges had
grown inconvenient in the course of time, and because of the
pains of excommunication attached, the chancellor, rector, and
doctors of the university were afraid to modify them. To remedy
matters, a commission consisting of the abbot of Saint Sernin
and the provost and vicar-general of the church of Toulouse
was named to correct and reform the statutes. It was over three
years later, apparently, before this commission acted. Then the
abbot and the vicar-general met in the house of the chancellor
within the cathedral close and published to a group of masters
there assembled certain modifications in the strict sumptuary
regulations for degree-taking celebrations.[1] In the following
year the commission again used its powers to allow two years'
audition or "reading" in civil law as one year's audition or
"reading" in canon law toward the grade of bachelor or licentiate in the latter faculty. This would have had the effect of
reducing somewhat the long years of study required of a civil
law degree holder who desired also the canonical grade. The
next spring there were two further modifications, one of which
authorized the chancellor to remit the public examination for
any *capitoul* of Toulouse who desired to undergo the private
examination for the license during his period of office.[2]

[1] Fournier, *Statuts,* I, no. 719, p. 679; and no. 731, p. 690.
[2] Fournier, *Statuts,* I, no. 735, p. 692; and nos. 737-738, pp. 693-694.

In 1404 the university discovered that one important clause
had been omitted in the bull of Innocent IV of 1245 whereby
the provisions of the famous *Parens scientiarium* privileges,
which had been granted to Paris by Gregory IX, had been
extended to Toulouse. At the request of the *studium,* this oversight was remedied by Benedict XIII. The missing clause had to
do with the university's rights of making ordinances concerning the manner and hours for lectures and disputations, and
also concerning academic garb, funeral ceremonies, the allot-
ment of hours and classrooms to regents and bachelors, and the
rates for hospices or even their interdiction. Furthermore, the
right of punishing rebels to its statutes by deprivation of association or by ecclesiastical censure, whether the culprits were
students or masters, was also conferred upon the *studium.*
Evidently the university was having difficulty enforcing its
statutes.[3]

The first new regulation after this confirmation seems to have
been the one directed towards ending disputes among the mendicant orders over precedence at the public ceremonies of the
university. This was settled by the drawing up of a seating plan
for each of the eight theological schools, whereby its own
bachelor in each case was last, and a Dominican and Franciscan
alternately held first and second places, while an Augustinian
and Carmelite similarly held third and fourth places. The order
for the remaining bachelors ran: school of the university, of
Saint Etienne, of Saint Sernin, and of Saint Bernard. These
statutes date from early September of 1404, but had evidently
been preceded by considerable disturbance, for Benedict XIII
had intervened to establish the precedence himself before he
learned of the official university regulations on this point. In
March of the following year, at the request of the Franciscans
and Carmelites, he ordered that the university ruling be observed, nullifying his own. These two orders, assigned second
and fourth places respectively in the pope's disposition, naturally
much preferred the other arrangement whereby they alternated
with their Dominican and Augustinian rivals in first and third
places. Perhaps even the reconfirmation of the university's right
of making and enforcing its own statutes had been called forth
by this mendicant quarrel, because it is especially stated in that

[3] Denifle, *Les universités,* no. xvi, p. 70. The bull of Innocent IV is found in
Fournier, *Statuts,* I, no. 523, p. 451.

document that even masters in theology might be punished for
failure to comply.[4]

The greatest activity of the university in reforming itself
did not come, however, until some three years had passed. The
years from 1407 to 1410 seem to have been particularly busy in
this respect. In the first place, elaborate new regulations were
drawn up to curb excessive display in dress among the students.
These were first arranged at a council meeting in the house
of the chancellor and published a few days later in a general
university congregation, where the chancellor merely sent a
deputy to represent him.[5] About this same time also many
additions to the ancient administrative statutes were made at
another congregation. Here were drawn up rules governing
precedence in the Saint Sebastian's day procession and regulations for deportment at the university Mass. Matriculation
procedure and the duties of the treasurer and councillors were
also specified.[6] In 1409 and 1410 there were further new statutes
compiled regarding the duties of beadles and the expenses permitted to magisterial and baccalaureate degree candidates.[7]

In 1411 the papal reform commissioners appointed in the
previous century drew up their fifth set of statutory dispensations, this time from degree requirements. A difficulty had
arisen because certain candidates, absent from the *studium*,
had lost their proper position for presentation for the public
examination. These and such others as were financially unable
to bear the expenses of such an examination were to be
excused. The chancellor was further permitted to admit worthy
bachelors to the private examination even if they had not
completed all the required class work. Such bachelors as
were unable to lecture because of the paucity of students in
this time of mortality, were authorized to have hearing of the
Decretum computed as reading.[8] In the same year, the king was
also called upon by the university for authority to license

[4] Fournier, *Statuts*, I, no. 754, p. 717; and Denifle, *Les universités*, no. xviii,
p. 72.
[5] Fournier, *Statuts*, I, nos. 764-766, pp. 726-728.
[6] Fournier, *Statuts*, I, no. 769, p. 730. The date is uncertain for the document
can be only approximately dated. Johannes de Gaurano is listed as the
absent rector. He was certainly rector in July and August of 1407, *ibid.*,
no. 764, p. 726 and no. 766, p. 728. This document may or may not date
from the same rectorship. Gaurano appears in university documents be-
twen 1403 and 1413, Denifle, *Les universités*, no. xv, p. 67, and Fournier,
Statuts, I, no. 779, p. 740, but never at other times is he designated as rector.
[7] Fournier, *Statuts*, I, nos. 771-772, pp. 732-733.
[8] Fournier, *Statuts*, I, no. 774, p. 735.

all medical practitioners. Because of wars, tribulations, and mortalities, many inexpert and unlicensed men and women had presumed to practice this science to the prejudice of all privileges, observances, and customs, so that many died before their time and others were rendered incurable. At the instigation of the university, the *capitouls* had decreed that no one be permitted to practice medicine in the vicarate, city, or diocese without the examination and approval of the masters. This act had been prohibited by the bishop's *officialis* on pain of excommunication. In response to the university's request, the vicar was commanded to aid in the enforcement of the statute by inflicting suitable penalties.[9] In 1306, it will be remembered, the examination of physicians had been entrusted to episcopal authority by the pope, which doubtless accounts for the intervention of the *officialis*.[10]

With the accession of Martin V and the healing of the Great Schism, the university in 1418 took the opportunity to have many of its administrative difficulties ironed out in a series of supplications to the new pope. These included such requests as to compel the rector to publish all matters touching upon the honor and status of the university on the first Sunday after his reception, to confirm the university's powers of visitation over the colleges, to permit all who had heard law for three years or had become bachelors to complete their courses up to the license even though beneficed, to forbid bachelors' granting vacations before Christmas, Lent and Easter, and to permit lawsuits concerning students to be tried in Toulouse or Avignon so that they might not be impeded in their courses. There was also complaint that the oath at licensing made to the chancellor not to receive the doctoral insignia save at Toulouse and not to seek dispensation from such an oath, had been frequently violated at the Roman Curia and elsewhere, to the great detriment of the doctors and masters at Toulouse. The request was granted by permitting the chancellor to compel such persons to satisfy first all the rights of Toulouse. The university also requested protection for its members from the inquisitor of Toulouse, asking that this officer be restrained from proceeding with the counsel of the rector and councillors. This was granted on condition that the accused was prepared to recant, so in reality was not much of a safeguard to academic freedom. At the same time

[9] Fournier, *Statuts*, I, no. 775, p. 736.   [10] See *supra*, p. 74.

confirmation was sought for the university statutes forbidding
the practice of medicine without the approval of masters of that
faculty, which was duly accorded. Finally the university expressed the desire that it be confirmed in the possession of the
parish church of Saint Anian which Pedro de Luna, the anti-
Pope Benedict XIII, had formerly given them. This was granted
too, for in the following year a special university congregation
was held to appoint syndics for filling the vacancy in the vicarate
of this church.[11]

The papal commissioners for university reform continued
to function in the matter of modifications of university statutes.
In 1413, 1414, and 1416 they authorized changes in such minor
matters as the extension of the chancellor's right of dispensing
from the public examination, the reduction of the time required
for licentiates in decrees or law to become bachelors in decrees
or law, and the broadening of the chancellor's privilege of ad-
mitting to private examinations before the completion of course
work.[12] The ninth statutes of reform by the standing papal
commission followed in 1425. This rectified the omission of the
canons of Saint Sernin from the earlier dispensation in the matter
of the remittance of public examinations.[13]

The university continued to legislate on financial matters,
for in 1423 it drew up statutes forbidding the remission of fees
for degrees in any faculty. A little later discord arose between
Jean Corneille, the chancellor, and Ramundus Serene, the rector,
over precedence and the emoluments and official title of the former. This problem was arbitrated by the bishop of Bazas, a former master, with the assistance of the provost of Toulouse, both
of whom were doctors in decrees. It is mentioned in the arbitral
award that these matters had been regulated by a former agreement between the chancellor and the university but that both
sides had agreed on the present arbitration.[14] Another minor
problem of administration arose in 1436, when there was a question of whether a master, after having once voted at the examina-

[11] Denifle, *Les universités*, no. xx, pp. 75-77; and Archives notariales de Toulouse, Assolent, no. 379, f°102.
[12] Fournier, *Statuts*, I, no. 778, p. 739; no. 780, p. 741; and no. 782, p. 743.
[13] Fournier, *Statuts*, I, no. 797, p. 769.
[14] Fournier, *Statuts*, I, no. 796, p. 767; and no. 805, p. 774. The day of the
month must be in error in the former document since the feast of the
Ascension fell on May 13 in 1423. The year has been omitted in the latter,
but the year 1430 is suggested in the *Histoire generale de Languedoc*, VII,
604, and is so given by Fournier. Bibliothèque Nationale, MS. Latin 4221C
places this document between one of 1425 and one of 1436.

tion of a bachelor, might change his vote. This problem was discussed before the vice-regent of the chancellor and decided in the negative. Another minor matter of precedence which concerned the theologians of the mendicant orders received papal confirmation in 1432. It rendered more precise the statute formerly confirmed by Benedict XIII on this point.[15]

In addition to these general reform measures for the *studium* as a whole, certain individual faculties also required attention. The first of these was a comparatively recent establishment, the faculty of theology. Authorized in 1360 by Innocent VI and organized with the assistance of Urban V in the years following, the faculty had grown rapidly. Its teaching personnel increased gradually during the last decades of the century. In 1378 the names of five regent masters occur in the supplication sent to the Avignon anti-pope, Clement VII, while two years later a supplementary set of statutes, made with the consent and unanimous counsel of all regent masters in theology, was subscribed by six masters of this faculty. In 1387 and 1392 other supplications list seven masters, which would indicate the progressive growth in the number of schools.[16] In this expanding faculty difficulties shortly arose, for in 1389 it was found necessary to draw up a third set of statutes and also to make revisions in certain portions of the primitive statutes.[17] These arrangements were made by the chancellor and rector who had probably acted rather abruptly, for the publication was made at a general university congregation at which only two regents in theology were present. The theological faculty as a whole undoubtedly resented this as interference, for a decision of the abbot of Saint Sernin and the provost of Saint Etienne acting as arbiters in a quarrel between the masters of theology on one part and the chancellor and rector on the other, has been conserved. The point in dispute was the right of emendation of statutes, which the arbiters confirmed to the chancellor and rector as need arose. This compromise was specifically stated to apply both to the second statutes and to the modifications and additions to the first set made at the same time.[18] Difficulties continued, how-

---

[15] Fournier, *Statuts,* I, no. 815, p. 794; and Denifle, *Les universités,* no. xxi, p. 77.

[16] For details of the organization of this faculty see *supra,* pp. 107-108. For the documents illustrating its growth, see Fournier, *Statuts,* I, no. 697, p. 631; no. 701, p. 660; and *ibid.,* III, no. 1909, p. 527. The *rotulus* for 1387 is in Vatican Archives, *Supplicationes* (Clemens VII) LXXII, f°ˢ344-364v°.

[17] Fournier, *Statuts,* I, no. 715, p. 677 and no. 670, p. 611.

[18] Fournier, *Statuts,* I, no. 714, p. 676.

ever. As has already been explained, the university in 1404 had had to seek rectification of a missing clause in *Parens scientiarum* in order to compel obedience to its authority in statute making, and thereafter immediately turned to regulating the disputed question of precedence in the theological schools.[19] In 1412 the validity of certain statutes of the theological faculty was still in question. A new set which was drawn up in that year is quite long and specifically denounces certain previous statutes made in the time of Aycardus de Quinballo which were without authority because they did not have the assent of the rector and university. As a whole, these new statutes legislate carefully for the general governance of the faculty.[20]

The arts and grammar faculties also had their difficulties within this period. In 1426 there was a quarrel between the masters of arts and grammar over the teaching of certain texts. This was arbitrated by the bishop of Bazas, assisted by two regent doctors of decrees and a master of theology. As a result the texts to be taught by the two inferior faculties were more strictly delimited.[21] Twenty years later trouble arose between the *capitouls* of Toulouse and the archbishop over the management of the school buildings used by the masters of grammar and arts. The *capitouls* obtained an arrest from the royal council which forbade the prelate or his *officialis* to take cognizance of matters pertaining to the schools, of their sites, or of the renting of houses for use as schools. These matters were attributed solely to the *capitouls*. As masters of grammar and arts alone are mentioned in the document, this probably had no reference to the quarters used by teaching members of the higher faculties. It is presumable that the city government contributed to the expenses of these elementary schools, hence claiming their direction in matters of physical appurtenances. It did not vitally concern the university as a whole, for its jurisdiction in this matter was probably supervisional only of the teaching and subjects taught.[22]

---

[19] See supra, p. 158.
[20] Fournier, *Statuts*, I, no. 776, p. 737. The reference to the invalid statutes that are to be superseded comes in paragraph 18 of this document. The scribe has obviously confused the citation, for he refers to the statutes made by Quinballo "with six masters then regent in 1389, June 3." The statutes of that year, *ibid.*, no. 715, p. 677, were officially sanctioned by the University in congregation so could not be the set intended. There are statutes of April 30, 1380, *ibid.*, no. 701, p. 660, which do answer the description, however, and which furthermore actually refer to the expedition of bachelors, the subject of paragraph 18 of the 1412 statutes.
[21] Fournier, *Statuts*, I, no. 798, p. 770.
[22] Fournier, *Statuts*, I, no. 825, p. 805, citing Lafaille, *Annales de Toulouse*,

The disorders in the colleges during this period arose only in part from the exigencies of the war. Difficulties in internal administration and disputes over the allocation of collegiate places also contributed their share of problems. There is also evidence for this same period of the normal functioning of college life, and the actual foundation of two new, small institutions.

The principal wartime difficulty of the colleges at Toulouse arose, as has already been explained, from the curtailment of revenues and the heavy taxation upon their endowment properties. The College of Saint Martial, one of the richest of these institutions, seems to have been particularly hard hit. In 1383 it made a convention with the consuls of Ganhac, where some of its real estate was located, in regard to the construction of a fortress there.[23] By 1396 its revenues were so depleted that the anti-Pope Benedict XIII wrote to the abbot of Saint Sernin and the *officiales* of Toulouse and Carcasonne, advising them to look into its financial condition, as it had sought his aid. The college alleged that it had suffered a great loss of rents because of wars and deaths, that many of its houses were in ruin because of a fire, and that many of its books and other belongings had been lost. In case the investigation proved the truth of this matter, the needs of the institution were to be supplied from funds derived from the episcopal courts.[24] The students of the college named their procurators for receiving such funds some six months later so their need must have been regarded as pressing. In the following year the pope united the priory of Miremont to the college to augment its endowment yet further.[25] The financial difficulties of the college at this time must have made the calls upon its conservators particularly numerous. The

---

I, 213, anno 1446. This passage reads as follows: "Les capitouls obtinrent un arrêt du conseil du Roi, per lequel il etoit fait défense à l'archevêque de cette Ville et à son officiel de prende connoissance du fait des écoles du lieu ou elles doivent être, ni des louages des maisons qu'il faloit pour cela; Sa Majesté attribuant aux capitouls uniquement la connoissance de tous ces faits. Il paroît par ce qui est exposé dans l'arrêt, qu'il y avoit alors dans cette ville deux regens en Grammaire, qui enseignoient la Jeunesse depous l'alphabet jusqu'à la Logique; et deux professeurs aux Arts, qui montroient la Philosophie." This document is cited by Lafaille as "aux archives sous la liasse K," but has not been found.

[23] Fournier, *Statuts,* I, no. 709, p. 674.
[24] Fournier, *Statuts,* I, no. 739, p. 694.
[25] Fournier, *Statuts,* I, no. 740, p. 695; and no. 744, p. 697. The latter information is given in a letter of October 29, 1398, whereby the archbishop of Toulouse announced the conferal of corporeal possession of the vicarate upon a priest of Mende—Bibliothèque Nationale MS. Lat. 4223, f^{s}59v°.

bishop of Pamiers, pleading his inability to fulfill his obligations as conservator and judge of causes, named his subdelegates in 1393, which the archbishop of Toulouse and the bishop of Carcasonne had already done over twenty years before. Two years later another archbishop of Toulouse likewise appointed subdelegates in matters of obtaining citations for the collegiates, as he himself was too occupied.[26]

During the first decade of the fifteenth century, Saint Martial's financial troubles continued. In 1400, it was having difficulties with the archbishop over the possession of its parochial church of Miremont; in that year, the archbishop had to be restrained from further action by letters from the cardinal of Vivarais. In 1404 the same college was collecting the sum of 800 *livres* from the *officialis* of Carcasonne on papal assignment. Court proceedings were also necessary in 1408 to compel the payment of gifts illegally distrained from pious causes, that affected this institution. The Cistercian abbot, judge-delegate of the abbot of Saint Sernin, as conservator of the college cited the executors of the will of a deceased benefactor of the diocese of Limoges to appear in Toulouse to answer to the college.[27] In 1410 Saint Martial was seeking royal safeguard against possible action on the part of the seneschal in punishment for its failure to send armed men to the host. The king ordered that in the future the college was not to be disturbed in matters of this sort.[28]

Other colleges at Toulouse were having similar difficulties. Among these was the College of Montlauzon, for Guigo Flandrin, a professor of canon law at Toulouse, received a papal commission in 1397 to make new statutes and reduce the number of students to two, since the college had suffered so seriously from the wars that it had had to be moved within the walls. As a result, the collegiates were reduced in number from six to three, two students and one priest being retained.[29] In 1421 and again in 1423 the College of Perigord, which had been so richly endowed by its cardinal-founder, was petitioning the pope to supplement its resources by sanctioning the union to it of a parochial church in the diocese of Toulouse, urging

[26] Fournier, *Statuts*, I, no. 726, p. 685; and no. 733, p. 691.
[27] Fournier, *Statuts*, I, no. 749, p. 702; no. 756, p. 717; and no. 761, p. 724.
[28] Fournier, *Statuts*, I, no. 773, p. 734.
[29] Fournier, *Statuts*, I, no. 741, p. 696; and no. 745, p. 697. See also Saint Charles in the *Mémoires de l'académie des sciences, inscriptions, et belles-lettres de Toulouse*, H., VI (1884) premiere partie, 57, for a description of the new site of the college.

the mortalities, wars, droughts, and inundations as reason for the great diminution of its revenues.[30] The College of Pampelune was also troubled by the disorders. Epidemics worked such havoc in the ordinary tenor of collegiate life that the members of this institution were given special permission in 1402 by Bishop Hugues of Agde, their provisor, to leave the city for such a period as should be deemed necessary, although this was in violation of its statutes.[31] The same college was also in financial difficulties in 1426 when it petitioned the pope for the union to the college of the church of Saint Julian in the diocese of Toulouse, explaining that due to mortalities, wars, droughts, and inundations, the means of the institution were so reduced that they scarcely sufficed to support the collegiates, and it would be necessary to reduce the number of students unless some provision was made. The pope sanctioned this arrangement, although without prejudice to a pending lawsuit.[32] In 1442 this college sought royal aid in its financial problems and was placed under special royal safeguard and accorded exemption from the lodgment and support of soldiers in all its properties.[33] Two years later the *capitouls* were forbidden to impose the *taille* on its revenues.[34]

Difficulties in internal administration seem to have been particularly dominant within the College of Pampelune. In 1394 Clement VII had appointed Guido and Guillaume, cardinals of Palestrina and San Stephano in Celiomonte, as commissioners for reforming this institution, the foundation of the late Pierre, titular of Santa Anastasia. These two cardinals were also executors of his testament. In addition the bishop of Agde, Hugues, who had formerly been appointed provisor of the college, was specifically forbidden interference, except at the will of the two cardinals. It was this prelate presumably who

---

[30] Denifle, *La guerre de cents ans*, I, no. 494, p. 210.
[31] Fournier, *Statuts*, I, no. 751, p. 702.
[32] Denifle, *La guerre de cents ans*, I, no. 495, p. 210.
[33] Fournier, *Statuts*, I, no. 822, p. 803 includes not only St. Catherine or Pampelune, but also St. Martial, Maguelonne and Perigord, for which I found no authority in the original document cited, i.e., Archives départementales de la Haute-Garonne, *Grand Inventaire des titres collège Sainte Catherine*, to which should be added the further reference, f°3. The inventory refers to liasse 1, numero 18.
[34] Fournier, *Statuts*, I, no. 734, p. 692. This is from the same inventory, and again there is no mention of St. Martial, Maguelonne, and Perigord. Furthermore the document is dated 1444—"1443 et le 17 mars"—and not 1395 as Fournier gives it. Three amortisements are referred to in the document, dated 1395, 1400, and 1407, hence the error.

in 1391 had dictated for the college the reform statutes which had not met with general approval.[35] At any rate the new statutes as drawn in July, 1394, entirely changed the regulations governing the priorship.[36] Hugues of Agde had to intervene shortly to aid the prior in compelling the priests and students of the college to help him with its business. Obviously the burden was too great on the prior, since the 1394 statutes forbade his deducting his year of priorship from the maximum years of residence permitted.[37] In 1402 again the bishop had to exert authority to restrain the students who would not obey the prior. For this purpose he extended the statutes given by Pierre of Santa Anastasia to the college of Saint Martial to his own college and added a few provisions of his own. This was evidently not effective in quelling the disturbance, for at a later date two commissioners, including the prior of the Daurade, and the chancellor had to appear in the college chapel to publish the said statutes of Saint Martial to the students there assembled.[38] In 1407 royal intervention actually had to be sought by the prior and students of the College of Pampelune to eject recalcitrant collegiates who had been expelled for the infraction of statutes. The king ordered that in the future the seneschal and vicar should not reinstate such student-complainants until the prior and three or four students had been heard.[39]

Other colleges at Toulouse escaped such protracted difficulties, but several of them required reform. The College of Saint Martial drew up lengthy new statutes governing the duties of its prior. The students in the College of Maguelonne, finding themselves so hampered by a regulation limiting the total residence in the college to ten years, sought papal dispensa-

---

[35] Fournier, *Statuts*, I, no. 729, p. 686. No. 732, p. 691 is the same document's inventory record, whose compiler misread the "xv kal. februarii" for "le 15 fevrier." For the reform statutes of 1391, see *ibid.*, no. 720, p. 679.

[36] Fournier, *Statuts*, I, no. 730, p. 687. The *Inventaire de Sainte Catherine*, f°1 remarks: "L'an 1394 et le 23 juillet les commissionaires déléguez par Hugues Eveque d'Agde, neveu du fondateur, le proviseur dudit collège Sainte Catherine reformèrent les statuts d'iceluy suivant l'acte reçu et expédié par Pierre Fabry notaire apostolique."

[37] Fournier, *Statuts*, I, no. 736, p. 693. This would indicate that Hugues had submitted to the 1394 statutes with good grace. Perhaps he had been consulted by the two cardinals in the first place? The date of this document should read 1396 instead of 1395, for it is before Easter. There is an enigmatic publication of reform statutes by commissioners in 1397 recorded in the *Inventaire,* but whose original has not been found—*Statuts,* I, no. 742, p. 697.

[38] Fournier, *Statuts*, I, nos. 752-753, pp. 702-707.

[39] Fournier, *Statuts*, I, no. 762, p. 725.

tion, complaining that the requirements for the doctorate could not be fulfilled in that time. Benedict XIII obligingly invalidated this ten year clause in 1407, but retained all others in these statutes of the cardinal of San Marco.[40] Some years later the college was subjected to papal reform. This was entrusted to the archbishop of Toulouse, who added an eleventh student to the college.[41] In 1418 the College of Narbonne required attention. Among the numerous university supplications to the newly elected Martin V was the request for confirmation of its powers of visiting, reforming, and placing and removing students in colleges. That of Narbonne was especially singled out because it had no prior at the time. The university asked that its rector might institute a new prior for the institution and administer oath to him.[42] This same college was also concerned in a financial problem. A general university congregation was held in 1421 to appoint a syndic for petitioning the heirs of Guigo Flandrin, who had acted as executor of two cardinals leaving bequests to this college, for certain sums of gold still owing.[43]

Appointments to collegiate places were another type of administrative problem that occasionally caused difficulties. There is record of an apparently normal award in 1388 of a place in the College of Perigord to a bachelor of law from the diocese of Limoges. That he was a councilor of the patriarch of Alexandria then administering the diocese of Toulouse must have made his appointment the more certain.[44] In 1407, however, there was litigation over an appointment to a place in the same college. The duke of Orléans, who was count of Perigord and patron of the college, had presented a student to a vacant place;

[40] Fournier, *Statuts*, I, no. 700, p. 657, dates it 1380, but the manuscript source bears no dating phrase. For the reform in the college of Maguelonne, see *ibid.*, no. 770, p. 732.

[41] From a copy of the *Catalogue des évêques de Toulouse dressé par Gaspard Sorèze* found in the Archives départementales de la Haute-Garonne, G. 366: "Dominique de Florence religieux des frères prescheurs succeda à Vital l'an 1412. Il eu commission du pape de visiter reformer et réparer l'èglise Saint Etienne, reformer pareillement les statuts du collège de Maguelonne, où il ajouta un onzieme collegiat perpetuel et confirma la fondation du collège du Mirepoix." Fournier, *Statuts*, I, no. 786, p. 751 refers to the same reformation with the citation "Saint Charles, Le collège de Maguelonne, p. 5," which I have been unable to locate. This citation does not refer to the pagination of the article of Saint Charles on this college in the *Mémoires de l'académie des sciences, inscriptions, et belles-lettres de Toulouse* Ser. H., V., (1883) 140.   [42] Denifle, *Les universités*, no. xx, p. 75.

[43] Archives notariales de Toulouse, Assolent, régistre no. 379, f°138.

[44] Fournier, *Statuts*, I, no. 713, p. 676. Bibliothèque Nationale MS. lat. 4223, f°92, gives the information not included in Fournier under this number.

but the college had refused to admit the candidate, alleging that the patron had not proposed within the term stated in the statutes, and had therefore lost his right. The case was argued before the *parlement* of Paris, and an inquest was ordered as to the truth of the statements. The duke's candidate was to have the place pending suit.[45]

Numerous other colleges had similar difficulties. In 1405 the bishop of Agde vacated the place of a bachelor of law who had contracted marriage in violation of the statutes of the College of Pampelune and ordered that in the future all places were to be considered vacant by contract of marriage, entry into a religious order, or the receipt of an ecclesiastical benefice.[46] Long absence and default of residence caused the patrons of the College of Montlauzon to fill vacancies on two occasions.[47] In 1424 the abbot of Saint Sernin invested a clerk with a place in the College of Narbonne because the rector of the university had failed to act within one month of the vacancy.[48] The collegiates of Saint Martial actually brought suit against the archbishop of Toulouse over the nomination to membership in their college. The points in dispute were several. The collegiates had the right to fill a vacancy on a two-third's majority vote. A candidate so chosen, according to the statutes, had to be presented to the archbishop if he were present in the city; but if not, the new candidate could take his place immediately. Such had been done, it seems, in the case of Jean Vital, who had been elected within eight days of the resignation of his predecessor and during the absence of the archbishop; but he had been impeded in possession of his place by a candidate chosen by the vicar of the archbishop. The vicar insisted that the two-third's majority must be based on a membership of twenty-three and not upon the existing membership of twenty-one. Furthermore, the election should have taken place, he argued, within eight days, computing from the absence of the member, and not from the date of his resignation. As the former member had been absent six months before his resignation, the college

[45] Fournier, *Statuts*, I, no. 767, p. 729.
[46] Fournier, *Statuts*, I, no. 758, p. 717.
[47] Fournier, *Statuts*, I, no. 790, p. 753; and Saint Charles, "Collèges" in the *Mémoires de l'académie des sciences, inscriptions, et belles-lettres de Toulouse*, Ser. H., VI, (1884) premiere partie, 59. The two documents date respectively from 1421 and 1425.
[48] Archives départementales de la Haute-Garonne, fonds Saint Sernin, H 183, f°12v°. Document dated August 7, 1424.

had thus lost its right of election, which devolved upon the archbishop. The college on its part denied that the archbishop had any right to delegate his patronage over them. Pending decision the court forbade either party possession of the collegiate place.[49] It is interesting to note that litigation over disputed places in collegiate establishments occurred not only in the richest institutions, where it might be expected, but also in the College of Saint Raymond. Students of this house were embroiled in a dispute with their patron, the almoner of Saint Sernin, over what they claimed to be an illegal presentation to membership in the college. The candidate had been installed over the protests of the collegiates, so the college appealed the matter to the *parlement*. The *juge-mage,* as lieutenant of the seneschal, was notified of this appeal as he was leaving the royal hall at Toulouse, and asked for a copy of the document. When this was presented to him an hour later, he refused to receive it as appeal.[50] The outcome in neither of these suits is ascertainable.

During this same period there is also evidence that the colleges of Toulouse were functioning normally and without difficulties. For example, the prior of the College of Maguelonne rendered his account of the receipts and expenses in connection with the execution of the testament of its founder in 1376.[51] In 1382 the Avignon pope, Clement VII, authorized the union of the parish church of Castaneto to the College of Pampelune when it should be vacated by the death of its incumbent. This property had been acquired by Pierre of Santa Anastasia for the endowment of his college some years before.[52] In 1386 the cardinal executors of Pierre, among whom was the prior of the college, appointed their procurators to transact the settlement of his affairs.[53] In a similar manner the will of Talleyrand, cardinal of Perigord, was in course of execution in 1382.[54] The College of Montlauzon was collecting the records of its foundation and confirmation in a *vidimus* of 1379. Papal confirmation of its

[49] Fournier, *Statuts*, III, no. 1914, p. 595.
[50] Fournier, *Statuts*, I, no. 827, p. 810.
[51] Fournier, *Statuts*, I, no. 696, p. 630.
[52] Fournier, *Statuts*, I, no. 708, p. 674. Both manuscript sources date this as of June 21, not June 19, as given in the text. Bibliothèque Nationale MS. lat. 4223, f°167 gives the information not recorded in the edited document.
[53] Bibliothèque Nationale MS. lat. 4223, f°175. "Acta fuerunt haec Avinioni in ecclesia Fratrum Minorum, anno . . . milesimo trecentesimo octuagesimo sexto, Indicatione nona et die viii Augusti, pontificatus . . Clementis . . septimi anno VIII."
[54] Fournier, *Statuts*, I, no. 705, p. 665.

foundation was sought and received by the College of Saint Martial in 1385.[55] All through this period the College of Saint Martial was apparently most active in its business affairs. An enumeration of its properties was drawn up in 1377.[56] Two lawsuits over financial questions were settled by accord between the college and its opponents. One of these was with the seigneur of Picacos over the payment of tithes, and the other was with the vicar of Colarède upon the subject of a house over which both parties pretended to have rights. A *vidimus* of the enumeration and homage made to the king by the prior for two seigneuries belonging to the college was enacted in 1397.[57]

The colleges of Toulouse were not forgotten by wealthy men when they prepared their charitable bequests. In 1385 there is record of payments made to the chapels of the colleges of Saint Martial, Pampelune, Maguelonne, Perigord, Narbonne, and Saint Raymond, in accordance with the testament of a noble lady. In the following year the will of a priest provided the chapel of the *studium*, and the colleges of Maguelonne, Perigord, Saint Martial, and Saint Raymond with a slightly smaller sum.[58] A discharge in favor of the executors of the will of Arnaud d'Avignonet of 1403, records gifts to the chapels of the colleges of Verdale, Narbonne, Saint Bernard, Saint Raymond, Perigord, and Saint Martial.[59]

The College of Saint Raymond was particularly active during these years, achieving a status approximating that of the other self-governing colleges. In 1403 exceedingly elaborate and all-inclusive statutes were arranged for it, and at about the same time regulations for the governance of its library were compiled.[60] In 1428 there is record of the oath to be taken by a new almoner of Saint Sernin on becoming the patron of the college, and also of new statutes drawn up by the college itself to regu-

[55] Fournier, *Statuts*, I, no. 699, p. 654; and no. 712, p. 676.

[56] Fournier, *Statuts*, I, no. 654, p. 598. The date at the end of this document in the manuscript is "1377, mars 24," not "1362, janvier" as given by Fournier.

[57] Fournier, *Statuts*, I, no. 717, p. 678; no. 727, p. 686; and no. 743, p. 697.

[58] Archives départementales de la Haute-Garonne, fonds Saint Sernin, H 98, f°324 and f°95v°.

[59] Douais, *Topographie des églises*, p. 25. The college of Narbonne is not named in this document but is designated as "collegii studii retro conventum fratrum Minorum Tholose."

[60] Fournier, *Statuts*, I, no. 754, p. 711; and no. 755, p. 715. Lahondès, *Les monuments de Toulouse, histoire, archéologie, beaux-arts* (Toulouse, 1920), p. 279, incorrectly interprets the first of these documents as foundation statutes.

late the oath to be taken by a prospective student before his admission.[61] In March, 1429, the college was officially inspected by the university rector, Raymundus Sebiende, on his rounds, and a report made to him of the provisions for the year, from which it is learned that the college had been successful in forcing the abbot of Saint Sernin to make certain annual provisions for the support of the college. The law suit had originally been heard in the court of the seneschal, but was later appealed to *parlement*.[62] Another patron was duly received in 1430, and the university gave recognition to the college in 1436 by declaring that the feast of Saint Raymond should be a holiday and officially placed upon its calendar.[63] The syndic of the college was prosecuting a suit on appeal against the syndic of the canonesses of the Eleven Thousand Virgins, an affiliate of Saint Sernin, in 1444 and the years following. The case had originally been tried before the *juge-ordinaire* of Toulouse and decision rendered in favor of the canonesses. It granted an annual payment of three florins of gold by the college to the abbess. The appeal was finally permitted, but as usual the judgment is missing.[64]

New collegiate foundations during this period were not numerous. The first of these was that of Guillaume du Puy, bishop of Mirepoix, who in 1415 commenced at Toulouse the foundation of a college that was to bear the name of his see. This document is an act of procuration by certain collegial students of Toulouse living at the expense of the bishop of Mirepoix, in order to receive the gifts of their founder. The students were ten in number at this time, two of them priests. Evidently they were not as yet in possession of their house, for the legal papers were enacted in the residence of one of their number.[65] About a year and a half later, the two collegiates of priestly rank who had been named in the above procuratorial act testified officially to the reception of the gifts of their founder and included a copy of the bequests of the bishop from an undated document. From this it is learned that Guillaume was endowing a college in his house at Toulouse for eight poor students who were to observe the statutes of the College of Pampelune. His nephew, a citizen of Rieux, and the canon-treasurer of his cathe-

[61] Fournier, *Statuts*, I, no. 801, p. 772; and no. 802, p. 773.
[62] Fournier, *Statuts*, I, no. 803, p. 774.
[63] Fournier, *Statuts*, I, no. 816, p. 795.
[64] Archives municipales de Toulouse, GG. 82. This document was kindly called to my attention by M. Galabert, the archivist.
[65] Fournier, *Statuts*, I, no. 781, p. 741.

dral church were appointed as first patrons of the institution, with the right of succession passing to the heirs of the former. The first students to enjoy membership in the new college were also named by the founder. Among these were his nephew and also the nephew of the canon-treasurer of Mirepoix. Aside from the house already mentioned and books to the value of 400 francs for the library, 1,000 pounds in cash had been turned over to the patrons for repairs on the house and other necessities, and the donor further promised the residue of his estate after his testamentary bequests had been paid. Right of future presentation to membership in the college was conferred on the *juge-mage* of Toulouse.[66] In 1420 the archbishop of Toulouse gave his permission for religious services in the college chapel, and at about the same time the cathedral chapter of Mirepoix sanctioned the gift of a parochial church of that diocese to the college, providing that its present rector be endowed for life with seventy per cent of the revenues, and that the college thereafter would maintain a rector on fifty per cent of the same. The matter was then referred to Rome.[67] Papal confirmation of the foundation of the college and the union of this parochial church to it was authorized in 1422. As the rector had already abandoned his church into the hands of his bishop, the bishop and chapter named their procurators for the official transfer and the college did the same.[68] Then, before the *officialis* of Toulouse a legal inquest was made on both points, and the foundation and union properly confirmed. Evidently no official act of foundation had been made, for at this inquest one of the witnesses deposed that the foundation of the college was common knowledge, and that he had slept, eaten, and drunk with the students in the said house.[69]

Later, the College of Mirepoix received further attention from its founder when he drew up his testament in 1431. In this document he ordered three copies to be made of his law work, called the *Memoriale,* one of which was to be given to the library of his college, along with his cope, stole, maniples, and alb for the college chapel. His former concession of books to the collegiates is reconfirmed, and his heirs are instructed to complete a library for the use of the students, where the books

[66] Fournier, *Statuts,* I, no. 783, p. 743.
[67] Fournier, *Statuts,* I, no. 788, p. 753; and no. 787, p. 751.
[68] Fournier, *Statuts,* I, no. 791, p. 754; no. 789, p. 753; and no. 792, p. 755.
[69] Fournier, *Statuts,* I, no. 793, p. 756 and no. 795, p. 763.

should be chained. Sixty *scuta* of gold are left to obtain papal ratification in the matter of the parish church to be united to the college, so evidently that was not yet entirely settled. The former rector of this church was further awarded 24 francs in gold in composition for releasing it. All arrears in rent of the bishop's property at Penne, if there were any at his death, should be paid to the college. He regretted his inability to increase the number of collegiates in his foundation from eight to twelve as he had hoped, but at the same time appointed two grand nephews to places in the college, stipulating that it should not be considered a permanent augmentation of the number. These two young men were to remain eight years, computing from one month after the day of the bishop's death. The prelate was probably merely insuring his young relatives' membership in the college in case he might die before they were ready for scholastic studies. As early as the original act of foundation, one of these grand nephews had been given special privileges to use the college's books. Finally the rights of patronage, formerly conferred on his treasurer and his nephew, were revoked in favor of his successors, the bishops of Mirepoix, and the college itself was authorized to fill vacancies by majority vote.[70] After the resignation of his see by the bishop in 1433, he appointed procurators to acquire rents for his College of Mirepoix, but retained the usufructs for himself during his lifetime. This act is dated from the college itself, so the bishop was probably there in person to inspect his foundation. At this same time, he drew up an elaborate set of statutes for the governance of the house.[71] In the following year, the bishop had a notarial document drawn up testifying as to his founding of the college, and his drawing up and publishing of statutes for it. The college itself testified that it had read these statutes and taken oath to observe them in accordance with the form laid down therein, on the sixteenth of May, 1435. Later in the same year official record was also made of inventory-taking in the college library in accordance with the statutes of its founder.[72] The bishop died soon after, for his executors began receiving quittance for the payments of certain sums as early as September, 1435, and the final quittance to the college as heir is dated in January of 1437. The college

[70] Fournier, *Statuts,* I, no. 807, p. 776.
[71] Fournier, *Statuts,* I, no. 810, p. 778; and no. 811, pp. 779-790.
[72] Fournier, *Statuts,* I, nos. 812-813, pp. 790-791.

received quittance for the completion of payments on a debt of its founder as late as 1444.[73]

The other new collegiate institution added at this time was very small. The College of Saint Girons was intended for only six students. Its founder was Jean Balguier, a doctor of both canon and civil law, who drew up his testament in 1430.[74] By the provisions of this will, the testator left his books to the consuls of Saint Girons, for the use of six clerks from the same region or its neighborhood, studying at Toulouse. He also provided for their residence by bequeathing to the consuls the house in which he resided or his house in another street, and endowed the college with the rents from other properties, but retained the usufruct during his own and his wife's lifetime. This property was to be inalienable in the hands of the consuls for the sustenance of the college, and they were also given authority to appoint the students with the advice of the *operarius* of the Dalbade and the prior of the Carmelite convent. In case the students proved unworthy, they could be removed by the same officials.[75] The exact date of the opening of this college is unascertainable. The founder was *capitoul* of Toulouse in the year of the drawing up of this testament, so it was probably not immediately organized.[76]

---

[73] Fournier, *Statuts*, I, no. 817, p. 795; and no. 824, p. 803.

[74] Jules Chalande, *Histoire des rues de Toulouse* (premiere partie, Toulouse, 1920), no. 104, who has neglected to correct the year to the new style.

[75] Archives départementales de la Haute-Garonne, fonds collège de l'Esquille, I, f°2v°.

[76] Lafaille, *Annales, sub anno* 1430.

CHAPTER 8

THE UNIVERSITY AND THE *PARLEMENT* OF TOULOUSE, 1434-1500

IN the years following on the settlement of the disturbing Saint Cricq affair, the University of Toulouse was still in difficulties trying to maintain its special royal privileges. All did not move smoothly on the resumption of academic life after the rather lengthy interruption, but our information as to the details of the disorders is fragmentary and allows for no very clear understanding of the course of events. There are references to uprisings which brought a condemnation of the *capitouls* before the *parlement* of Paris.[1] For certain abuses in criminal jurisdiction they were fined 10,000 *écus d'or* at this time, but in 1434 Charles VII reduced this sum to 6,000 because of the heavy charges that the city had been put to in repairing its walls. At the same time their criminal jurisdiction was restored.[2] When the royal letters authorizing these changes were presented in the court of the seneschal, they were opposed by the syndic of the university who maintained that the *capitouls* by virtue of their criminal jurisdiction should not have power to capture students or other members of the university, either clerk or layman, whether or not they were to be remitted to their judge. This objection was overruled by the seneschal and the university syndic and royal procurator immediately appealed to the king and *parlement,* but the appeal was denied.[3] As the

---

[1] A. du Bourg, "Episode des luttes de l'université et du capitole de Toulouse," *Mémoires de l'académie des sciences, inscriptions, et belles-lettres de Toulouse* (1889) J., I, 358-374 seems to believe that the outcome of the earlier case had been in favor of the *capitouls,* but offers no very conclusive proofs. He records that the second parlementary suit was due to an uprising against the prerogatives of the royal officers, but it would seem that the University was also concerned from the later developments.

[2] Letter cited in a *vidimus* of the same King, "Donné à Thoulouse ou mois de mars l'an de grace mil quatre cens quarante deux, et de nôtre le vingt ungiesme" (March, 1443). The enclosure was dated at Vienne, "mois d'avril l'an de grace mil quatre cenz trente et quatre" (April, 1434). Archives municipales de Toulouse, AA5 (no. 127).

[3] Letter cited in the same *vidimus* and dated February, 1435, "Donné à Poictiers au mois de fevrier l'an de grace mil quatre cens trente quatre."

sum of 6,000 *écus d'or* was not paid by 1437, the king took over the administration of the city. It was only during Charles VII's visit to Toulouse in 1443 that this matter was settled. He then restored administration of the city to the *capitouls* and reconfirmed their criminal jurisdiction. At the same time he confirmed the quittance of the amend of 10,000 *écus d'or* formerly charged against them, because of the heavy charges the region had borne owing to the presence of the royal army in the past season, and because a fire had destroyed a fourth part of the city in the same period. He again denied the appeals of the university and royal procurator, and testified as to the payment of 6,000 *réaulx d'or* therefore.[4]

Meanwhile the university was also having difficulties maintaining its royal privileges even in matters of civil jurisdiction. In 1437 it appealed to the king on this score. It would seem that members of the *studium*, both masters and students, were having difficulties in the transfer of their revenues from distant home communities to Toulouse without suffering pecuniary loss. When they had applied to the vicar as conservator of university privileges and had acquired the proper letters for legal action, they found that the persons cited refused to obey because certain royal officers of cities, villages, and towns, particularly in Languedoc, gave authority to refuse, alleging certain royal privileges that had been conferred on the inhabitants of such places. Thus the university found itself unable to draw cases into the court of the vicar. In response to the plea of the chancellor, rector, and syndic of the *studium*, the king renewed his former safeguard over it and instructed his vicar to include a *non obstante* clause in his letters of citation that would nullify such privileges that might have been given to cities, towns, and villages of his realm which did not have express mention of this instance.[5] At the same time Charles VII officially reconfirmed the letters of his father of 1392, quitting the chancellor or rector, the corporation itself, its students, two notaries, two stationers, two parchmenters, and treasurer from all subsidies

---

[4] Same *vidimus*. On October 31, 1444, this letter was published and registered in the court of the seneschal.

[5] This document is vaguely summarized in Fournier, *Statuts*, I, no. 818, p. 798, as letter patent taking under safeguard students stranger to Toulouse. As authority he cites Vaissete, IV, 504. This reference is to the old edition of the *Histoire générale de Languedoc*. In the new edition, IX, col. 1156, the same document is found. Fournier malquotes Vaissete's citation as "Reg. Senesch. de Toulouse, no. 12," which should read "no. 22," and reports the document as missing. Gadave, no. 176, has located the docu-

and impositions on wine, grains, and vegetables, even for war or defense.[6]

It would appear from these confirmations that financial problems concerning university members were not being successfully litigated in the court of the vicar. The record of one such suit before that tribunal for the year 1439 gives details of a typical instance.[7] Helyas Brolhet, the advocate who had pleaded so eloquently for the *capitouls* in their suit before the *parlement* of Béziers in 1427, was now the plaintiff in a case against them. Since the former time he had become syndic for the university. In fact he seems to have been a professional advocate rather than a professor, although he did hold a doctor's degree in civil law.[8] On the second of November, 1438, the rector of the university had designated Brolhet, one of the two university syndics who enjoyed the royal privileges, to assume and defend a case newly arisen in the court of the vicar. This case concerned the rights of the university, its syndics, and other officers and servants, so that they not be compelled to respond before any judge other than the said vicar, and especially concerned their exemption from contributing to any *tailles* or subsidies for the cause of the war. Brolhet was further instructed not to recede from the appeals of the university against the *capitouls* which had already been interposed; to protest the innovations and attempts against them; and to require that the vicar as conservator not permit but prohibit under severe penalties that the

ment in two manuscript sources, Archives municipales de Toulouse, GG., 75, f°8 and GG., 76, f°5.

[6] Fournier, *Statuts*, I, no. 809, p. 778, misdates the document in his heading as of September 4, but the manuscript text cited, Bibliothèque Nationale, MS. lat. 4222, f°109, reads September 14. "Datum Supra Secanum decima quarta die Septembris anno Domini MCCCCXXXIII et regni nostri xiv." As the year of the Lord and the regnal year do not agree, this looks suspiciously like a garbled version of the same dating phrase that appears on the document cited *supra*, footnote 5, which reads; "Datum Braii supra Secanum die decima quarta Septembris anno Domini millesimo quadringentesimo tricesimo septimo, et regni nostri decimo quinto." In this the regnal year agrees with the year of grace. The *Ordonances*, XIX, 526, also gives the text of the quittance from royal subsidy but dates it September 14, 1439. This is, however, a document of Charles VIII of 1483, in confirmation of one of Louis XI of 1462, which confirms in turn that of Charles VII, so is liable to be in error, being so far removed. Furthermore the original documents of Charles VI which are being confirmed in the letters of Charles VII are both of the same date—October 17, 1392—so it is presumable that the confirmations also should be of the same date.

[7] Archives municipales de Toulouse, GG., 76, a volume of 50 paper folios.

[8] Aside from his pleadings in defense of the *capitouls* in 1427, in 1439 he was one of the procurators of the College of St. Martial to act in Toulouse —Archives départementales de la Haute-Garonne, fonds Saint Sernin, H. 99, f°200.

university, its officers, and servants be compelled to litigate or be vexed in any way.[9]

On the sixth of September of the following year, the case was brought up on appeal in the court of the vicar. The formal appeal of Brolhet was directed to the king or his *parlement* or to the vicar himself, and asked protection from compulsion and capture of goods, and from the application of a demand for great and impossible sums of money, or that he should in any manner be held by the *capitouls* of Toulouse. Furthermore, the appeal included the case of the subsidies and the royal privileges conceded to the university and asked restraint from further acts to the aggravation and vexation of the appellant. In response to this appeal, Brolhet obtained letters of adjournment from the vicar setting the ninth of September for a hearing. On that day Brolhet stated his complaints in the presence of the syndic of the *capitouls*. He alleged that in spite of his special privileges as university syndic, the *capitouls* had tried to compel him to pay an enormous sum. The syndic of the *capitouls* responded that what had actually been done was to try to collect the arrears owed by Brolhet before he was syndic and the assessment on his wife's property since that time. He thus demanded that Brolhet pay expenses of the court as the case was wrongly appealed. Brolhet replied in defense that his wife had but a very small dot, whereas the sums assessed against him were enormous. He further asserted that all arrearages had been paid. At the next session of the court on September 12, only Gibbert, the capitular syndic, appeared. He presented royal letters of April, 1438, by which the *capitouls* were authorized to collect taxes on all lands, goods, and possessions, not belonging to nobles, and also an itemized account in Provençal of the arrearages of Brolhet from 1423. Gibbert then repeated that the case against the former was only for these sums and for his wife's goods. The suit was continued on the fifteenth of September, when Brolhet pleaded that the letters of the defense were old and had been superseded, delivering all the documents necessary to his own case.[10] With these was presented Brolhet's brief of his suit, stating that he had enjoyed the privileges of university syndic for about eight years and that it was manifest

---

[9] From a mandate of the rector quoted in the records of the case.

[10] These are copied into the record and include the mandate of the rector already cited, and letters of Raymond Serene, rector in 1431, testifying as to the legal appointment of Brolhet as University syndic at a University congregation of that date.

and noteworthy that as such he was subject to the royal safe-guard and free from *tailles* and the imposition of subsidies for the war. Therefore he appealed to the king and the *parlement* of Paris.

On September 17 the suit was continued, Brolhet complain-ing that he had been ordered anew to pay large sums by the *capitouls* and demanding his privileges. On the nineteenth of the same month a royal officer, Fabri by name, appeared before the court notary with a letter, a *rotulus*, and a brief. The first was from the king ordering his sergeant to collect the sum of 2,040 *livres,* 5 *sous tournois,* from the *capitouls* and citizens of Toulouse, stipulating that if they did not pay immediately he was empowered to collect the same, as it was sorely needed for use against the English.[11] The *rotulus* contained a list of names with sums assessed in Provençal vernacular, among which "Helyas Brulhet" appeared for "singuanta livras," by far the highest individual assessment. The brief stated that Fabri with other royal officers, armed with the letter and the *rotulus*, had called at the house of Brolhet on September 4 and had de-manded payment on the pain of seizure of means. Brolhet had claimed exemption as university syndic; but nevertheless they had placed the *fleur-de-lys* on his house and left a guard there, so that he could not remove any property. On the following day Fabri revisited Brolhet, but the latter refused to pay. The next Monday Fabri was summoned to appear before the vicar. Brol-het again appeared in court on the twenty-sixth of September, this time at the citation of Fabri. He presented a receipt in Provençal for all arrears up to the time he had become syn-dic, that is to August, 1431; but his opponent still insisted that it was for his wife's property that he was assessed since that date and asked that he be compelled to pay the costs of the suit. Brolhet again denied that his wife had anything other than her dot and that the property described on the syndic's list did not belong to him, appealing his case as before. He also declared that the letters of execution made no mention of the arrears, their years, or their amount, and requested that they be nullified by reason of the royal safeguard, and that the court costs be assessed against the *capitouls.* The court ruled that the case proceed, and quashed the plea that expenses arising from delay in payment be charged to Brolhet. At the next session

[11] This letter is dated at Toulouse, August 27, 1439.

of the court on October 9, the syndic of Toulouse denied the
jurisdiction of the vicar and sought dismissal of the case. Brolhet, on his part, claimed that he held the lieutenant of the
vicar suspect, who then refused to concern himself further with
the case. However, the case dragged on until the third of
November, when the court finally ruled that it was competent
to give judgment; and the record closes, as usual, without the
actual decision.

During this period of the gradual reconquest of France from
the English under Charles VII, the university manifested its
patriotic joy. In April 1436, a solemn procession, Mass, and
sermon were celebrated to honor the return to obedience of
the city of Paris.[12] On several occasions it was given the opportunity to welcome the king in person when royal journeys
brought him to the city. Charles VII, accompanied by the
dauphin, entered Toulouse in November, 1441, leading his army
for the conquest of Aquitaine. He seems to have been in the
city again in June, 1442, for he exempted the members of five
colleges from contributing to the *ban et arrière-ban* for the
expedition to Tartas. Also in the spring of 1443 Charles was
present in Toulouse, when he ruled on the matter of the return
of criminal jurisdiction to the *capitouls*.[13] Another procession
and solemn Mass took place in the Augustinian convent in 1451
to celebrate the return of the city of Bordeaux to royal obedience and the capitulation of the city of Bayonne.[14] On the
death of Charles VII in 1461, the university gave further testimony of its loyalty to the house of Valois. A solemn requiem
was celebrated in the convent of the Dominicans for the repose
of the soul of the late king. Over the commemorative bier, bearing the arms of the king, was placed a splendid golden pall. The
university and colleges contributed twelve candles each to
flank the sepulchre, and the university presented wax candles
to all regents, collegiates, and mendicants attending the ceremony. Afterwards a funeral repast, costing the university 4
scuta, was served "so that they should pray the more fervently
for his soul," as the rector's account reads. The university
did not delay long in requesting reconfirmation of its royal

12 Fournier, *Statuts*, I, no. 814, p. 794.
13 Bertrand, *Gestes Tolosains*, Q. ii; *Histoire générale de Languedoc*, IX, 1144;
  and Archives municipales de Toulouse, AA5 (no. 127) and Bertrand, Q ii.
14 Fournier, *Statuts*, I, no. 830, p. 811. The dating phrase in the document
  itself should be corrected to read MCCCC°LI° instead of VI°. The heading gives the date correctly as 1451.

privileges. Letters of October, 1461, and of March, 1462, conveyed the desired information.[15]

The university, as might be expected, continued to take some interest in the conciliar movement. It was asked to send its deputies to the Council of Basel in 1432, and had the resolutions of the council addressed to it in 1438. In the following year, it was asked to send its representatives to a royal assembly called for the fifteenth of October, to find a means of ending the quarrel between the pope and the council.[16] The count of Armagnac, in addressing a letter to the council in 1434 over a disputed election to an abbacy, requested that the response be given to Raymundus Darens, Doctor of Decrees and prior of the Daurade at Toulouse, who was probably the deputy of the university.[17]

After the middle of the century a new influence came to have great authority over the affairs of the university. This was the *parlement* of Toulouse, an offshoot of the *parlement* of Paris, which had long been the ultimate judicial body of the realm. The *parlement* of Paris had had its origins in the thirteenth century when Louis IX had nominated commissioners from among the knights and clerks of the *curia regis* for this purpose, under the nominal presidency of a prelate and a great noble or one of the high officers of the court. The number of commissioners varied from session to session at first, and the personnel of the delegations was constantly changing. Originally the court held four sessions annually to care for judicial business; but these were subsequently reduced to three, then to two, and finally, after 1292, to a single session beginning at All Saints and usually lasting longer than the primitive four terms combined. Ordinarily the court sat at Paris *in domo regia*, but occasionally sessions were held in the Temple or at the Hotel de Nesle, or even outside Paris at Vincennes, Pontoise, or Poissy.

[15] Fourner, *Statuts*, III, no. 1916, p. 637, contains the rector's account. *Ibid.*, I, no. 859, p. 859; and no. 845, p. 849 are the reconfirmations. No. 859 is misdated and given without citation in Fournier. Gadave no. 200 supplies the missing reference to the *Ordonances*, but gives an incorrect volume number. The document can be found in *ibid.*, XV, 171-172. Fournier has neglected to correct for a date before Easter in his no. 845.

[16] Gadave, no. 169 and nos. 178-179. See also A. Thomas, "Lettres closes," in *Ann. Midi* (1915-1916), 188, who calls attention to the incorrect dating given by Gadave for the last document.

[17] Martène, *Amplissima collectio*, VIII, 781. Raymundus Arenxis appears frequently in University documents. He is mentioned as regent doctor in 1420 and 1421 (Archives notariales, Assolent, régistre 379, f°102 and f°138), and again in 1439 (Archives hospitalières, B.20.).

The term *parlement* in the sense of general assembly was applied to these meetings; but gradually, owing to the frequency and quasi-periodicity of this judicial assembly the term came to be reserved almost exclusively to designate this high court. By the end of the thirteenth century the *parlement* had taken on a more definite form, being subdivided into a *chambre des plaids,* a *chambre des requêtes,* and towards 1307, a *chambre des enquêtes.* Regulations of 1345 gave it a permanent organization with three presidents and thirty *maîtres* for the *grande chambre,* and forty *maîtres* for the *chambre des enquêtes.*[18] After 1271 when Languedoc was united to the crown, the *chambre des requêtes* was divided into two sections, one for the *Langue d'oïl* and the other for the *Langue d'oc,* and at about the same time an *auditoire du droit écrit* was instituted to judge appeals from the southern area where the Roman Law was followed. The latter had a hectic existence and was several times suppressed and reëstablished. Meanwhile itinerant courts sent out from the *parlement* of Paris were occasionally used to facilitate judicial business in the provinces, such as the *échiquiers* held periodically in Normandy, the *grands jours* similarly held in Champagne, and the *parlements* held at Toulouse between 1278 and 1280 and again between 1287 and 1291.[19] The first provincial *parlement* to be given permanent and separate jurisdiction was that of Toulouse which was created in 1420 by the Dauphin Charles. It was intended as successor to the ephemeral *parlement* of Poiters which had been established during the time that the Dauphin was living at Bourges. The *parlement* of Toulouse, however, continued to function after the recovery of Paris and was reorganized as a special court to receive the pleas of Languedoc in 1443. At first the counsellors for this body were mostly drawn from the north, but gradually they attached themselves to the province through acquiring large properties in the area.[20] As early as 1452 three degree holders, presumably of the University of Toulouse, were named as candidates for the position of counsellors to this *parlement.* In that very year the university recognized the new court as arbiter in its future legal difficulties.[21]

18 Lavisse, *Histoire de France,* III:II, 327-329, and IV:I, 81.
19 *Ibid.,* III:II, 329-330 and 346-347.
20 *Ibid.,* IV:II, 236-237, and the *Cambridge Medieval History,* VIII, 264 and footnote.
21 Fournier, *Statuts,* I, no. 829, p. 811. The citation is incorrectly given by Fournier as "Arch. municip. de Toulouse, B. I, f°181." It should read to

Nor was there any lack of dissension in university affairs to delay an appeal to the *parlement*. Financial difficulties brought about by the long war were still pressing sorely, although the conflict itself was at last over. The very controversy which brought forth the recognition of the *parlement* by the university as a source of arbitration in 1452, had been a financial matter. In that year Nicholas V had united the parochial church of Osville of the diocese of Toulouse to the treasury of the university, for the *studium* had complained that the revenues of its treasury were so diminished by the wars and mortalities that it was not capable of providing a competent salary to the doctors and masters.[22] Over this augmentation in revenues conceded by the pope to the university a controversy with the archbishop of Toulouse was shortly under way. In September of that year the prelate and the university reached an agreement over the division of rents from this property, and declared that all future processes on the subject of benefices or other matters should be remitted to the *parlement*. Similar difficulties again arose over the appointment of a new pastor for this church when a vacancy occurred in November of that very year. An accord was then reached whereby the archbishop was to appoint and the university to support the successor of the deceased ecclesiastic.[23] There are other indications that the financial situation of the university was far from satisfactory, although they have no particular bearing on the relations between the university and the *parlement*. The first of these,

the Archives du Parlement. Jean de Saines who is mentioned among the newly appointed counsellors is presumably the Johannes de Saxis who appears as lieutenant for the judge of appeals on March 17, 1452 (Archives municipales de Toulouse, GG. 82). He is qualified there as *milite et legum doctore Tholose*. His appointment as lieutenant dated from December 2, 1451. Gaillard Dahus may be Galhardus Dancii (Danssii, Daucii or Dantu) whose name appears on several University records. In 1421 he was named syndic at a University congregation for a special piece of business (Archives notariales, Assolent, régistre 379, f°138). He was capitoul in the same year (Lafaille, *Annales*). In 1427 he was judge of Villalonge (Fournier, *Statuts*, II, no. 1915), and appeared in court on behalf of Garrigia, his brother-in-law, in the St. Cricq affair. His name occurs again in 1423 in the statutes for degree payments (*Ibid.*, I, no. 796, p. 767.). Pierre Sans Vesiau may be the licentiate in canon law who is listed as capitoul for 1468. Lafaille lists him simply as *Vesian* without given name. The document whereby the University agreed to submitting certain cases to the *parlement* is found in the Archives notariales, Assolent, régistre 379, f°64, and is cited by Gadave, no. 193.

22 Denifle, *La desolation des églises monstères et hopitaux en France pendant la guerre de cents ans*, I, no. 496, p. 211.

23 Archives notariales, Assolent, régistre 379, f°s64 and 56; listed in Gadave, nos. 193 and 194.

which dates from August, 1454, is the new university statute which required all bachelors to swear at the hands of the chancellor and rector that they would attain the rank of licentiate or doctor only at Toulouse, and in case of dispensation to receive these grades elsewhere, that they would pay all fees integrally to the doctors, beadles, and treasurer at Toulouse.[24] The general economic difficulties of this period are also illustrated in the grievances of the Estates of Languedoc for the year 1456. Here the university is mentioned in the complaint because its students had permitted their relatives, children, and parents, to use their scholastic privileges to give vexation to others, and especially to withdraw their possessions from the *taille* and other charges. Many of these so-called students, the complaint continued, were not really students at all, but married laymen in business, who had attended classes for fifteen days in order to have a certificate of matriculation, and who thereby exempted their property from taxation. As the Estates of Languedoc's most important function was the apportionment of taxes, it is easily understood why they should be concerned over these abuses. The response to these articles of complaint referred the Estates to the court of the seneschal, and informed them that they could also demand application of statutes made against such fraudulant transactions of students at Paris.[25] Even the provost and chapter of Saint Etienne were complaining to Calixtus III in this very year, that possessions of Stephanus Pastell, the late chancellor, and of another deceased canon of the monastery, were being maliciously and secretly detained by unknown persons to the great detriment of the chapter.[26]

To this financial stringency arising from the disorders of the late war were added the calamities of fire and pestilence. In the first week of May, 1463, a great conflagration broke out near the Carmelite convent and raged for several days. The wind was so strong that nothing could be done to extinguish it. It continued until it had burned to the walls in the vicinity of the *studium*. Three-fourths of the city was destroyed by this disastrous fire. Louis XI appeared in Toulouse shortly after and remitted the *tailles* for one hundred years to permit the city to recuperate. He also pardoned the unfortunate bakers who had been hastily condemned to death as responsible for the con-

---

[24] Fournier, *Statuts*, I, no. 835, p. 812. [25] Fournier, *Statuts*, I, no. 837, p. 814.
[26] Archives départementales de la Haute-Garonne, 4G XIX, liasse quatrième, titre sans numero.

flagration.[27] Both before and after this calamity Toulouse was harried by successive outbreaks of the plague. The records of the *parlement* note that body's frequent removal from the city to escape contagion. In August, 1451, the sessions of this court were prematurely closed because of the high mortality rate. In December, 1455, the sittings were suspended for a month for the same reason. After the great fire in 1463 a recurrence of the epidemic in Toulouse caused the *parlement* to transfer its seat to Albi, only returning in January of the next year.[28] In 1468 the *capitouls* of Toulouse had to send a special commission to the king to recover the *parlement* which had been moved to Montpellier. In this they were successful, but again in 1472 the court was moved to Albi, and then later to Réalmont, because of the plague. In July of 1474, the *parlement* was at Revel on account of the epidemic. Both the fire and these constantly recurring epidemics must have injured the university. There was even a famine recorded for 1473, when wheat became very dear and scarce. These calamities perhaps explain the infrequence of university records for this period.[29] Toulouse continued to be disturbed by recurrences of epidemics in the last quarter of the century. In 1482, 1490, and 1494, the sessions of *parlement* were suspended or transferred to other cities, and there are references also to the mortality again in 1497 and 1498.[30]

As time went on the university came to rely more and more on the *parlement* of Toulouse for settlement of its administrative

[27] Catel, *Histoire des comtes de Tolose,* 168, citing *Chronicon ecclesiae Sancti Pauli Narbonensis.* "Anno millesimo quadringentesimo sexagesimo tertio, et prima septimana Maii, fuit diruta per tres partes meliores civitas Tolosae per ignem: erat ventus validus de altano, et marino, et non potuerunt extinguere donec fuerunt ad muros villae, a parte studii." Charles Roques, *Inventaire des Archives de la Haute-Garonne,* (Toulouse, 1903), I, under HG., Ser. B, refers to B2, f°s279 and 280 for "measures prise à suite d'un incendie que avait détruit les trois quarts de la ville de Toulouse (samedi 7 mai, 1463)." See also Bertrand, *Gestes tolosains,* S iᵛ and Qiiᵛ.

[28] Roques, *Inventaire,* "clôture anticipée des séances du Parlement à cause de la mortalité (23 aout 1451, B1 f°179)"; *ibid.,* "suspension des séances de la Seneschausée de Toulouse jusqu'au dernier janvier, à cause de la mortalité (29 decembre 1455, B1, f°284)"; and *ibid.,* B2, f°s287 and 312.

[29] Bertrand, *Gestes tolosains,* Q iiᵛ; Roques, *Inventaire,* "determination prise par la Cour de se transporter à Albi 'pour fuyr et obvier au dangier et peril de l'impidimie qui ja grandement à commence en ceste ville de Tholoze' (2 mars 1442, B3, f°419)"—the court transferred itself to Réalmont on July 30 of the same year, B3, f°434; and *ibid.,* B4, f°69.

[30] The court was at Saint Félix de Caraman in July, 1482 (Roques, *Inventaire,* B6, f°76). It was moved to Bourg-Saint Bernard in September of the same year (*ibid.,* f°89). Seances were suspended in July 1490 (*ibid.,* B8, f°s251-252), while the court was at Montauban in August 1494 (*ibid.,* B9, f° 349). The mortalities of 1447 and 1498 in Toulouse are referred to in B10, f°349 and B11, f°s5-6.

problems. Where in the thirteenth century the intervention of the pope would have been sought, and in the fourteenth either that of the pope, the royal officers of Toulouse or the *parlement* of Paris, now the *studium* seems to go directly to the local court of supreme authority whose seat was within the walls of the city itself. Arrests were handed down by that tribunal that regulated in minute detail the purely internal administration of the *studium*. This should not, however, be taken to signify that the *parlement* was unwarrantedly injecting itself into academic matters. As in the case of the earlier papal intervention, the court seems to have acted only in lawsuits actually brought to its attention. It had the great advantage of proximity to the problems concerned over the papal Curia of the thirteenth and fourteenth centuries. *Parlement,* on the scene, could actually observe and investigate matters, whereas, the pope could only delegate commissioners to investigate or render decisions on the pleas of interested parties.

The quarrels, which in this period were so frequently litigated before the *parlement,* arose from differences in opinion between masters and students. This litigation was made possible by the presence of the court in Toulouse itself. If the students had grievances in the earlier period, they were economically unable to prosecute their suits in places as far distant as Avignon and Rome. Instead they would necessarily have to rely on someone in authority to present their views in the matter. Now they had only to organize and choose a procurator, for definite and final decision could be obtained in Toulouse itself.

In 1470 a rather bitter quarrel arose between masters and students, apparently over the payment of fees. The matter was adjudicated in the court of the seneschal but not to the liking of the parties concerned, who appealed to the *parlement.* The dispute had grown so heated that the students had been excommunicated at the request of the masters. For relief the students turned to the *parlement,* and as a result the order was forthcoming that they be immediately absolved; but at the same time they were admonished to pay the sums due to the doctors and *banquerius* of the schools for the Easter term, according to the form of the sentence rendered in the court of the seneschal. This they were to continue to do without prejudice to their case on appeal, until it should be otherwise ordered by the court.[31] The final decision in this suit was rendered September

[31] Archives du Parlement, B3, f. 267, signaled by Gadave, no. 202.

13 of that year. This arrest of *parlement,* aside from the elaborate regulations for fees at all stages of the academic career, included corrections of certain malpractices, such as the selling of magisterial chairs, the omission of solemn doctoral repetitions, and the absence of student-councillors at the congregations and assemblies. The garb of the student was also regulated with strictures forbidding ostentation. It would appear the *parlement* was attempting to be strictly impartial, guaranteeing the university suitable revenues and restoring to the students a share of control in general university administration through the revival of their counsellors.[32] Three years later the *parlement* also intervened in a student matter for the proper administration of justice. Three students were charged with the homicide and murder of a merchant of Bigorre in one of the principal streets of Toulouse. The charges having been examined by *parlement,* that court ordered that the prisoners should not be returned to the immunity of the church in which they had taken refuge, and from which they had been extracted by officers of the king at the command of the seneschal and vicar, but should be remitted to the court of the archbishop as the court of privileged cases. Because of the enormity of the crime, the *parlement* ordered the archbishop to delegate as his vicars two or three of its ecclesiastical counsellors to assist his *officialis* and loaned its palace to the archbishop for the conduct of the trial. Furthermore, the prisoners should not be freed before communication with the *parlement* itself.[33] The decision in this case as included in the parlementary record under a date two days later, condemned two of the accused to amends of 1,000 *livres tournois* and the third to amends of 100 *livres.* Half this sum was to go to the king and the other half was to be divided equally between the widow and children of the murdered man and the foundation of an *obit* for the repose of his soul in the church of Saint Sernin, where he was buried. Furthermore a pillar of stone or tile with a cross and inscription and sculptured relief should mark the spot and record the manner of this murder. The condemned were not to be released from prison by the archbishop until all this had been done on pain of recovering them and on pain of seizure and retention of his temporals in the hand of the king, until entire payment was made. A priest, detained on this same

[32] Fournier, *Statuts,* I, no. 858, p. 855.
[33] Archives du Parlement, B3, f.489, signaled by Gadave, no. 204.

matter but found innocent, was released by the same arrest.[34]

In 1480 the *parlement* was again called upon for intervention in a controversy within the university. The trouble between the students and masters seems to have concerned a recurrence of the question of student representation in the university council, for the court laid down a new statute on that subject. Furthermore, on the complaint of the students, the regent doctors were ordered to restore a statue of Saint Sebastian to its accustomed place before the next Christmas. The court was also evidently looking into the observance that had been accorded to its decision of 1470, for other matters settled at that time were again taken up. For instance, investigation was ordered concerning magisterial chairs sold since the last statute had been authorized; and the masters were again forbidden substitutes and warned to summon student-councillors for all academic assemblies. Furthermore, the court confirmed an old statute regarding the university Mass, and forbade the masters to withdraw students from one another on pain of 200 *livres* applicable to the king quite aside from the penalties already prescribed in university statutes. Students were similarly obliged to half the sum, applicable as above, and a prison term. In order to enforce its earlier decision in regard to student garb, the *parlement* commanded that the vicar of Toulouse, the conservators of the university, their lieutenants, and other royal officers should arrest any student wearing a harness, unless it could be proved that he was going or returning from outside the city. The rector and doctors were to enforce this ruling on pains of privation of scholarity or by 10 *sous* applicable to the university treasury. These might be further enforced by ecclesiastical censure. In regard to financial matters, the court discovered that its earlier ruling had been far from satisfactory, so it revoked its 1470 statute and reënacted an old one from the ancient university statutes. In response to the plea of the royal procurator against both students and masters and university conservators, the court ruled again on the legal aspects of letters of scholarity. Evidently abuses in this matter were still of frequent occurrence. At any rate the conservator and sub-conservator and their notaries were forbidden to cite persons without letters testificatory of scholarity from the student-complainant.[35]

---

[34] *Ibid.*, f°491, signaled by Gadave, no. 205.
[35] Fournier, *Statuts,* I, no. 860, pp. 859-862.

Two years later a case on appeal from the court of the seneschal was brought up in *parlement*. This was a suit of a regent master in theology against the administrator of the monastery of Saint Sernin. Evidently the theologian of the schools of Saint Sernin was having difficulty obtaining the perquisites of his office during a vacancy of the abbacy. *Parlement* set the case for the next week and ordered that certain quantities of wheat and wine and 8 *livres* for a habit and other necessaries be immediately paid.[36] In 1483 the same administrator of the abbey, Laurens Alamand, who was qualified as counsellor of the king in the previous document but who is now entitled bishop and perpetual administrator of Saint Sernin by apostolic appointment, selected Jacques Menon, a doctor of decrees, as subconservator of university privileges. The new subconservator was a regent doctor of the University and also prior of the College of Perigord.[37]

In 1486 the students of law and decrees backed by the procurator general and syndic of the city of Toulouse, were suing in the court of *parlement* six regent doctors of the same faculties over the question of the misuse of substitutes as lecturers. *Parlement* ruled that the doctors should read personally at all times, as the statutes ordered, on pain of deprivation of salary to be applicable to the other regents. As three specified regents had read but little during the past three years, this penalty was ordered invoked against them by the others if they did not follow the statutes in the future. Doctors were also forbidden to remit fees save to a poor student with the consent of the other regents. Bachelors and students were warned against lecturing for pay in private places, convents, or colleges; but collegiates were permitted to read to members of their own colleges at hours not conflicting with the ordinary classes in the schools.[38] In this same year a quarrel between two canons of the cathedral chapter that had intimate bearing on university affairs was also settled by *parlement*. Pierre de Rosergue, who had been provost since 1475, was maintained in possession of the office and perquisites of chancellor, by the renunciation of Guillermus de Aula, another canon of Saint Etienne. Pierre, who was nephew of Bernard de Rosergue, a famous master of Toulouse who had been success-

---

[36] *Ibid.*, no. 862, p. 868.
[37] Archives départementales de la Haute-Garonne, fonds Saint Sernin, H 183, fascicule XXV, livre 114, f°3ᵛ. See also Fournier, *Statuts*, I, no. 864, p. 869, and no. 866, p. 870.
[38] Fournier, *Statuts*, I, no. 866, p. 270.

ively provost of Toulouse, bishop of Bazas, and then archbishop of Toulouse, was very ambitious to follow in the footsteps of his illustrious uncle. His character was presumably rather turbulent, for in 1471 the *parlement* had confirmed letters patent that annuled the penalty of banishment which had been pronounced against him and authorized his reëntry into the realm. He is the first provost, as far as can be learned, who held concurrently the office of chancellor, although his famous uncle may also have held this double rank.[39]

In August of the same year, 1486, *parlement* handed down another decision on the vexed question of the proper use of the matriculation roll. The process for procuring letters of scholarity was again set down in detail. A merchant and an apothecary, who had presumably been using such letters illegally, were ordered to desist molesting anyone with excommunication and to have absolved at their own expense those whom they had caused to be excommunicated by the conservator and sub-conservator.[40] The troubles between masters and students also had not ended, but continued to excite the *studium* for months. In November at the request of the masters, *parlement* attempted to restrain the students from excesses. It would appear that the latter had been holding congregations and assemblies and had been impeding the doctors in their lectures and scholastic acts in an attempt to win their points. At the same time the court ordered its *hussiers* to inquire into these alleged excesses, and required the students to send ten or twelve representatives to the *parlement* on the following day. The priors of colleges were

---

[39] Archives du Parlement de Toulouse, B7, f°102ᵛ. Pierre's election as provost dated from September 24, 1475, Du Mège, *Histoire des institutions*, III, 134-147. Charles Roques, *Inventaire*, B3, f°388, lists the "entertainment des lettres patentes qui cassent et annulent la peine du banissement prononcée contre Pierre de Rosergue, et l'autorisent à rentrer dans le royaume (10 sept. 1471)."

[40] Fournier, *Statuts*, 1, no. 867, p. 871. No. 799, p. 771 is probably a summary of some part of the same decision. As dated by Fournier in 1426 it is nearly twenty-five years earlier than the earliest conserved arrests of the *parlement* of Toulouse. As source Fournier cites La Roche Flavin, *Arrets notables du parlement de Toulouse*, a copy of which I was unable to locate, so could not verify the year. As both documents date from August 14, it is possible that the year of no. 799 has been garbled either by Fournier, La Roche Flavin, or the latter's source. The omission of an *LX* in the dating phrase would account for this discrepancy, and the two documents were almost identical. The chief differences are that no. 799 omits all references to personal names, uses the word *bédeaux* where no. 867 uses *notary*, and adds a few Latin phrases that are missing from the latter. The penalties also vary slightly. Fournier comments that no. 799 is not otherwise found than in La Roche Flavin.

likewise to be assembled.[41] From an arrest of February 1, 1487, the details of this quarrel are elucidated. It would seem that the dispute included many points upon which the *parlement* had already ruled, to which both masters and students objected. The students were still of the opinion that their councillors were not being allowed a due voice in administrative matters and were refusing to pay the fees that the court had arranged in 1470. The masters, too, seem to have failed in the observance of some of the *parlement's* earlier decisions, for the prohibition against selling chairs is also repeated; and it is again ordered that a student-councillor be given one key to the *archa*. Complaints in regard to the reading of the *Decretum* were deferred for later judgment, but the arrest of July 21, 1486, was to be followed meanwhile. Settlement of the dispute between the beadles and the students was also deferred and likewise the difference between the masters and students over the ancient form and manner of the election of the rector. Points in regard to the fees of bachelors were given further interpretation by the court, and all books seized for non-payment of fees were to be returned when the students had complied with the present regulations. The archbishop and the chancellor also injected themselves into this suit and secured their ancient rights to representation in the university council. The royal procurator likewise took advantage of the opportunity for the correction of abuses that had arisen in the colleges. As a result the selling of collegiate places was forbidden by the court. The seller was to be liable to loss of his own place, and the purchaser was to lose the purchase price, half to the college and half to the king. Furthermore, collegiates were ordered to matriculate like other students in order to enjoy university privileges.[42]

In 1490 there occurred a famous disputed election to the archiepiscopal see of Toulouse. The university took the part of the ambitious Pierre de Rosergue, provost and chancellor, and elected him over the minority candidate, Hector de Bourbon, bishop of Lavaur, who was brother of the seneschal of Toulouse and supported by the nobility of the region. The king intervened on behalf of Hector and had him officially recognized. This dispute caused great disorder in the city as late as 1493, and the rector and professors had to be enjoined to impede the

[41] Archives du Parlement de Toulouse, B7, f·137, signaled by Gadave, no. 214.
[42] Fournier, *Statuts*, I, no. 868, pp. 872-873.

students from assembling in arms on behalf of Rosergue. The Dominicans were likewise ordered not to permit the bell of the university, which hung in the tower of their church, to be sounded. A few months later the *capitouls* were likewise ordered to guard well the bells of Saint Etienne.[43]

Even after all this great éffort on the part of the *parlement*, the affairs of the university seem to have remained constantly snarled. The court had to enjoin two regent doctors to proceed to the nomination of a candidate for the chair of the recently deceased Jacques Menon, who had risen in the legal profession to the office of royal judge of Cominges. It was ordered that on this point the court's former arrest be followed. A few days later the court had to command the regents of the university to elect councillors from among the bachelors according to the statutes, and then to proceed to fill the vacant chair of law on pain of 100 marks of gold and deprivation. The beadles were forbidden to interfere in the election on the same penalties. This same chair by September was in dispute between two claimants. A bachelor of laws, who claimed to have had possession of the chair but who was afterwards dispossessed by a licentiate of both laws, was given a day to present his suit. Meanwhile the licentiate was given the regency with all its emoluments during the course of the suit, although without prejudice to the claims of the plaintiff.[44]

The records of the *parlement* at other times contain references to minor matters that concerned the university. For instance, in 1490 the court ordered the archbishop's *officialis* to take the advice of the masters in theology and other doctors of the university before rendering judgment in the matter of prohibiting the great cross of the Daurade from being placed in the Garonne on the last day of Rogations. It would seem that such a prohibition was contemplated on grounds of superstition. When the king issued letters in July, 1498, confirming the ancient privileges, franchises, and liberties of the *pays de Languedoc*, the *parlement* enregistered and published them "without prejudice, however, to the privileges of the University of Tou-

[43] See the article by Rodière in the *Receuil de l'académie législative de Toulouse*, X, (1861) 168, and Lafaille, *Annales*, I, 261 ff. The arrests of *parlement* in this matter date from November 23 and December 17, 1493, and are signaled by Gadave, no. 221. They are found in register B9, f.s188 and 197 of the Archives du Parlement de Toulouse.

[44] Gadave, no. 217 and no. 220, citing the register of the Archives du Parlement de Toulouse, B9, f°s114 and 170. Menon is mentioned as judge in B8, f°278. See also Fournier, *Statuts*, I, no. 870, p. 875.

louse." Similarly, letters presented by the syndic of the faculty of medicine at Montpellier were confirmed with reservations in regard to the king and also in regard to the privileges of the University of Toulouse and other universities.[45]

Evidently the protracted disorders in the city of Toulouse had set in motion a royal commission for the reformation of justice, since the *parlement* registered letters of the bishop of Albi on this point in 1499, with injunctions to all magistrates. A similar injunction was made at the same time to the rector, regent dcotors, chancellor, conservators, and sub-conservators of the University of Toulouse to guard and maintain the new ordinances.[46] Abuses by students in the use of their legal privileges were also being investigated. Both the king and the *parlement* of Paris issued regulations upon the employment of letters of scholarity in May of the same year. The parlementary decree in the first place insisted that a student to employ letters of scholarity must be a true student and have resided in the university six months before obtaining his testimonial letter from the rector. Because of the numerous frauds which had been perpetrated, an absence of six months was to constitute a loss of such privileges. Students were not to use their privileges for others by virtue of any transfer made to them, except it be from father to son, brother to brother, or uncle to nephew. Students who entered suits in which they had no interest should be condemned for the costs. If a student were legally associated in a suit, once it had begun he might not claim reversion to another court. Nor might any scholar or master enjoy these legal privileges unless they remained daily in the *studium* as regent or student. The edict further stipulated the number of years that this legal privilege might be enjoyed, which varied according to the faculty in which the degree was to be taken. Regent masters were to profit from this privilege as long as they actually taught, and after twenty years' teaching could have it perpetually. Fraud in matters of scholarity was to be punished by the assessment of costs and amends. Louis XII's letters from Romorantin included four of the clauses recounted above, but in addition had provisions of its own. The king ordered that the students, at the sound of a trumpet, be warned to use their privileges justly; and that the conservators be for-

[45] Archives du Parlment de Toulouse, B8, f⁸222; B11, f.117ᵛ (Gadave, no. 226); and *ibid.*, f⁸150, dated January 4, 1500.
[46] Gadave, no. 225, citing Archives du Parlement de Toulouse, B11, f.115.

bidden cognizance in criminal matters of churchmen, divorce, the sacraments, or hospitals, and be denied the use of general monitions.[47] On publication of this royal letter by the *parlement* of Toulouse, the university syndic, the archbishop and his *officialis,* the abbot of Saint Sernin, the seneschal and vicar as conservators and sub-conservators, and the religious of the Hospital, of Cluny, of Saint Bernard, of the Dominicans, the Augustinians and the Carmelites, all objected. A hearing was set for a later date, but meanwhile the abbot of Saint Sernin was not forbidden to take cognizance of suits based on university privileges, as long as they were justly used, and according to the form outlined in the previous arrests of *parlement.* The archbishop was forbidden to take any cognizance in university affairs and, with the abbot, seneschal, and vicar was denied jurisdiction in cases of the Cistercians, Cluniacs, and Franciscans. Ecclesiastical notaries were forbidden to cite persons from outside the diocese, but students might do so on proving six months' residence. Conservators of university privileges were forbidden jurisdiction over students in criminal cases, where the delicts were committed in other provinces or dioceses. Nor might they confirm elections appertaining to other judges, nor absolve from pains of excommunication incurred in such cases. The *parlement* further ordered that all abuses of university privileges be investigated, and summoned for hearing on the same matter the conservators, sub-conservators, and regent doctors of the universities of Montpellier and Cahors, which also belonged to its jurisdiction.[48]

On one occasion in 1487 the *parlement* took cognizance of a matter that concerned the colleges, *capitouls,* and the ecclesiastical court of appeals in Toulouse. The sum of 400 *livres* had been conceded by the clergy of Toulouse towards the repair of the bridges, walls, and ditches of the city, against which the judge of ecclesiastical appeals had issued impeditive letters for a certain chaplain. It was against this action that the *capitouls*

---

[47] Isambert, *Recueil des anciens lois francaises* (Paris, 1827) XI, 301 and 395. The two documents differ considerably in contents. That of the *parlement* is dated May 17, 1499 (Gadave, no. 223 incorrectly "1498, aout 31"), while that of the King is dated May 12 of the same year from Romorantin. The arrest of the *parlement* of Toulouse in publishing the latter on August 21, cites the royal letters as of May 22, 1499, Fournier, *Statuts,* I, no. 874, p. 876, which is apparently the correct date, for a copy of this document from an ancient register of the *chambre d'enquêtes* of the *Parlement* of Toulouse, conserved in the Archives municipales de Toulouse, MS. 147, no. 102, p. 667 is dated May 22, 1499.   [48] Fournier, *Statuts,* I, no. 874, p. 876.

complained. The judge of appeals explained that this case had
not yet been heard and excused his action on that score. As a
date was set for its hearing, the *capitouls* were satisfied. Then
the syndic of the colleges complained that although the *officialis*
of Toulouse had been warned by the court not to assess the
colleges with any part of this sum, still he had sent them admonition to contribute. The syndic requested that the court instruct
the judge of appeals and *officialis* to revoke these letters. The
decision of the *parlement* advised the judge not to impede
further the collection of the sum since there was evident peril
and instructed him to inform the *officialis* to look into the request
of the colleges. This was evidently a reiteration of the old plea
that a college was not an ecclesiastical corporation, but a spe-
cially exempted charitable institution.[49]

There is evidence from the last years of the fifteenth century
as to the use of letters of scholarity in protecting the property
of students from taxation by the city. Indeed, some of these
records may have been the cause for the commission in reformation of justice in 1499 that has been considered above. During
the first year of his reign Charles VIII had reconfirmed for the
university the cherished privilege of quittance from subsidies
and impositions for its members and officers, as had his two
immediate predecessors.[50] Charles de Bourbon, the seneschal of
Toulouse and university conservator, seems to have been very
busy with lawsuits in regard to student exemptions from taxation. Five of his letters on such subjects during the period of a
single year have been conserved. The first of these dates from
May 27, 1498, and was directed to the justices, officers, and
royal servants to whom it might be exhibited. Therein is recounted how Guillermus Masset, a bachelor in decrees, had
pleaded exemption from paying the *taille* on his patrimonial
goods, based on his scholarity. This was conceded by the court
of the seneschal, and the case was judged without appeal. Since
that time, however, and in spite of the seneschal's inhibition,
the *capitouls* of Toulouse and their treasurer had again assessed

---

[49] Archives du Parlement de Toulouse, B7, f.206.
[50] Fournier, *Statuts*, I, no. 863, p. 869. The date is here given as 1483 without precision as to the month and day, which are missing in the manuscript
source cited (Bibliothèque Nationale, MS lat. 4222, f°s109-111ᵛ). Gadave,
no. 210 gives an additional manuscript source as Archives municipales de
Toulouse, GG. 75, f°59, where the date reads March 1484. "Datum Tu-
ronis in mense Martii anno Domini millesimo quatercentesimo octuagesimo
tercio. Regni nostri primo."

the property of the student and seized his goods. The seneschal ordered the citation of the *capitouls* and their treasurer for the following day and forbade further molestation of the student on this account. In December of the same year, the same official had to summon the treasurer again on a similar matter appealed to his court by Johannes de Michaele, a bachelor in decrees. On the fifteenth day of January following, the *capitouls* and their treasurer were duly ordered to return the illegally seized goods. A similar plea for exemption by Johannes Bonihominis, a simple student, had been allowed by the seneschal on the previous day. Other letters of adjournment for the municipal treasurer were sent out a few days later on behalf of Raymundus Valade, a bachelor of law. The court of the senescal was certainly functioning smoothly in protecting the students' privilege of exemption.[51]

Lawsuits regarding the university in general during the late fifteenth century had fallen to the jurisdiction of the *parlement* or the seneschal, but one interesting matter was adjudicated in the ordinary municipal court. Printing had first appeared in Toulouse in 1476 and, as nearly everywhere in Europe, had begun to flourish almost immediately.[52] This did not occur without the dislocation of the traditional arts and crafts that had prospered before the new method had been instituted. In Toulouse it was the book illuminators who were aggrieved and who petitioned the *capitouls* in 1479 to accord them the very necessary protection for their livelihood. Five illuminators, residents of the city, were the complainants. They explained that formerly books which had been composed in Toulouse by several doctors and nobles had been written by hand, and had given the illuminators sufficient employment for their art. Now, however, no books were so written in Toulouse nor in any other cities of the realm; all were printed. Since the university maintained two stationers, whose function was to bind and sell all sorts of books, and since these officials, unlike the complainants, were exempt from all *tailles* and subsidies, the illuminators felt especially aggrieved. One of these stationers, Guyot Brisson by name, had been particularly charged with the sale of printed books, imported from distant places, such as Germany, Rome,

[51] Gadave, no. 222, citing the Archives municipales de Toulouse, GG (Supplement. Exemption des tailles-Université).
[52] Desbarreaux-Bernard, "Barthelmy Buyer" in *Mémoires de l'académie des sciences, inscriptions, et belles-lettres de Toulouse*, (1875) Ser. G., vii, 230-238.

Venice, Paris, Lyons, and other cities. To the great distress of
the illuminators, he had begun also to decorate such works,
a thing which in no way pertained to the office of stationer.
This practice Guyot had been undertaking for three or four
years, so that their livelihood was being deliberately destroyed.
He had even drawn from them several journeymen to aid him
in this work, taking from the complainants all the trade in the
city. This had been done in violation of the city ordinance
passed several years before whereby each artisan was to have
but one trade, and not to concern himself with work that did
not properly belong to it. All members of crafts had been compelled to draw up and swear to statutes and ordinances for
their governance at that time. To prevent further unjust competition of this sort, the *capitouls* were requested to verify and
confirm as municipal statutes the articles and ordinances in
Latin which accompanied their request, so that the illuminators
might be guarded and maintained as were the other crafts.[53]

The only matter of an administrative nature during this
whole period in which the university acted by its own powers
was an arbitral sentence of the rector on a point disputed by
masters of arts and grammar in 1489. This was in regard to the
exclusive use of certain texts in their respective courses and
was decided in accordance with the decision handed down in
1426 by four commissioners, including Bernard, bishop of Bazas.
The artist was not content with the award and appealed, but
this was denied by the rector.[54] This seems to be almost the
only matter in which the *parlement* was not called upon to
interfere during the entire period. That court was not to be
quit of intervention in university disputes even after the turn
of the century. In 1532 it handed down an arrest whereby the
capitouls were ordered to provide that the students should be
properly treated by hospice-keepers and were not to suffer
undue exactions, and to see to it that the doctors continued to
lecture under pain of arrest.[55]

During the last half of the fifteenth century there was only
one new collegiate foundation at Toulouse. Pierre, cardinal-
bishop of Albano, had been given permission by Eugenius IV in

[53] Archives municipales de Toulouse, HH 2, f°323ᵛ.
[54] Fournier, *Statuts*, I, no. 869, p. 873.
[55] Archives municipales de Toulouse, AA5 (no. 162). "Capitularii . . . . pro-
videant . . . . et ut scolares Tholose studentes tractentur debite ab hos-
pitibus sine exactione indebita . . . et doctores universitatis continuent et
continuare faciant lecturas et actus eorum regentie sub penis arresti . . ."

1440 to found a college in the university. This prelate as son of the count of Foix had been created cardinal at the age of twenty by Benedict XIII in 1409, and was named bishop by Alexander V in the same year. He had served as legate in Spain under Martin V and Eugenius IV and was to continue in this capacity under Calixtus III and Pius II. He had worn the Franciscan habit from birth, and had received his education in Toulouse.[56] Eugenius IV, in authorizing the foundation of this college in 1440, gave Pierre free hand in selecting the students during his lifetime and guaranteed future patronage over the college to the counts of Foix. At the same time he conferred on the new institution all privileges and prerogatives held by the other colleges. On the same date, the pope wrote to the bishop of Saint Lizier, ordering him to unite to the college which was about to be founded three priories of the orders of Saint Augustine and Saint Benedict which pertained to the bishop of Albano. In return for this sanction, two students from each of the three dioceses of Tarbes, Rieux, and Lombes would be maintained in the college. The college was not yet established when Nicholas V came to the papal throne in 1447, for he confirmed the two bulls of his predecessor even in spite of this fact.[57]

The erection of the College of Foix proceeded very slowly. Between 1450 and 1452 several properties were purchased in way of endowment, among them an auditorium or school that had belonged to Petrus de Trilha, a doctor of laws. In 1454 Charles VII amortized these acquisitions of the cardinal for his college, and the archbishop of Toulouse favored its chapel with rather wide spiritual indulgences, but still the plan remained inchoate.[58] The cardinal-founder continued to work toward his goal. Calixtus V confirmed the bulls of his predecessors in favor of the college in 1455, and the cardinal himself finally drew up the act of foundation in 1457. Pierre at this time was resident in Avignon as papal vicar-general in temporalities and legate for the provinces of southern France. Recalling his long held intention of founding a college, dating, as he said, since his assumption of the cardinalate over forty years back, he records the progress of his endeavors. The special love he bore Toulouse came from the studies he had made there at that

[56] Baluze in Bibliothèque Nationale MS. lat. 4223, f°s195-201.
[57] Fournier, *Statuts*, I, no. 819, p. 798; no. 820, p. 799; and no. 826, p. 805.
[58] Fournier, *Statuts*, I, no. 828, p. 811; no. 831, p. 812; no. 833, p. 812; no. 834, p. 812; and no. 832, p. 812.

time. Having acquired a suitable site for his proposed foundation in the *Rue de l'Orme Sec,* near the Franciscan convent, he had united several houses in that area and had had them amortized by the king. His foundation was to be dedicated to Saint Jerome and Saint Francis and was to house twenty-five students, including four priests to attend their spiritual needs.[59] A few months later the cardinal acquired another house in the vicinity to enlarge the college properties. Shortly after, an elaborate set of statutes was arranged for the institution, which was to be called the College of Pierre Cardinal of Foix; and a canon of Cominges, Guillermus de Subvilla, was named its rector for life.[60] The first collegiates were not installed until May 22, 1458, when two more priests were named. The college was not completed at the time so was not ready for its full complement of students. The three ecclesiastics meanwhile were given full powers of transacting its business. In June, Subvilla and Bernardus de Garlenis accepted on the part of the cardinal 600 *cannae* of wall, according to specifications, and a mason-contractor of Toulouse testified as to receiving 4000 *scuta* of gold and gave quittance therefore.[61]

On the death of the cardinal in the following year, Subvilla was given procuration by the college to raise the sums due to it as heir, from the archbishop of Auch and the bishops of Oloron, Dax, and Cominges, and to collect the books, utensils, and other gifts that had been bequeathed it.[62] Evidently the death of its cardinal-founder left the college in a sad financial plight for it was shortly supplicating papal assistance in many matters. The college as heir had incurred considerable debt for the upkeep of the palace at Avignon and feared that everything would be consumed to its detriment unless something were shortly done. Although 6,000 ducats had been expended by the college for this purpose, the governor of the city had conceded only 40 *scuta,* and the college would be destroyed unless His Holiness were more liberal. Furthermore, certain citizens of Avignon were vexing the college for repayment of a sum borrowed for the conservation of that city. The pope was asked to pay the 1,500 *scuta* or to declare the college not liable for the sum. It also asked for confirmation of the concession of the fruits of the late cardinal's benefices to the college as heir for the period

[59] Fournier, *Statuts,* I, no. 836, p. 813 and no. 838, p. 815.
[60] *Ibid.,* nos. 839-840, pp. 817-845.
[61] *Ibid.,* no. 843, p. 847.   [62] *Ibid.,* no. 849, p. 849.

of one year that his debts might be paid and the foundation of the college completed. The confirmation of a concession of 1,000 ducats from the goods of the cardinal's palace was also requested, and likewise the union of benefices made or to be made. The cardinal, as was frequently his wont in time of need, had pawned a gilded crystal chandelier for 500 ducats. If the pope desired this object would he be pleased to redeem it.[63] Paul II in response to this request exempted the college from the vexation of creditors for the period of a year and appointed two bishops as commissioners to confirm its statutes. This confirmation was duly accomplished in 1467 and the *officialis* of Toulouse was empowered to absolve from sentences of excommunication incurred by the violation of the statutes. At the same time Gaston, count of Foix, as patron of the college designated the judge of appeals of Toulouse, the judge of Verdun, and a bachelor in law to decide on the honesty of life, suitability, and good morals of the four priests and twenty collegiates then in residence, since so many suits and differences had arisen among them over places, titles, and collations.[64] A month later the count had to write again to urge the collegiates to peace among themselves, stipulating that none included by name in his previous letters was to be disturbed or molested since he had confirmed them all. Anyone who continued to do so was to be deprived. In 1468 the *officialis* of Toulouse, as judge-commissioner of Paul II, issued letters to constrain the debtors of the cardinal to pay the sums owed to the college as heir. The vice-regent of the Apostolic Chamber at Avignon also assisted the collegiates to recover the means, furniture, and other possessions of the cardinal. On two occasions during the later years of this century additions were made to the original statutes of the college.[65] Among the most unusual privileges conceded the cardinal during the preparation for the founding of this college was that of creating licentiates in theology and law, and even doctors of law and decrees. The latter were to be given the same privileges as doctors of the university and were authorized to the number of twelve. These papal gifts are dated from 1431 and 1447, but it is not known whether the cardinal ever made use of such extraordinary powers.[66]

---

[63] Fournier, *Statuts*, I, no. 849, footnote 1.
[64] *Ibid.*, nos. 850-851 and 853-854, pp. 849-852.
[65] Fournier, *Statuts*, I, no. 855, p. 853; no. 857, p. 855 and footnote; and III, nos. 1917-1918, pp. 637-638.   [66] *Ibid.*, I, no. 806, p. 776.

The other colleges seem to have been functioning normally during this period. The College of Saint Martial had a church, formerly of the diocese of Cominges, united to it in 1462 by Paul II, and was also given a priory with permission to alienate one of its seigneuries—presumably in exchange. In the following year the chapel of Saint Jean de Picacos, a testamentary foundation, was intrusted to the chaplaincy of a student of this college with the provision that the college itself should become perpetual patron with power of collation after his decease.[67] In 1484 it purchased a house, an agricultural domain, and a vineyard in the neighborhood of Toulouse, and in 1498 concluded a transaction with the religious of Saint Pantaleon, whereby the nuns were given a house and garden in the city as compensation for the house leased by the college which had been burned in the great fire.[68] The business transactions of this institution between 1489 and 1493 have been conserved in a manuscript register of the notary, Louis Palanquin. In this volume are records of some forty-three transactions of various sorts within the space of three and one-half years. Their range is great. Several of them regard the fiefs of the college, and many have to do with the leasing of property to various individuals.[69] Others record debts owed by or owing to the college. In one case this was for a field that the college had purchased. In another, the college testified as to the reception of rent for which no record of lease had been made. Numerous transactions for the purchase of wood during the winter of 1490 are also included under the headings of "purchase and debts."[70] Syndics were appointed on two occasions by the collegiates, once for an exchange of rents in 1489, and again in 1490 for the peaceable settlement of a dispute between the college and the consuls of Blagnac. At another time a suit between the college and one of its priests over a violation of statutes, that had come before the seneschal, was compromised out of court by the parties. A former college

---

[67] *Ibid.*, nos. 846-848, p. 849. The college already had a priory at Picacos, conferred by its founder in 1360—*Ibid.*, no. 647, p. 596.

[68] Fournier, *Statuts*, I, no. 865, where the date is incorrectly given as 1481. "M°CCCC°LXXXIII et decima tertie mensis Martii" is the reading from the register of the College of St. Martial, no. 68, p. 531, in the Archives départementales de la Haute-Garonne. For the latter transaction, see *Statuts*, I, no. 871, p. 875.

[69] Archives départementales de la Haute-Garonne, fonds Saint Sernin, H. 142, f°s2, 2ᵛ, 3ᵛ, 5ᵛ, 6, 6ᵛ, and 7ᵛ for the fiefs; 10, 10ᵛ, 12, 12ᵛ, 14, 14ᵛ, 19ᵛ, 20, 20ᵛ, 21, 22ᵛ, 23 (two documents), 23ᵛ and 24 for the leases.

[70] *Ibid.*, f°s3, 11ᵛ, 16, 17ᵛ (two documents), and 18 (two documents).

prior was given general quittance for his stewardship in 1490 at a college assembly, although he had rendered his statement on vacating the office in 1488.[71] From this series of documents some idea of the occupations of a college prior can be gained. His name appears on every document, although frequently the presence of one of the priests of the college lends additional authority to the transactions. The number of students resident in the college can be estimated from the number present at the congregations for important business. On five occasions during a period of two and one-half years such assemblies were held, with an average of fourteen members present.[72]

The records are not so full for the other colleges during this period. The abbot of Saint Sernin as provisor for the College of Narbonne commissioned two members of his court to confer a collegiate place in this college in 1454.[73] The countess of Perigord communicated with the seneschal of Toulouse in 1458 over her right of presenting students to the College of Perigord and was presumably recognized, for she appointed to such places in 1468 and 1471. Relics of Saint Front, titular patron of the college, were transferred from Perigueux to the chapel in Toulouse in 1464.[74] On the death of the countess in 1483, the college was relieved of the payments that had formerly been made at the presentation of each new student, on condition that the sum be applied to an anniversary Mass on December 18 of each year. In 1497 the college appointed syndics for receiving gifts from the bishop of Bazas, authorizing them to oblige the college for the celebration of an anniversary Mass for the repose of his soul after the bishop's death. From a quittance given the bishop in 1500, it is learned that the bequest consisted of books, always a thing of great value to a medieval college.[75] The College of Saint John was still in existence in 1478 because

---

[71] Archives départementales de la Haute-Garonne, fonds Saint Sernin, H. 142, f°s1ᵛ, 6ᵛ, 8, and 13.

[72] They date from November 7, 1489, with 14 present (f°1ᵛ); April 4, 1490, with 17 present (f°6ᵛ); April 25, 1490, with 19 present (f°8); May 18, 1490, with 12 present (f°13); and May 4, 1491, with 7 present (f°19ᵛ).

[73] Archives départementales de la Haute-Garonne, fonds Saint Sernin, H. 133, fascicule without page numeration found in above volume at f°5, and having at the bottom of its first page, *XXV livre 109*.

[74] Fournier, *Statuts*, I, no. 844, p. 818, and Bibliothèque Nationale MS. lat. 4223, f°129 bis, citing "Ex libro obitum colegii Petragoricensis Tolosae, f°151ᵛ, and f°155ᵛ. For the translation of the relics, see Saint Charles, "Collège de Perigord" in the *Mémoires de l'académie des sciences, inscriptions, et belles-lettres de Toulouse*, (1886) Ser. H. VIII, 198.

[75] Fournier, *Statuts*, I, no. 864, p. 869; no. 872, p. 875; and no. 875, p. 878.

it was mentioned in the tax cadastre of that year.[76] The Cistercian College of Saint Bernard had fallen on evil days. In fact, it had been reduced to a single student and was sadly in need of repair. In 1482 a commission of nine abbots arranged a reorganization of the institution, appointed a new prior, and drew up elaborate statutes. George of Amboise, the apostolic pronotary, later cardinal archbishop of Rouen, donated 150 *livres tournois* for the very necessary repairs on the dormitory, cloisters, and other edifices.[77] A quarrel between the almoner of Saint Sernin as provisor and the College of Saint Raymond that had been litigated in several courts and finally reached the *parlement*, was settled out of court in 1485 by a compromise on the several points raised. It was provided that the keys of the college should be turned over once annually to the almoner by the prior, but that the former must return all of them with no retention. The almoner on his part agreed that the college should have its customary prior and that when a new collegiate was to be presented, it should be done through a bailiff chosen by the almoner from among the collegiates. The right of removal for cause or of punishing collegiates was recognized as pertaining to the almoner. The collegiates on their part agreed to take steps for the parlementary confirmation of this private agreement.[78]

---

[76] Jules Chalande, *Histoire des rues de Toulouse*, (Toulouse, 1920), première partie, no. 42.

[77] Fournier, *Statuts*, I, no. 861, p. 863.

[78] Archives départementales de la Haute-Garonne, fonds Saint Raymond, XV, sac AF, liasse 1, titre 6. A partly illegible copy of this legal transaction.

CHAPTER 9

THE UNIVERSITY OF TOULOUSE
IN THE MIDDLE AGES

T HE University of Toulouse in the Middle Ages was important in many aspects of its history. Its very foundation marked an almost new departure among medieval universities, and the purpose behind it was unique. After its early years, the *studium* had significance for its city and diocese, for the sub-Pyrenean area, and ultimately for the whole of the Midi. It came to have great attraction even for students from Aragon. The university played an important rôle in the history of the Avignon papacy; it was deeply affected by both the Great Schism and the Hundred Years' War. Even its constitutional arrangements as a corporation, its grouping of faculties, and its participation in the academic collegiate movement were of moment in the growth of the medieval university system.

The University of Toulouse was almost the earliest and certainly the most enduring of the thirteenth century universities which had papal and royal authorization for their foundations. Only Palencia and Naples antedated it slightly, and the latter had only royal approbation. Palencia had but an evanescent existence and Naples was never too prosperous. Although Toulouse was founded on papal and royal authority, and protected by both throughout the Middle Ages, it was not dominated by either patron. The kings of France never intervened in its internal administration as did the kings of Sicily at Naples. Unlike the Italian foundations of this epoch which had municipal backing, Toulouse never had the official patronage of the government of the city in which it was located. Even the endowment of its teaching staff by the count of Toulouse lasted only ten years. Once established it was left very much to its own devices.

The purposes of Gregory IX and the French royal government in establishing the University of Toulouse are apparent from the Treaty of Paris of 1229. The new *studium* was intended to assist in the eradication of heresy, and in the pacification of Languedoc

205

after the long Albigensian wars. The papal representative, Romano, would naturally have been more interested in the first of these two objectives, and the royal advisers of young Louis IX in the second. Indeed the royal government was definitely preparing by other provisions of this treaty for the eventual acquisition of Languedoc as royal domain. Both the papal and royal objectives were in fact obtained in the course of the thirteenth century, but the effectiveness of the university in contributing to these ends is not definitely clear. The early masters at Toulouse certainly suffered from their connection with the victorious parties in the long conflict, and were decidedly unwelcome in the city.

Just how the *studium* overcame local prejudice and managed to persevere can not be ascertained, but it obviously succeeded. The count of Toulouse can have had no real interest in the survival of the university. His obligation to pay magisterial salaries for ten years was merely an additional burden to his already heavy obligations as the defeated party. There is no evidence that Alphonse of Poitiers as Raymond's successor took any interest in the *studium,* nor that the city government of Toulouse did anything to further its growth. The obvious fact remains, however, that it did grow steadily in the thirteenth century. By the opening years of the fourteenth century, it was in flourishing condition. In some fashion it had won the approbation of the local community, for its graduates were to be found even among the *capitouls,* the chief magistrates of the city; and many others had become prominent officials in the local ecclesiastical establishments. The citizens of Toulouse were at least enthusiastic about their schools of law, and the city government actually joined the officers of the university in petitioning unsusccessfully for the establishment of a new theological faculty in 1346.

From the supplication rolls dating from the last quarter of the fourteenth century, which the university sent to the Avignon Curia requesting favors for its students, a clear idea of the approximate distribution of its student clientele can be obtained, and hence the extent of the drawing power of the *studium,* and of its meaning for the peoples of the surrounding areas. An analysis of these lists reveals that the dioceses located between the Garonne and the Pyrenees, and those of the central highlands to the northeast sent by far the largest groups of students to Toulouse — far more than the neighboring dioceses in the area southeast of Toulouse or those north of the Garonne on the western coastal plain of France. The University of Montpellier would, of course, offer heavy competition to Toulouse in attracting students from the southeastern sector, but no reason can be offered for the comparative paucity of students from the Atlantic coastal plain north of the Garonne, unless for them the University of Orléans was easier of access. In the major areas of southern France, Toulouse had little competition from other *studia*. Only that of Montpellier was of prior foundation in all southern France. The fourteenth century foundations in this area were of minor moment. Neither Cahors nor Perpignan really prospered, nor did they prevent students from Cahors and the diocese of Elne from enrolling at Toulouse.

It is perhaps a bit surprising that students came in such considerable numbers from the Iberian peninsula, particularly from Aragon. Far more came from there than from France north of the Loire or from the area east of the line of the Rhone and Saône. In 1378 students in small numbers came to Toulouse from Portugal and Castile. By 1387 they no longer came from Portugal, and by 1394 Castile was represented by students from but a single diocese, Murcia in the far southeast of the peninsula, which contributed a few students from Cartagena. Portugal of course had a *studium* of its own dating from the late thirteenth century. The constant shift of its seat between Lisbon and Coimbra in the fourteenth century may account for the presence at Toulouse in 1378 of Portuguese students from three dioceses. Castile, in addition to the *studium* at Palencia which never prospered, had two thirteenth century foundations of its own which were almost coeval with Toulouse. Their continued existence would account for the small numbers of Castilian students ever enrolled at Toulouse. The kingdom of Navarre had no *studium* of its own, so was represented consistently on the rolls of fourteenth century Toulouse. The kingdom of Aragon acquired *studia* only in the fourteenth century when Jaime II founded Lerida in 1300, and Pedro IV founded Perpignan in 1349 and Huesca in 1354. None of these establishments apparently detracted much from the drawing power of Toulouse for Aragonese students. The diocese of Urgel sent over thirty students to Toulouse in 1378, and sprinklings of students came from eight other dioceses in that kingdom, including Lerida, Elne, and Huesca. In 1387 students from additional Aragonese dioceses were listed on the rolls of Toulouse.

These students were attracted to Toulouse in the late fourteenth century by the opportunities offered for instruction in six different branches. The distribution of students from the various areas within the different faculties indicates broadly what brought them to the university. Students from the city of Toulouse itself in 1378 were attracted primarily to the study of canon law, and only in lesser numbers to arts and grammar, though both these faculties drew more than the faculty of civil law which ranked a very poor fourth in popularity. The faculties of grammar and arts of course offered basic preparation for the higher faculties, and unless civil law students did not enroll themselves on supplication rolls because of poor expectancy of ecclesiastical benefice, the civil law faculty was certainly of lesser importance. Canon law was also by far the most popular faculty to students from the dioceses of the southwest, but the attraction of the arts faculty was greater in this instance than that of grammar. Grammar schools must have been available locally in these dioceses, which would account for the smaller numbers of grammarians sent to Toulouse. Students from the northeastern highlands found canon law and grammar almost equally compelling, and arts and civil law exactly so, though in only about half as great numbers. Students from the southeastern section again favored canon law, but grammar and civil law were tied for second place at about half the total of students in canon law, and the students in arts were not appreciably less. The northwest coastal plain sent students in about equal numbers to all four faculties. The students from the Iberian peninsula dominantly favored canon law, but civil law, arts, and even grammar each drew a few students from this area. From the peripheral area in the north of France, and from the regions east of the Rhone and Sâone, came very few students at any time and strangely enough in 1378 they preferred grammar and arts to the two legal branches which were precisely equal in drawing power in this instance.

The faculty of theology had its first considerable listing of students in 1394. At this time, the enrollment within this faculty was almost equally apportioned among Toulouse itself, the southwest, and the northeast. The only other area represented at all in this faculty was the northwest. Of course the students of the religious orders were not normally listed in supplications, and they may well have been the majority of the students in this faculty.

The Avignon residence of the papacy throughout the greater part of the fourteenth century created a demand for canon lawyers, which may account for the popularity of the canon law faculty at Toulouse. The Avignon papacy also contributed to the general importance of the university. French popes favored the *studium* in many ways. Especially were its masters and alumni singled out for offices at the Curia, and as candidates for sees in southern France. The university so appreciated and profited from the favors of Avignon that, on the removal of the seat of the papacy back to Rome and the ensuing Great Schism, it did its utmost to support the French claimant. It continued to do so to its own detriment after the University of Paris took the lead in trying to heal the Schism through the subtraction of obedience from Benedict XIII. With the healing of the Schism in 1417, Toulouse ceased to enjoy any special favor from the papacy.

The campaigning in the Hundred Years' War did not approach Toulouse too closely, but it did cause the university economic distress because of the need for financing French military efforts. Students from English areas such as Bayonne, Bordeaux, and Saintes are listed in the supplication roll of 1378. By 1387 Bayonne had ceased to send any students and Bordeaux and Saintes had reduced their complements of students almost to the vanishing point. In 1394 Bordeaux sent but a single student, and other dioceses in the western part of the area between the Garonne and the Pyrenees were also sending many fewer students to Toulouse. In this latter group, were included the dioceses of Dax, Oloron, Lescar, and Aire. Their close proximity to the chief English areas and the exigencies of the warfare may have accounted for the decline, but the Schism probably had more vital influence. The roll of 1378 was in the first year of the pontificate of Clement VII, that of 1387 was for his ninth. Those students listed in the first roll were present at Toulouse before there was a schism, those of the later list were definitely of the obedience of Avignon.

There are many aspects of the history of the medieval University of Toulouse that have not been touched upon in this volume. As explained in the preface, only about one-half of the work as originally planned, namely the chapters recounting the foundation of the university and the narrative of its growth to 1500, is being published at this time. Other chapters, written but not yet in definite form, include essays on the constitution of the *studium* in theory and in practice; on its standing committees, lesser officers, and servants; on the organization and functioning of its faculties; and on the history and organization of its medieval colleges. The chapters on masters and students are yet to be written. All these materials will complete topically what could not be treated in the chapters devoted to the general growth of the university to 1500. Lest the omission of such important matters be regarded as an oversight, perhaps a few general conclusions without argument or proof may be proffered here in summary.

There is no definitive evidence as to the model followed at Toulouse in its earliest constitutional arrangements. That the founding masters were from Paris would suggest that *studium* as its probable model. The provisions of the Treaty of Paris of 1229 which govern the payment of magisterial salaries stipulate theology, canon law, arts, and grammar as the subjects to be taught at Toulouse. All these were to be found at Paris, though masters of grammar never formed part of the official corporation. The extension of the privileges of *Parens scientiarum* to Toulouse in its early years would support the same assumption, although as time went on Toulouse developed basic features that were different from Paris. Her theological faculty certainly did not endure long, for it had to be reformed officially in 1360. A faculty of civil law was also acquired at Toulouse some time in the thirteenth century, which greatly differentiated it from Paris, where the study of civil law was forbidden. Exactly when this faculty appeared at Toulouse however can not be determined. By 1311 the first set of general statutes for the *studium* gives evidence of such a faculty, and those of 1314 actually request the bishop, in applying the provisions of *Parens scientiarum* to include the legists among the doctors of decrees there mentioned. Thus Toulouse in the early fourteenth century possessed faculties of civil law and grammar which were not to be found at Paris and faculties of canon law and arts which were. The university was also apparently in process of seeking theological and medical faculties at this very time, faculties which Paris had long possessed. That the university had a chancellor and rector, as Paris did, is attested by a document of 1290, directed to those officials by the Dominican prior provincial of Provence in reply to a request for the appointment of a master of theology from the order for the local convent at Toulouse. The rectorship at Toulouse changed four times annually, as at Paris, but rotated among the masters of the four major faculties. This again was far different from the situation at Paris where only masters of arts could hold the rectorship. Though Toulouse became important as a legal university there is no hint of any borrowing from the Bologna model. Like Paris, again, the University of Toulouse had its rivalry between rectors and chancellors, but for the most part these officials functioned with a minimum of friction despite the anomoly of the *studium's* two heads which the statute-makers seemed anxious to keep on a basis of strict equality.

The autonomy of the corporation in directing university affairs is amply demonstrated from its activity at statute making in the fourteenth century. This independence was vigorously maintained from 1309 to 1329, when the *studium* found itself in grave difficulties by having too many conflicting statutes all to be observed by the most solemn oaths. A way out was found by applying to the pope for a commission to disentangle matters. Thereafter the corporation continued to draw statutes as they were found to be necessary, but in 1353 the same difficulties appeared again and Innocent VI at the request of the university, named the archbishop of Toulouse to revise the conflicting statutes. In 1378 and 1391, the same problems had to be corrected. To meet this last occurrence of the problem, a permanent commission of local ecclesiastical dignitaries, which functioned when called upon to do so on nine occasions between 1395 and 1425, was named by the pope. As a corporation, the masters continued to legislate for themselves during this period for their autonomy was in no way curtailed. They even appealed to Benedict XIII, the Avignon claimant, to intervene in other matters in 1404, but after the Schism had been healed with the election of Martin V, the requests almost ceased. Eugenius IV did confirm, when asked, university statutes submitted to him in 1432. Papal intervention in the *studium* came in nearly every instance at the request of the corporation or of a particular group of its members and was not undertaken at papal initiative. Even the changes accomplished were not the decisions of the popes themselves, but of especially designated commissioners. Though reforms seem to have been amicably accomplished, they had the effect of reducing the initiative of the master's corporation which gradually ceased to legislate. The last statutes to be drawn by the masters themselves date from 1454, though an arbitral decision of the rector in a dispute between masters of arts and grammar was still rendered as late as 1489.

In the last half of the fifteenth century, however, the corporation suffered a diminution of its autonomy at the hands of the *parlement* of Toulouse. This was a much closer authority to which to appeal than either the pope or the king. Prior to this time the university had sought royal intervention only in the matter of enforcing royal privileges which bestowed exemption from local jurisdictions and from taxation levies. From 1470 to the close of the century, there was constant turmoil within the *studium*, and the university or some of its members were frequently appearing before the *parlement* for settlement of their grievances. These quarrels were occasionally appealed from a lower court, but at other times seem to have originated before the *parlement* itself. Most of its decisions were undertaken judiciously, with the obvious intention of maintaining order in the distraught atmosphere. All actions seem to have been at the request of disputing factions, and the *parlement* at first tried patiently to judge and reform on the basis of existing university statutes. In the end, however, with patience exhausted, the *parlement* ruled on such diversity of subject and with such stringency of detail that it left little or nothing to the university itself, whether in the maintenance of former judicial privileges, in the arranging of lectures and schools, or even in the keeping of its own matriculation records. This would imply the inability of the *studium* to guide itself effectively in a trying period of rapid social change. That its difficulties were so largely financial would seem to confirm the assumption. Furthermore, its cooperative organization, with lack of continuity in the rectorship, seemed to discourage any self-reform. Even the basic idea of an association of masters and students as a self-governing body, achieved and perfected in the thirteenth century, was clearly in the process of decay in the fifteenth, and not only at Toulouse.

The participation of Toulouse in the academic collegiate movement of the Middle Ages was of considerable significance. The endowed hospice for deserving students first appeared at Paris in 1180, and rapidly developed there in the early thirteenth century before other *studia* showed any tendencies to imitate. Indeed Toulouse has fair claim to be the first to follow the example of Paris in this matter. At least two of her establishments are earlier than any known at Oxford, Bologna, Montpellier, or Cambridge. It is known that Cardinal Romano ordered the bishop of Avignon to pay the expenses of twelve poor scholars in theology from the revenues of the tithe of that city in 1227. He may also have suggested to the monastery of Saint Sernin at Toulouse a new use for its Hospital of Saint Raymond, for it was being used for students as early as 1233. Innocent IV in 1245 ordered the bishop of Toulouse to admit poor students to all the hospitals of his city. The plan was similar to that which had been inaugurated at Paris, except at Toulouse there was apparently no permanent endowment of beds in the hospitals by individual donors as there was in the *Dix-Huit*, in Saint Thomas of the Louvre, and in the *Bons Enfants* of Saint Honoré at Paris. That there were such later at Toulouse is indicated by a clause in the University Reform Statutes of 1329 requiring monastic houses to observe the conditions of testamentary bequests.

Another inspiration for the later medieval college came from the houses of study maintained by religious orders in university cities. The Dominicans and Franciscans had established houses at Paris and Oxford between 1217 and 1224. The Dominicans had a house at Montpellier by 1250, and the Franciscans founded one at Toulouse before the end of the thirteenth century. They even maintained such houses at Bologna, despite its emphasis on legal studies. These all were private institutions and in no sense charitable hospices of the normal collegiate type. They did serve as examples for collegiate organization, however, and stimulated other religious orders to provide for the training of their own members. A house was acquired in Paris by the Cistercians in 1227, but its purpose as a house of studies was only clarified in 1239. In 1263 they set up a house in Montpellier, and in 1281 the General Chapter of the Cistercians ordered such establishments at Oxford and Toulouse. The Canons of Saint Augustine and the Cluniacs also followed this example in establishing houses of study for their members at Paris in 1229 and 1261. The Augustinian Canons of Saint Etienne and Saint Sernin maintained such student establishments at Toulouse for their own membership before 1279 and 1306 respectively, and the Cluniacs from Moissac did the same before the early fourteenth century. These were houses of much more normal collegiate type than the Mendicant and Cistercian establishments which did not permit their students to follow courses in the ordinary university schools. The Augustinian and Cluniac colleges also differed from the secular colleges in not being self-governed.

Strictly speaking, neither the charitable endowment for pauper students in existing hospitals nor the houses of study for religious orders constituted the type for the later secular college, whose distinguishing feature was corporate autonomy. Several of the earlier Parisian establishments of the first type tried to acquire a measure of autonomy in the course of the thirteenth century, as did the Hospital of Saint Raymond at Toulouse in later times. The normal secular college began to appear in the second half of the thirteenth century with founders who had actually studied in the schools. Hence they were men familiar with scholastic conditions, and not merely merchants making pious bequests for the repose of their souls. In 1254 Robert de Sorbon started work on the college which was later to bear his name in Paris. A document of 1264 first qualifies him as provisor of this college. Similar autonomous foundations followed at Paris in swift succession for students from specific dioceses or particular foreign countries. Two founded before 1300 were for students from specified Norman dioceses, and two were for students from Denmark and Sweden. At Toulouse the autonomous college may actually have appeared in the College of Vidal Gautier in 1242, for it was not connected with any religious hospital but had its house and endowment quite simply intrusted to episcopal supervision. Unfortunately this college is never mentioned again in later documents. It probably collapsed within a short time. Several colleges of this new Parisian type were founded at Oxford during the thirteenth century and were preceded by such benefits for poor students as the chantry foundation of Allen Basset in 1243 and the penitential endowment of a group of poor students for a few years by John of Balliol. Three secular foundations, however, were made at Oxford between 1262 and 1268 — those of Walter of Merton, William of Durham, and Balliol College founded by the widow of John of Balliol. Peterhouse was founded in 1284 at Cambridge, and the College of Avignon at Bologna, established by the occupant of that see for students from his diocese, was the solitary foundation in Italy during this century.

In the fourteenth century, nine autonomous colleges were founded at Toulouse which causes it to rank high in comparison with other universities, exception being made of Paris which had thirty-eight foundations. In this century, there were five new foundations at Oxford; seven at Cambridge; six at Padua;

and four at both Bologna and Montpellier. Italian, German, and Spanish universities acquired them, as did the new French *studia* of this age. In the fifteenth century, there were only three new colleges founded at Toulouse, but new foundations at Paris showed almost the same percentage of decrease. At that, the Hundred Years' War had surprisingly little deterrent effect on new foundations, for the greatest decline is noticeable in both Paris and Toulouse for the period after 1460. In England the war had no perceptible effect, for at Oxford there were five new foundations all dating before 1450 and Cambridge had five founded after 1440. Elsewhere in Europe the decline in the number of collegiate establishments is amply clear. Among the older universities, Avignon is the one exception with seven new foundations, though new fifteenth century *studia* did acquire colleges.

Although the roster of medieval colleges at Toulouse totaled fifteen, quite exclusive of houses of study for the regular orders and the semi-collegiate, charitable institutions, it is impossible to estimate with any accuracy just how many houses for students were in existence in any given time. There were six listed in 1329, and a document of 1409 sets the total at ten though it names only seven. A document submitted in the Saint Cricq affair in 1426 refers to eighteen colleges.

Most of the founders of colleges at Toulouse were former professors or alumni, as in the instances of the colleges of Montlauzon, Verdale, Narbonne, Saint Martial, Montrevel, Mirepoix, Foix, and Saint Girons. It may also have been true that the two nephews of Innocent VI, and of the Cardinal of Perigord, were alumni but this is never stated. Another striking fact is the number of founders who were prelates. This was true of all the colleges mentioned above except Verdale and Saint Girons, and the founder of Verdale was named bishop of Maguelonne shortly after making his foundation. Four of these prelates were cardinals, and one was a pope. Only Montpellier, Bologna, and Turin could actually boast papal founders for colleges on the type of Saint Martial at Toulouse.

The University of Toulouse, of course, did not cease to perform its functions after 1500, but continued as an institution of importance for all southern France. After the interruption of the French Revolution it was reëstablished and continues to this day as one of the national universities of the French Republic. As in the past, it especially encourages the attendance of students from the Iberian peninsula and has even attracted them in some numbers from a far more distant region which was an unknown wilderness until shortly before the Middle Ages had run their course. Although of continuing interest, this further history of a venerable university lies outside the field of a medievalist and hence cannot be included in this study of the origin and early development of the University of Toulouse.

BIBLIOGRAPHIC ESSAY

Interest in the history of medieval universities in general—with the exception of a few of the most outstanding, such as Paris, Bologna, and Oxford—is of comparatively recent growth. This is particularly emphasized when bibliographical research is undertaken on any of the numerous institutions which trace their origins to that epoch. It matters little whether they have long since ceased to exist or whether they have continued to this day in more or less modified form.

To trace the historiography of the University of Toulouse, one has to look but little in advance of the year 1850. Prior to that date there are but two works containing even scattered references to the history of the university, the monumental *Histoire générale de Languedoc* of de Vic and Vaisette and Percin's *Monumenta*. At the epoch when the learned Benedictines labored, writers of history were still primarily interested in politics, so that it is not surprising that the pages devoted to the development of an academic body are scattered and few in number. What is included there, however, although of slight content, is accurate on the whole if not in any sense complete. The Dominican Percin, while primarily interested in the history of the mother-convent of his order, devoted one entire section to the *Academia*. A few valuable documents are inserted, but the treatment on the whole is no longer adequate.[1]

Toward the middle of the last century the first of the numerous scattered articles on various special phases of the history of the University of Toulouse began to appear. As might be expected, the earliest essays were written by men interested in local history. In 1847 Benech published his essay on the teaching of French law in the University of Toulouse, which was reprinted ten years later in the posthumous collection of essays entitled *Mélanges de droit et d'histoire*. As the chair of French law at the university was instituted under Francis I, this work falls entirely outside the Medieval period. Indeed, Benech began his treatment only with the age of Louis XIV.[2]

---

[1] Dom Claude de Vic et Dom Joseph Vaisette, *Histoire générale Langue-doc* (Paris, 1730-1745); 5 vols. in folio. Jean Jacques Percin, *Monumenta Conventus Tolosani Ordinis Fratrum Praedicatorum* (Tolosae, 1693), in folio.

[2] Benech, *De l'enseignement du droit français dans l'ancienne université*

217

In 1857 Gatien-Arnoult, a professor in the University of Toulouse, began a series of lectures on various phases of the early history of the university, which stretched over a period of twenty-five years. These were published as articles in the organs of local historical societies. Those dealing directly with the university appeared between 1857 and 1882 in the *Mémoires* of the Academy of Toulouse. They were intended as preliminary essays for certain chapters of a history of the university that he proposed writing, but are not of a consecutive nature; for many chapters were inserted merely in skeleton form to fill in between those printed in full. Originally written for lecture purposes, they are popular in style and are re-enforced only rarely by citations of sources. On occasions when original material is cited to fortify his statements, he is guilty of excessive squeezing, frequently reading into isolated words and phrases great volumes of hidden meaning.[3]

While Gatien-Arnoult was still in the midst of his not inconsiderable work on the university, Rodière, a professor of law in this same institution, began publication of a series of articles on the teaching of law at Toulouse. Between 1860 and 1866, four essays on various phases of this subject appeared in a legal periodical of that city. In the earliest of the four, he treated the subject of law instruction at Toulouse before the founding of the university—a very hypothetical subject at best—gave an edition of the statutes of 1314, and listed the doctors and masters who had studied or taught there, deriving his information mainly from Savigny and Lafaille. The next year a similar treatise on the period between 1334 and 1540 was published, with a few generalizations on the university as a whole. The two later articles deal with the period from 1540 to 1789, and therefore fall entirely outside the scope of this work.[4]

de Toulouse (Toulouse, 1847). The posthumous essays were published in Paris in 1857.

3 Adolphe Félix Gatien-Arnoult, "Note sur les commencements de l'université de Toulouse et sur une pièce relative à ces premiers temps" in *Mémoires de l'Académie des sciences, inscriptions et belles-lettres de Toulouse*, E. I (1857), 202-220. The chapters for a proposed history of the university appeared in the same periodical in Series G. IX (1877), 455-494; X (1878), 1-34; Ser. H, I:I (1879), 1-32; III:I (1881), 1-36; and IV:I (1882), 1-26.

4 Rodière, "Recherches sur l'enseignement du droit dans l'université de Toulouse" in *Recueil de l'Académie de législation de Toulouse*, IX (1860), 244; X (1861), 153; XII (1863), 216; and XV (1866), 210. In 1869 he seems to have recast the same articles under the title, "Des études juridiques dans l'université de Toulouse du XIIIe au XVIIIe siècles" in *Revue de Toulouse*, XXX (1869), 22-43.

In 1862 Charles Jourdain, in the *Revue des sociétés savantes,* published a report upon the university made by royal commissioners in 1668, which gives information as to the state of the university in the seventeenth century but nevertheless has a few references to the period before 1500. Interest in this subject continued in local circles for the next decade. Vaïsse-Cibiel published an address that he had made upon the history of the university in 1865, and Pessemesse presented an article on the same subject to the Archaeological Society of Southern France. In 1867 Antoine Baudouin made an even more elaborate address upon this subject before the Academy of Sciences and Inscriptions.[5] Between 1882 and 1886 a series of articles by St. Charles appeared in local scholarly journals on the history of individual colleges of the University of Toulouse. These articles commenced very modestly with a bare two-page report of a paper he had read on the College of Narbonne before the Academy. The other four are complete essays devoted to the College of Maguelonne, to a group of ten colleges only five of which dated from the Medieval period, to the College of Foix, and to the College of Perigord. Of these, the latter two are very well done.[6]

The first orderly and scientific treatment, however, of any particular aspect of the university's history came with the re-edition of Vaisette's monumental *Histoire générale de Languedoc* between 1872 and 1904. At that time the editing commission added many new notes to the original edition as well as considerable new documentary material as proofs. The note upon the University of Toulouse was entrusted to Emile Molinier, who carefully edited all the statutes and then published a brief but scholarly essay upon the university organization of the fourteenth and fifteenth centuries.[7]

---

[5] Charles Jourdain, "L'université de Toulouse au XVIIe siècle" in *Revue des sociétés savantes,* 2nd Series, VIII:II (Sept.-Oct. 1862), 314 and 405; Vaïsse-Cibiel, "L'ancienne université de Toulouse" in *Revue de Toulouse,* XXVI (1865), 328; Pessemesse, "Sur l'ancienne université de Toulouse" in *Bulletin de la société d'archéologie du Midi de France,* XI (1875-1876), 4; and Antoine Baudouin, "Discours sur l'ancienne université de Toulouse" in *Mémoires de l'Académie des sciences, inscriptions et belles-lettres de Toulouse,* in Series G. VIII (1876), pp. xix-xxv.

[6] St. Charles in *Mémoires de l'Académie des sciences, inscriptions et belles-lettres de Toulouse,* in Series H. IV (1882), 176; H. V (1883), 140; H. VI:I (1884), 57; H. VII:I (1885), 259; and H. VIII (1886), 158.

[7] Dom Claude de Vic et Dom Joseph Vaisette, *Histoire générale de Languedoc,* 2nd edition (to 1790), (Toulouse, 1872-1904), 16 vols. Emile Molinier, "Etude sur l'organization de l'université de Toulouse au XIVe et au XVe siècle" in *ibid.,* VII, 570-608.

In 1885 the learned Dominican, Heinrich Denifle, published his epoch-making work on the origins of medieval universities. He gave a good brief account of the beginnings of Toulouse and pointed the way to many hitherto unknown but extremely valuable sources. Seven years later Marcel Fournier—after putting together his companion-piece to the *Chartularium universitatis Parisiensis* of Denifle and Chatelain, under the title, *Statuts et privilèges des universités françaises*—produced in a rather careless fashion his *Histoire de la science du droit.* His seeming dread lest anyone anticipate him in the use of the *Statuts* made speed rather than accuracy of prime importance. Although specifically interested in the legal faculties, this work includes also a brief sketch of the development of French universities in general. As a bare outline, his account of Toulouse is adequate; but he wrote in such haste that there are occasional statements in contradiction of documents that he had published in the *Statuts*. The section on the legal faculty itself is of poorer quality. Although the statutes are translated at length, few explanations are proffered, so that one is really not much the wiser for having read the volume.[8]

In 1895 appeared a work in English which treats of the University of Toulouse. Hastings Rashdall, in his monumental work on medieval universities, devoted some few pages to this institution. His treatment is fuller in scope than Denifle's, which considered only the origins; but owing to the broad field in which he worked, his account is brief.[9]

The early twentieth century saw continued interest in various phases of the history of this medieval university. Antonin Deloume, also of the law faculty of Toulouse, published his brief history of that body in 1900. This work is for the most part a compilation from the earlier secondary works on this subject written in French. Five years later he issued a revised edition under a different title. During the interval he had discovered the

---

[8] Heinrich Denifle, *Die Universitäten des Mittelalters bis 1400* (Berlin, 1885). This is the only volume completed of a proposed five volume work, and bears the special title *Die Entstehung*. The essay on Toulouse extends from page 570 to 608. Marcel Fournier, *Histoire de la science du droit en France* (Paris, 1892), 3 vols. The third volume bears the special title, *Les universitiés françaises et l'enseignement du droit en France au moyen âge*. The section devoted to Toulouse extends in that volume from page 209 to page 340.

[9] Hastings Rashdall, *The Universities of Europe in the Middle Ages* (Oxford, 1895), two vols. in three. The sketch of Toulouse is in *ibid.*, II:I, 158-170.

works of Gatien-Arnoult, from which he quoted copiously. He also refers to the *Statuts et privilèges,* but apparently did not make use of them. In the same year Dr. Barbot produced his chronicles of the faculty of medicine of Toulouse. This two volume work was a thesis for the faculty of medicine of Toulouse. Although very critical of his contemporaries, the work is marked by a strong anti-clerical bias and lack of knowledge of the Middle Ages.[10] In 1909 Jules de Lahondès published his article on the College of Pampelune, thereby completing the work of St. Charles.[11]

The Reverend Louis Saltet of the *Institut Catholique* at Toulouse published in the organ of that institution two brief articles on the history of the ancient university in 1912 and 1916 respectively. Only the former deals with the Medieval period, for the latter is devoted to its sixteenth and seventeenth century history. The first article, however, is based on consultation of the best printed sources, though its restricted scope of seventeen pages does not allow for any detailed consideration of the development of the university.[12]

The seventh centenary celebration of the foundation of the University of Toulouse inspired several publications on the history of this venerable institution. In 1928 Louis Vié, the librarian of the university, published certain chapters and fragments of his proposed history of the university in the April, May, and June issues of the *Bulletin de l'Université et de l'Académie de Toulouse.* Seven chapters of this work were reprinted in the memorial volume issued at Toulouse by Privat in 1929 entitled *L'Université de Toulouse, son passé, son présent.* Only three of the seven chapters contributed by Vié concern the Medieval period. His materials are drawn primarily from the works of Gatien-Arnoult and Saltet. Likewise included in this memorial volume are articles by professors of the university on various special aspects of its history. M. Picavet traces the general historical development of the university; MM. Paul Thomas and

[10] Antonin Deloume, *Aperçu historique sur la faculté de droit de l'université de Toulouse : Maîtres et escoliers de l'an 1228 à 1900* (Toulouse, 1900), and *Histoire sommaire de la faculté de droit de Toulouse fondée en 1229: centenaire de la réorganization de 1805* (Toulouse, 1905). Barbot, *Les Chroniques de la faculté de Médecine de Toulouse du treizième au vingtième siècle* (Toulouse, 1905) 2 vols.

[11] Jules Lahondès, "Le Collège de Pampelune," *Bulletin de la Société d'archéologie du Midi de France* (1909), 488.

[12] Louis Saltet, "L'ancienne Université de Toulouse," *Bulletin de littérature écclésiastique,* 3rd Series, XIV (1912), 16-32; and XVII (1916), 50-65.

Georges Boyer describe that of the faculty of law; M. Gerber, that of the faculty of medicine; MM. Charles Lécrivain and L. Delaruelle, that of the faculty of letters. None of them has made any particular study of the Medieval era. The coverage of that period in these essays varies from one chapter in the section devoted to the law faculty to one page in the section on the faculty of letters. Similarly inspired by the centenary is the article by Joseph Calmette published in that year and the small volume by Moses Bensabat Amzalak in Portuguese published in 1930.[13]

In 1930 Juliette Puget published an essay entitled "L'Université de Toulouse au XIVe et au XVe siècles" in the *Annales du Midi*. This essay was based on her thesis prepared under the direction of M. Calmette, which bore the much more appropriate title, *L'Université de Toulouse et les juridictions séculières*. The essay is divided into two parts to correspond with the two centuries included in the title, and deals primarily with the relations between the university and the civil government, a fact not indicated in the title of the essay as printed. She has carefully consulted the archive materials on her subject both in the municipal and departmental archives. She has used and referred to all the secondary materials in her documentation; she lists the printed primary source collections but rarely uses them. Her synthesis regards the fourteenth century as a period when the university was overbearing in its attitude toward the city government; and in the fifteenth century as one in which the *parlement* of Toulouse reduced the university to disciplined submission.[14]

In the decade following this centenary celebration at Toulouse, two general histories of medieval universities were published. By far the more scholarly was the two-volume work of Stephen d'Irsay on the history of universities in both the Middle Ages and modern times. In the first volume he traces the origins of the movement and the history of universities through the sixteenth century. Save for Paris, Bologna, and Montpellier, no individual university is accorded so much as a whole chapter. In-

[13] Louis Vié, "Histoire de l'Université de Toulouse," *Bulletin de l'Univrsité et de l'Académie de Toulouse*, (April-June 1928). These seven chapters are reprinted in the memorial volume published by Privat, *L'Université de Toulouse, son passé, son présent* (Toulouse, 1929). Joseph Calmette, "Les sept siècles de l'Université de Toulouse, 1229-1929," *Bulletin des Amitiés; Franco-Etrangères*, No. I (1929), 25 ff. Moses Bensabat Amzalak, *Universidades de França: a Universidade de Tolosa e o sen ensino* (Lisboa, 1930).

[14] Juliette Puget, "L'Université de Toulouse au XIVe et au XVe siècles," *Annales du Midi*, 30, t. 42 (1930), 345-381.

stead, the major part is divided into chronological epochs describing the chief developments in the history of universities. For this reason materials on the foundation of Toulouse occupy about three pages, though there are other scattered references elsewhere on special aspects of its history. The work as a whole is meticulously done and a real contribution in its field. Its synthesis is far more complete than Rashdall's, and the second volume carries the story of universities to the middle of the nineteenth century. The scholarship involved is everywhere apparent. The second general history of medieval universites should scarcely be mentioned in juxtaposition to the work of d'Irsay. Though published in 1938, Schachner's *Medieval Universities* is an almost perfect antithesis. D'Irsay's work is not even included in his bibliography. His work is vulgar popularization, written with an eighteenth century "enlightened" disdain for the medieval. He admits at times that he can find no authority for some of his idiosyncratic interpretations. He draws most heavily on Rashdall for his facts, and obviously has not used the printed primary sources he lists in his bibliography.[15]

Aside from these secondary works, articles on special incidents, biographies, and other peripheral materials have been consulted which would take too much space to evaluate here and which have only slight bearing on the history of the university. These are always acknowledged in footnotes in due course. Similarly acknowledged are details drawn from sixteenth, seventeenth and eighteenth century chroniclers who wrote on the city of Toulouse. The secondary works used in the chapter on backgrounds are also duly cited in appropriate footnotes. For the sake of brevity all such works are omitted from this bibliographical essay.

Turning from the secondary material to the printed primary sources, aside from isolated documents in various collections, the first actual attempt to assemble materials relating to the history of the University of Toulouse was the collection of statutes of this university edited by Molinier in the new edition of the *Histoire générale de Languedoc*. This collection of statutes, although based almost entirely upon manuscripts of the Bibliothèque Nationale, is most carefully edited. In marked contrast is the larger collection of sources by Fournier which appeared soon after;

[15] Stephen d'Irsay, *Histoire des Universités françaises et etrangères des origines à nos jours* (Paris, 1933-1935), 2 vols.; and Nathan Schachner, *The Medieval Universities* (New York, 1938).

for even in borrowing from his predecessors, he showed himself incapable of avoiding serious error. Its imperfections have been castigated by both Denifle and Chatelain.[16]

For all its imperfections, however, the *Statuts* is valuable, if merely from the point of view of convenience. Its most besetting fault is its pretentiousness. All of Fournier's claims to completeness were mercilessly exposed as vain by Denifle, who published many important Vatican documents unknown to Fournier. From references drawn from Fournier, I have found several new documents of interest even in the Bibliothèque Nationale manuscripts; while at the Municipal Archives of Toulouse and at the Departmental Archives of the Haute-Garonne there was new material in embarrassing quantities. He cannot even claim to have exhausted previously printed documents, for I have drawn materials from so well known a work as Martène's *Thesaurus*— which, by the way, has a usable index. As excuse for this lack of completeness in replying to Denifle's criticism, Fournier has tried to minimize the importance of his omissions, and proffered the great quantities of hitherto inedited material that he had included, in comparison with that contained in the first volume of the *Chartularium*. This unfortunate defense calls down even more criticism upon his head, for whereas the *Chartularium* is graced with a beautiful critical apparatus, the *Statuts* could not be more entirely innocent of one. The hundred odd footnotes with which Fournier has seen fit to equip the four hundred pages of documents on Toulouse in his first volume are about as utterly valueless as they could possibly be. A number of them contain documents he did not consider worthy of insertion in the text proper, others are identifications of Biblical and legal quotations, but by far the major part are simply a series of cross-references. On several occasions he offers critical suggestions that can be proven false by reading further in the documents he publishes. He seems to have been ignorant of even the most elementary ideas of good editing, for he has assigned undated documents in a most arbitrary fashion. He publishes resumés of documents in great numbers, quoting neither the address nor the dating phrase. This is the more blameworthy in that on numerous occasions

---

[16] Marcel Fournier, *Les Statuts et Privilèges des Universités Françaises depuis leur fondation jusqu'en 1789* (Paris, 1890-1894), 4 vols. See also Heinrich Denifle, *Les universités françaises au moyen âge : avis à M. Marcel Fournier* (Paris, 1892); and Denifle and Chatelain, *Les Délégués des universités françaises au concile de Constance : Nouvelle rectifications aux ouvrages de M. Marcel Fournier* (Rennes, 1892).

when the documents are given *in extenso,* the editor's dating and the dating phrase are entirely irreconcilable. Under purely typographical errors, the jumped lines and omitted words are innumerable.

To supply in some measure the deficiencies of Fournier, Gadave, in 1910, presented a thesis at the faculty of law of Toulouse upon the sources of the history of the university with particular reference to the legal faculties. This is neither a history nor a collection of sources, but a calendar of documents arranged in more or less chronological order, with elaborate references to both printed and manuscript sources. Although errors of Fournier are here corrected and many additional documents cited, Gadave—as M. Antoine Thomas justly remarks—is entirely innocent of any knowledge of diplomatics. For him, the fifth *kalend* of September was September 5, and the year very conveniently commenced January 1. There are also several municipal documents misattributed to the university because of the use of the word *universitas.*[17]

Among other collections of source material in which I found scattered references to my subject, the most important were the *regesta* of papal registers for the thirteenth and fourteenth centuries as published by the French School of Rome and Athens; the *Analecta Vaticano Belgica* published by the Belgian School of Rome; the *Bullarum Romanum,* and Martène's *Amplissima collectio* and *Thesaurus.* References to the individual documents are cited in footnotes as used. In the background chapter contemporary chroniclers and original documents from other standard collections of sources are similarly cited.

The manuscript material for the history of the University of Toulouse in the Middle Ages is of considerable bulk. Fournier, in both the *Statuts* and the *Histoire,* has printed a short essay upon his sources, and Molinier and Gadave have carefully described those which they have employed in their respective works. Although my material is taken in general from the same sources and depots, still a recapitulation of what they have reported, with a few personal observations, may not be out of place.

---

[17] René Gadave, *Les Documents sur l'histoire de l'université de Toulouse, et spécialement sa faculté de droit civil et canonique* (Toulouse, 1910). See Antoine Thomas, "Lettres closes de Charles VI et de Charles VII addressées à l'université de Toulouse," *Annales du Midi: Revue archéologique, historique et philologique* (1915-1916), 176.

The documents from which the early history of the University of Toulouse has been obtained are of various sorts and are distributed somewhat unequally among three European cities— Toulouse itself, Paris, and Rome. Since the university was of papal foundation, it is only natural to suppose that the Vatican Archives would be a most important repository for material dealing with its history—which to a certain extent is true. There Denifle—and after him Fournier—transcribed from pontifical registers many bulls and letters having to do with this university. There also in the registers of *Supplicationes,* numerous requests of masters and students for benefices and other gifts within the bestowal of the pope are to be found. Although of very standardized nature, these documents give information of all sorts and are really deserving of a detailed study from the point of view of the personnel of the medieval university, a study to which my two months' visit in Rome permitted only a most cursory introduction. There are ninety-nine registers for the incomplete series of the fourteenth century alone, hence years would be necessary for any comprehensive view of this collection. At Paris, in the Bibliothèque Nationale, one finds several manuscript volumes containing the statutes of the university at various epochs and of several of the colleges. Among the former, three are of primary importance, Latin manuscripts 4221D, 4221C, and 4223A.

The first is a volume of sixty-seven paper folios, and has its first twenty-four devoted to a copy of university statutes.[18] These contain documents dated from 1245 to 1329, arranged in no particular order. Aside from the papal letters conferring privileges, none is previous to the year 1309. The hand is clearly one of the fourteenth century; and, at the end of the first set of statutes, after quoting the date, the copyist has added: "Et per me, hoc XV die septembris, anno M°CCC°XLI°." As 1341 is well after the date of the latest document included, it is very probable that this reference is to the actual date of the writing of that portion of the manuscript. As the hand is the same throughout, the compilation of the chartulary as a whole can probably be assigned to that period. This is further confirmed by the fact that there is no record of general university statutes having been enacted between 1329 and September 15, 1341. On September 20 of that year, there is record of a new university statute. If the scribe was at work after that date, this document too, would

[18] Bibliothèque Nationale, Ms. Lat. 4221D.

surely have been included. Perhaps this volume was a *liber statutorum* of the rector, as provided by the statutes of 1313, although no reason for its transcription at this particular time can be offered, unless the earlier volume has been lost, or, in the interval of twenty-eight years, had become too worn for convenient use. The margins are decorated with drawings of a crude nature. Near regulations concerning mimes and *joculatores* are pictures of young men in elaborate costumes, wearing skull caps. Another page is ornamented with a bearded gentleman in hood and *cappa,* carrying a staff, while still another shows a stone house with an open door, opposite a paragraph on hospices.[19]

The second of the three manuscripts, Number 4221C of the Latin *fonds,* is a parchment codex of forty-eight folios written in fourteenth and fifteenth century hands. Although of a more complex nature, one of its earliest sections contains a copy of the same documents that are given in 4221D, in the identical order. Immediately thereafter appear the statutes of 1341, not included in the other manuscript, and a series of documents in chronological order to the year 1390. Then, in a later cursive hand, were added the long series of reform statutes and other related documents down to 1436.[20] Fournier, in transcribing the last document of this series, has copied the scribe's dating phrase as a last paragraph for his Number 815. From these two sentences it is learned that Johannes Textoris, Doctor of Canon Law and chancellor of Toulouse, had written these statutes in his own hand and that he had made a true copy of them from a book which had belonged to Bernard Rosergue, then chancellor of Toulouse, during his chancellorship. This subscription is dated the fifteenth of November, 1459. That this volume had belonged to a chancellor is quite evident, for the marginal notes in a cursive hand call particular attention to the privileges of that officer. On the flyleaves, too, are found a long series of *formulae* for oaths to be

---

[19] The dating phrase of the scribe is on f° 3. The statutes of September 20, 1341 are reproduced in Fournier, *Statuts,* I, no. 596, p. 561. The reference to the Statute Book of the rector is found in *ibid.,* no. 544, xv, p. 478. The crude illustrations are found at f°17v°, f°20v°, f°21v° and f°22.

[20] Bibliothèque Nationale, Ms. Lat. 4221C. The copy of the documents from the previous manuscript extends from f°9 to f$34. The additional statutes 1341 to 1390 extend to f°48. Fournier, *Statuts,* I, no. 714, p. 676 is mis-dated as of 1389. From internal evidence, it is really posterior to no. 715, p. 677, which is dated June 3 of that year. Because of the movibility of Easter, the year 1389 had two days designated April 12, so this document is obviously of the year 1390 N.S. The documents written in cursive script extend to f°48.

taken before the chancellor by candidates for various degrees, written in a fifteenth century hand. The upper part of the verso of folio two has been erased to allow for continuing this series; for it is headed, "Sequentur Juramenti forma prestandi," but the copyist evidently changed his mind. Instead of continuing to scrape the rest of the page, he merely drew lines through it, leaving some very interesting notes—very probably also in the hand of a chancellor—assigning dates for vespers and *aulae*. These are all for the years 1404 and 1405. Aside from these materials, the manuscript also contains an elaborate university calendar with richly decorated initial letters and borders. The original hand is of the fourteenth century, but there are later cursive insertions of added vacations and references to university sermons.[21]

The third of these manuscripts, 4223A, is a register of statutes of the University of Orléans. On folio ten verso, a rubric announces that the following documents are copied from a letter of the officials of Toulouse, containing the privileges of that *studium*, all of which are conceded to the University of Orléans. This *vidimus* contains copies of eight papal bulls from Innocent IV to Clement V and is dated at Toulouse, the sixteenth of January, 1309.[22]

Among the other manuscripts at the Bibliothèque Nationale containing material on Toulouse, are two seventeenth century copies. One of them—Latin Manuscript 4222—is Baluze's concordance of the three manuscripts just described. The other—4354C of the same *fonds*—is a collated copy, dated 1630, of a volume of statutes of 1573, of which I can find no trace. The seventeenth century copyist of this volume avers that he found it in the archiepiscopal archives of Toulouse, and had transcribed and collated it at the request of the king.[23]

---

21 Fournier, *Statuts*, no. 815, p. 794. The marginal notes in the manuscript calling particular attention to the Chancellor are found at f°15v°, col. 2; f°23v°, col. 2; and f°25. The *formulae* for the oaths to the Chancellor occupy all of f°1; and are reproduced in Fournier, *Statuts*, I, no. 748, p. 699. The University Calendar is edited by Molinier in *Histoire générale de Languedoc*, VII, 617-619; and reproduced by Fournier in his footnote to *Statuts*, I, no. 46. The cursive insertions in the calendar are found at f°3 and f°8v°.

22 Bibliothèque Nationale, Ms. Lat. 4223A, f°10v° to f°15, col. 2. It is reproduced in Fournier, *Statuts*, I, no. 25, p. 25 in abbreviated form where he gives cross-references to the papal bulls in his documents for Toulouse, and omits the witnesses of the *vidimus*.

23 Bibliothèque Nationale, Ms. Lat. 4222, is Baluze's collated copy of the three manuscripts commented on above. It is a codex of 123 folios which, from f°114 on, contains printed material after 1500. Ms. Lat. 4354C is a collated copy made in 1630 of an old Statute Book of the Uni-

In addition to these manuscripts, two others are preserved in the Bibliothèque Nationale which contain documents relating to the various colleges. Latin Manuscript 4222A is evidently a sixteenth century copy of records pertaining to the College of Pampelune. The latest document included is for the year 1542. Latin Manuscript 4223 is a collection of Baluze of transcriptions and also of original pieces having to do with the colleges of Toulouse. Being a former collegiate of the College of Saint Martial, he was primarily interested in that college; but a few documents for other colleges are included.

At Toulouse the manuscript material having reference to the university and colleges is dispersed in three principal depots, with a few scattered documents in two others. In general, most of the documents for the relations between the university and the city are conserved at the municipal archives. These consist in bound books, for the most part records of lawsuits, a few rolls, usually complaints to the royal authorities or briefs submitted in a law case, and of isolated documents—letters, summonses, and the like. Fournier has published some of this material, Gadave has cited a great deal more; but there were left a few interesting pieces that had escaped both.

At the Departmental Archives of the Haute-Garonne, are conserved enormous quantities of valuable material. The Series D— that category reserved for the university and colleges—I was unable to consult as it was in the process of reclassification. The archivist assured me, however, that there was no material for the period before 1500, thereby confirming Fournier's similar dictum. I was permitted, however, to glance through certain ancient registers, classifying the documents of several of the colleges, and was thus able to control some of Fournier's dates. The valuable *Livre Blanc de l'archevêché*, a manuscript of various epochs, threw considerable light, not so much on the university itself as upon ecclesiastical affairs in general during the thirteenth century. Another codex, Number One of Series D, proved to be a copy of the *Livre Rouge*, the original of which is conserved in the university library. In the *fonds* Saint-Etienne, that of the cathedral chapter and diocese of Toulouse, there was considerable new material, above all on the office of chancellor. The *fonds* Saint-Sernin contained an astonishing amount of new

versity belonging to the archbishop (f°140v°). The manuscript is headed: "Haec sunt statuta universitatis Tholosanae 1573" f°1).

material and was so vast even for the period before 1500, that I was able to do little more than glance through it. The abbot of that great monastery had been conservator of university privileges and as such had acted as judge in many cases where that institution was a litigant. Also from an early time this monastery had taken a vital interest in the university itself, and later had even transformed its Hospital of Saint Raymond into a college for poor students. My researches in the Dominican *fonds* did not prove so valuable, but there was an occasional document in that of the Daurade that gave new information.

At the Palais de Justice in Toulouse are conserved both the notarial archives and those of the *parlement*. Guided by Gadave's citations, I copied several documents of interest from both collections, but did not attempt further research. Two documents in the hospital archives were also signalized in the same manner. At the university library, where I was admitted through the kind interest of Dr. Gerber of the faculty of medicine and pharmacy, I glanced over the famous *Livre Rouge,* a sixteenth century manuscript containing a nearly complete set of university statutes. The hoped-for variant readings for irreconcilable dates did not materialize, for I found that, as far as dates were concerned, the numerous copies of this manuscript were true ones. Among the fine manuscripts of the Municipal Library of Toulouse are several that had been made or purchased by students. Molinier's excellent catalogue of this collection was invaluable.[24]

[24] Emile Molinier, *Catalogue général des manuscrits des bibliothèques publiques des départements, Toulouse-Nimes* (Paris, 1885).